GENESIS AND JUDAISM

Number 108
GENESIS AND JUDAISM
The Perspective of Genesis Rabbah
An Analytical Anthology
Translated and Edited by
Jacob Neusner

GENESIS AND JUDAISM

The Perspective of Genesis Rabbah
An Analytical Anthology

Translated and Edited
by
Jacob Neuser

Scholars Press
Atlanta, Georgia

GENESIS AND JUDAISM

The Perspective of Genesis Rabbah
An Analytical Anthology
Translated and Edited by

Jacob Neusner

Library of Congress Cataloging in Publication Data

Midrash rabbah. Genesis. English. Selections.
   Genesis and Judaism : The perspective of Genesis
rabbah.

   (Brown Judaic studies ; no. 108)
Bibliography: p.
   Includes index.
   1. Midrash rabbah. Genesis—Commentaries.
I. Neusner, Jacob, 1932–   . II. Title.
III. Series: Brown Judiac studies ; no. 108.
BM517.M65A3   1985a   296.1'4   85-26210
ISBN 0–89130–940–3
ISBN 0–89130–941–1 (pbk.)

Printed in the United States of America
on acid-free paper

For

The Faculty of
Hebrew Union College-Jewish Institute of Religion
in Los Angeles
in general

and for

SAMSON LEVEY
in particular

The only rabbinical faculty in the world
from which I have enjoyed a fair
hearing
in twenty-five years

These colleagues, persons of honor and dignity,
prove that we can believe
and also doubt:
with perfect faith believe in God and in the Torah,
but receive with skepticism
the assertions of mere humanity.

They demonstrate that Reform Judaism,
in founding modern Judaic learning,
really did make a difference.

CONTENTS

Preface

The sages of third and fourth century Judaism who created Genesis Rabbah teach us an important lesson. It is to bring to the book of Genesis our deepest concerns as individuals and as a society -- but to listen to the Scripture's abiding judgment. The book of Genesis, today a battlefield among contending forces of science and philosophy, religion and historical study, for the ancient sages of Judaism as for us formed the arena for sorting out and settling critical issues of human destiny and national history. That fact testifies to the enduring power of Genesis to speak to the human condition, but also to lay down a judgment of that condition. Genesis tells the story of humanity's beginnings and (to the sages of Judaism) of Israel's redemption. We do well to encounter the response, to Genesis, of sages who through the truth they found there taught an entire people the meaning of their lives.

In this book I propose to address a new generation of readers, of a sort without precedent in the history of Judaism. To them I present a fair sample of how the ancient sages of Judaism teach us how to confront the story, in Genesis, of human beginnings as the Hebrew Scriptures record that story. These readers are both Jew and gentile. In prior ages no one expected non-Jews to take an interest in the words of the ancient sages of the Talmud and the midrash-compilations. Everyone took for granted that Jews knew these words in the original Hebrew or Aramaic. So the audience at hand is both new and without parallel.

Asking a new generation to read Genesis the way the sages of Judaism have done so so strikes me as urgent. Why?

First, because the sages before us present a paradigm of creative and profound response to the biblical record.

Second, because today we witness debate on that same story.

Third, the picture of humanity and of the cosmos presented by Genesis retains abiding relevance to our understanding of ourselves. Genesis does not sit on a library shelf, nor should it. It is a gripping, moving, deeply wise account of us: "in God's image, after God's likeness." We therefore cannot ignore the account of human origins presented by the book of Genesis.

But we also cannot permit the meaning of that account to reach us as though we alone, for the first time this morning proposed to consider it. Why not? Because we stand in a long tradition of encounter with Scripture. The civilization of the West reaches back to the book of Genesis in order to make sense of itself and has done so for the entire history of the West in its Christian expression and in its Judaic formulation, to mention the two great traditions of Western civilization. That is why ours is the task of listening, before we speak, to the vision of others, if also to say our word as well. Here we see the choices made by Israel's sages in times past. They present us with an alternative but also a challenge -- see things as we did, or in the model of how we framed our vision, or perceive nothing worth knowing. So they offer both a method and a message, and ours is the work of appropriating each for our own purposes. That I think defines the challenge at hand: to see things as others saw them and, through their vision, to perceive a perspective otherwise not visible to our eyes. It is the perception of our beginnings as humanity different from the one we ordinarily form, thus, in a curious way, in this book we see ourselves as others see us, but by comparison and contrast.

What precisely do the ancient Judaic sages who produced Genesis Rabbah, flourishing in the Land of Israel from about 200 to about 400 of the Common Era, have to teach us? They demonstrate the power of Scripture to speak to our immediate circumstance, they illustrate the right of Scripture's people (among whom, today, are all who revere the Hebrew Scriptures) to listen to Scripture as the word reaches the here and the now. Once more they offer a model, a method, and a message. The model takes precedence, then the method, and, for all Israel, finally the message.

That does not mean they invented for the moment, any more than that we make things up as we go along and call it God's word. But it also does not require us to wait for scholars of comparative Semitic philology to mediate the word of God to the world we know. What we are about to confront is a generation of sages who, because they revered Scripture as God's word, also insisted that God spoke to them about their deepest concerns. The lesson we here may learn concerns a Scripture employed today to intimidate science, on the one side, and embarrass belief, on the other. We learn, specifically, from the model of sages who found in Scripture profound and diverse layers of meaning, messages from God to their own hearts. To them God spoke a single word, but humanity heard many messages. There was therefore no single and "fundamental" message, which all must believe on pain of losing salvation.

To speak directly, the sages at hand knew nothing of rigid fundamentalism. They found many and diverse meanings in a text they read in many dimensions. But they also would have found incomprehensible the uncomprehending insistence of another kind of fundamentalism, that which assigns to the text only the "original" meaning, the one determined by a long-dead context of obscure and unimaginative philology. The lesson of the sages is simple. They exercised the freedom to ask many pressing questions, but also exhibited the patience to attend to answers. Above all they manifested the initiative to explore the Scripture's deepest layers of meaning.

So I propose in this analytical anthology to show, through a rich repertoire of detailed examples, exactly how Judaic sages brought their questions to Scripture and also listened to Scripture's answers. I deem the task urgent. Why so? Because the sages at hand have the power to teach us how to read Scripture their way, which, in Judaism, is the only right way. What is that way? It is the route that leads us to return to Scripture carrying the burden of all all our anguish and our hope, to reflect through Scripture, that is, through the perspective of the Torah, upon our condition as human beings, and -- to speak bluntly and as a religious Jew, -- to listen to and learn what God has to say about us: "in our image, after our likeness." We human beings are in God's image and after God's likeness. What can that possibly mean? Genesis, as the sages of Genesis Rabbah read the book, answers that question in very specific ways.

Why this compilation of biblical exegeses (called, in Hebrew, *midrashim*) in particular? Because it is the first and the best. Genesis Rabbah presents the first complete and systematic Judaic commentary to the book of Genesis. In normative and classical Judaism, that is, the Judaism that reached its original expression in the Mishnah, ca. A.D. 200, and came to final and full statement in the Talmud of Babylonia, ca. A.D. 600, Genesis Rabbah therefore takes an important position. Specifically, this great rabbinic commentary to Genesis, generally thought to have been closed ("redacted") at ca. A.D. 400, provides a complete and authoritative account of how Judaism proposes to read and make sense of the first book of the Hebrew Scriptures.

Genesis Rabbah also may claim to constitute the best of the midrash-compilations. Why so? Because sages' way of reading the first book of the Bible shows that faithful exegetes uncover deep layers of meaning and discover truth entirely consonant with the concerns of a given age. That is the fact, whether it is the fourth century, in which our sages did their work, or the twenty-first century, to which, with God's help, I hope to hand on these books of mine. Let me now spell out the character of this translation and anthology and what I hope to contribute by doing it.

This analytical anthology of Genesis Rabbah takes as its text and systematic commentary J. Theodor and Ch. Albeck, *Midrash Bereshit Rabba. Critical Edition with Notes and Commentary* (Berlin and Jerusalem, 1893-1936) I-III. That text is critical, so far as contemporary Judaic scholarship can produce a critical text, and I have treated it as authoritative in every detail. I have furthermore had the advantage of an excellent translation, already available, and have made ample use of it. I systematically consulted H. Freedman, *Genesis*, in *Midrash Rabbah. Translated into English with Notes, Glossary, and Indices*, ed. by H. Freedman and Maurice Simon (London, 1939: Soncino Press) I-II. Where I have adopted Freedman's translation verbatim or nearly so, I have indicated by adding his name in square brackets. But I have taken full account of his rendering of nearly every line. I learned from him on each occasion on which I consulted him. It is a splendid piece of work. As to the translation of verses of Scripture, I took an eclectic approach, sometimes copying Freedman's, sometimes relying on the fine English of the RSV, and sometimes making up my own translation.

My principal interest in the present text, by contrast, focuses upon the authors' or compositors' recurrent points of polemic. I take for granted that where there are problems in the meanings of words and phrases, Freedman and the commentators whom he follows have given us as likely an account of the sense of a passage as we are apt to have. What I wish to display here is how the people who made the document as we know it made an important statement through both what they presented and how they presented it. This anthology draws from the entirety of Genesis Rabbah to demonstrate the recurrence of specific points, the presence of an encompassing and fundamental system: a world-view, expressed in a concrete way of life, addressed to the people, Israel -- a Judaism. So I wish here to show the Judaism of Genesis Rabbah. In Protestant and Catholic circles what I propose here would be called "a theology of Genesis Rabbah," though in the present context theology claims more order and system than I allege we find in Genesis Rabbah.

Whose Judaism do we describe? That is to say, precisely who speaks to us here? Genesis Rabbah is a composite document, as I said, generally regarded as the work of compilers of the period ca. A.D. 400. Much of the material in the compilation, however, can be shown to have been put together before that material was used for the purposes of the late fourth century compilers. Many times we shall see, for example, that a comment entirely apposite to a verse of Genesis has been joined to a set of comments in no way pertinent to the verse of Genesis at hand. Proof for a given syllogism, furthermore, will derive from a verse of Genesis as well as from verses of other books of the Bible. Such a syllogistic argument therefore has not been written for exegetical purposes particular to the verse at hand. The ones who selected that completed composition made the decision of what to include. Hence they are the ones who speak through their selection. We find in the work of redaction, and only in that aspect of the text before us, our point of entry into the mind and imagination of the compositors of Genesis Rabbah. So if we want to know about the mind and imagination of fourth-century rabbis in the Land of Israel, we have to pay close attention to what the sages at hand have selected, to how they have arranged the document at hand, and to the points of stress and emphasis they repeatedly locate in the verses that are subject to their explanation.

Here therefore we venture into the inner life, the world-view, of Israel's sages in the Land of Israel in a critical age. For at the time at which our document reached closure, the Roman empire in general, and the Land of Israel in particular, went from pagan to Christian rule. The political situation of the Jews and of the Judaism presented by the sages of the document at hand and of the canon of which it forms a part radically changed. Now we see how Israel's sages proposed to read the book of Genesis for purposes important in their circumstance and context. When we know the answer to that question, we may gain entry into the way in which the sages at hand thought about, and responded to, the world in which they lived. And understanding how they read Scripture as a statement in particular to them and their age, we gain access, also, to Scripture as a statement to us and ours.

I have provided the document at hand with a complete system for identifying its smallest whole components of thought. I have made it possible to identify and classify those minima -- the bits and pieces of evidence. Let me briefly explain the reference-system. It is quite simple. I have labeled each sentence, paragraph, and larger composite, so as to facilitate ready reference to the entire document. The first Roman numeral refers to the *parashah*, or chapter; the second, to the paragraph of the *parashah*. These two matters are already signified in the printed text and in Freedman's translation. Many of the so-called paragraphs in fact are made up of two or more complete and autonomous thoughts. In my use of an Arabic numeral after the Roman, I indicate the divisions within paragraphs as I propose to differentiate them. I then indicate, by a letter, each individual stich, that is, the smallest whole unit of thought. Thus I:I.1.A stands for the first parashah, the first paragraph of the first *parashah*, the first complete composition of the first paragraph of the first *parashah*, and the first sentence of the first complete composition of the first paragraph of the first *parashah* -- and so on.

To conclude: the interest and importance of their reading of Genesis transcend the age in which the sages did their work. For how the great Judaic sages of that time taught the interpretation of the stories of Genesis would guide later Judaic exegetes of the same biblical book. So when we follow the work before us, we gain entry into the way in which Judaism in its normative and classical form, from that day to this, would understand the stories of the creation of the world. These concern Adam's sin, Noah, and, especially, the founding family of Israel, in its first three generations, Abraham, Isaac, and Jacob, as well as Joseph. In an age in which the book of Genesis attracts remarkable interest and in which a literal mode of reading enjoys the authority of true religion, the supple and creative approach of the ancient rabbis, founders of Judaism, provides a valuable alternative. The sages show the profound depths of the story of the creation of the world and Israel's founding family. How so? They systematically the history of the people Israel to the lives and deeds of the founders, the fathers and the mothers of this book of the Torah.

Once we have read Genesis the way "our sages of blessed memory" teach us to, we gain the freedom to follow our imagination as they arouse it. We no longer need to deal with those who claim to dictate how in what they deem a literal and fundamental sense we must receive the story of the creation of the world and of Israel. What to some proves fundamental to us, having heard the story as the third and fourth century sages of Israel retell it, appears shallow.

What these sages find in the text opens our minds to possibilities beyond imagining.

Let me close with a personal word. As I carefully translated the work at hand, I found myself gripped by the stories of Genesis as though I had never heard them. On occasion I came near tears. So in hand is no mere record of ideas held long ago. Here I find myself as a Jew. My hope is that for today I make help possible for Christians and Jews alike to see themselves as another sees them, specifically, as God, in the understanding of the sages of Judaism, in Genesis sees them: "in our image, after our likeness." What can that possibly mean, in the beginning? In the pages that follow, I propose to report the answer of Judaism, as its original statement spelled matters out.

Jacob Neusner

Program in Judaic Studies
Brown University
Providence, Rhode Island U.S.A.

March 4, 1986
Suzanne's forty-fifth birthday: onward to 120!

Introduction

1. Method and Message: How the Sages Read the Book of Genesis, What They Found There

Once we understand the method that tells the sages how to approach a verse or a story, we know how they derive meaning from the message of the Torah. So the proper route directs us first to the literary-critical question: exactly what does a sage see when he looks at a verse of Scripture? Only then shall we turn to questions of meaning, that is, sages' results in the explanation and amplification of a text. The fundamental method of sages is simple and familiar: they persistently see one thing in terms of another thing, one story in the light of another.

By method I mean a very simple thing: what tells a sage to ask one sort of question, rather than some other? How does a sage know what to look for? What will strike the sage as noteworthy? For example, a sage may want to know about the connection between one story and some other story, because the sage takes for granted that stories form a connected narrative and so relate to one another. So one point of method will be the sages' interest in tying tightly the threads of narrative and the strands of a story.

To take another, more telling example, the sage takes for granted that Scripture speaks to the life and condition of Israel, the Jewish people. God repeatedly says exactly that to Abraham and to Jacob. The entire narrative of Genesis is so formed as to point toward the sacred history of Israel, the Jewish people: its slavery and redemption; its coming Temple in Jerusalem; its exile and salvation at the end of time. The powerful message of Genesis proclaims that the world's creation commenced a single, straight line of events, leading in the end to the salvation of Israel and through Israel all humanity. Therefore a given story will bear a deeper message about what it means to be Israel, on the one side, and what in the end of days will happen to Israel, on the other. So another point of method will be the sages' persistent search in Scripture for meaning for their own circumstance and for the condition of their people.

Now these two points of persistent methodological concern, seeing one thing in terms of something else, exemplified, first, in the narrative, second, in the substantive meaning of what is narrated for Israel's coming redemption, will help us understand how the sages of Genesis Rabbah received and read the book of Genesis. But these points prove important, not merely illuminating, when we realize that the sages who are our teachers in our effort to read the book of

Genesis also set the pattern and defined the model for generations to come. For Judaism the sages at hand presented the definitive response to the book of Genesis: this then is how Judaism reads the story of humanity.

So when we understand how the sages of Genesis Rabbah read the book of Genesis, we also learn what is right and proper for us to do when we take up that same fundamental document of the Torah.

The negative result? We are not bound to read the book of Genesis as a tale of things that happened long ago -- or that never happened. Nor is the book of Genesis to remain merely a source for the study of ancient Semitic philology or long-dead Israelite history. The scholars of Semitics and history have had their say on this book. Now let us listen to the believing Jews who revered the book and found in it God's message.

The positive? We are free, as they were free, to bring to Scripture a free and open imagination, a tormented and troubled spirit, the concerns of an age of trial and tribulation.

Once we realize that in Judaism as defined by the sages before us Scripture, that is, the Torah, addresses the living, we confront the living word of God to us, here and now, just as they did, and for the same reason.

So how may we define the basic problem as to method? It is to see how many layers of meaning the sages penetrate, on the one side, and to describe the types of meanings they uncover, on the other.

Ours are two tasks. First, to discover for ourselves some of the methods that tell them how to read the book of Genesis. Second, to determine the basic message they wish us to derive from the encounter with the text. If we succeed in this work, we shall endow ourselves with the freedom to read the book of Genesis as they did: in a way we find relevant to the world we know, but also we know congruent to the will of the Torah's source and authority.

2. One Tale, Many Meanings

A quartet in an opera joins four voices, each telling its own singular story, into a harmony, so that, at one moment a diversity of messages forms a single song. If I had to specify the dominant method of scriptural understanding revealed by the sages of Genesis Rabbah, it is the power to hear Scripture's harmonic music, to perceive each of its distinct melodic lines, all at once, all together, and all in deep union of ultimate meaning. The one important, exemplary fact of Scriptural interpretation we learn from the sages at hand is to permit the Torah to tell us all that it wishes, saying many things by the act of speaking a single word.

It is one thing to say so in the abstract. It is quite another to provide a concrete example of how the sages hear much in little. For that purpose, I present a passage in which the sages face a simple task. It is how to find meaning in a story of merely domestic consequence.

We recall that, square in the middle of the tale of Joseph and his brothers, in Genesis 38, is intruded a story of how Judah, one of Joseph's brothers, got himself involved with a woman whom he thought was a prostitute but who turned out to be his daughter-in-law. How shall we read what is to follow? We begin with the literary convention at hand. Sages love to juxtapose two seemingly unrelated verses of Scripture and to show how one illuminates the other. The problem will be the explanation of what I call "the base verse," that is, the verse that demands unpacking. Then the verse intended to open up the matter, which I call "the intersecting verse," will be quoted, and the meaning of the two verses brought into collision will be spelled out, ordinarily only by implication.

The interpretation of our story begins with a statement quoted at the outset of the passage to follow. Then the exegete cites another verse, unrelated to the former. This other verse will open up the interpretation of the tale at hand. Why do I call the verse under examination" the base verse"? Because it is the foundation for all that follows. Then comes the second verse, the one drawn from some other passage of Scripture entirely, which I call, as I said, "the intersecting verse," meaning, the verse that will serve to intersect with, and to open up, the base-verse.

LXXXV:I.

1. A. "It happened at that time that Judah went down from his brothers [and turned in to a certain Adullamite, whose name was Hirah. There Judah saw the daughter of a certain Canaanite, whose name was Shua; he married her and went in to her]" (Gen. 38:1):

    B. "Judah has done treacherously [and an abomination is committed in Israel...for Judah has profaned the holiness of the Lord which he loves and has married the daughter of a strange god]" (Mal. 2:11).

    C. [God] said to [Judah], "You have denied, Judah, you have lied, Judah."

    D. "...and an abomination is committed in Israel...for Judah has profaned," which is to say, Judah has become unconsecrated.

    E. "...the holiness of the Lord which he loves and has married the daughter of a strange god."

    F. "It happened at that time that Judah went down from his brothers [and turned in to a certain Adullamite, whose name was Hirah. There Judah saw the daughter of a certain Canaanite, whose name was Shua; he married her and went in to her]."

2. A. "I will yet bring to you, O inhabitant of Mareshah, him who shall possess you, the glory of Israel shall come even to Adullam" (Mic. 1:15).

    B. The reference is to the Holy One of Israel.

    C. "...to Adullam shall come" the King of Israel.

    D. "To Adullam he shall come:" "It happened at that time that Judah went down from his brothers and turned in to a certain Adullamite, whose name was

Hirah. There Judah saw the daughter of a certain Canaanite, whose name was Shua; he married her and went in to her."

3. A. R. Samuel bar Nahman commenced discourse by citing this verse: "'For I know the thoughts that I think toward you, says the Lord' (Jer. 29:11).

B. "While the fathers of the tribes were taken up with the sale of Joseph, Jacob was taken up with his sackcloth and fasting, and Judah was taken up with finding himself a wife, and the Holy One, blessed be he, was creating the light of the king messiah.

C. "'It happened at that time that Judah went down from his brothers [and turned in to a certain Adullamite, whose name was Hirah. There Judah saw the daughter of a certain Canaanite, whose name was Shua; he married her and went in to her].'"

4. A. "Before she travailed she brought forth" (Is., 66:7):

B. Before the final persecutor was born, the first redeemer was born:

C. "It happened at that time that Judah went down from his brothers [and turned in to a certain Adullamite, whose name was Hirah. There Judah saw the daughter of a certain Canaanite, whose name was Shua; he married her and went in to her]."

The interest of the exegete, No. 1, in the statement that Judah went down from his brothers, becoming less than they, is that he did so by marrying a Canaanite woman. So his first point is that people who marry Canaanite women lower themselves. No. 2 then follows up with attention on the place mentioned in the base verse. No. 3 draws the ironic contrasts among the activities of the heroes of the narrative. Here is where the analogy to the operatic quartet becomes apt. The Messianic theme derives from the fact that the offspring of Judah and Tamar would be the messiah. No. 4 goes over the same ground. Obviously, the linkage of the lives of the patriarchs to the history of Israel accounts for the point of special interest to the exegete. In some ways, as I said, we have the equivalent of an operatic quartet, in which each character sings about a single strand of the drama, and in which all the strands form a whole greater than the sum of the parts. The messianic theme will now infuse all to follow, with contrasts and comparisons outlining the tragedy and the triumph of Israel.

To return to the point at which we began, the one striking fact before us is how many layers of meaning the sage's eye discerns. Any claim that the text at hand bears only a single sense and significance must give way to the sage's insistence to the contrary. So the first principle of the sages' way of reading Genesis dictates that none can impose limits. That is not to say whatever we wish to find there will be there. It is only to force open -- for all time, I think -- the boundaries of meaning, to insist we read a many-splendored story.

3. Explaining Connections

If sages find diverse layers and levels of meaning, we wonder where they start. The question carries with it a second: do we make things up as we go along, or are there correct, therefore also incorrect, ways of proceeding?

The answer begins to emerge when we consider systematic and recurrent ways of addressing a given tale or verse. Once we discern patterns of explanation and amplification, we also may define the rules that guide sages in explaining and amplifying a story or saying. For, working back, the pattern reveals the rule. And the presence of rules assures us that there is a right way, therefore also a wrong way, of doing things. But the right way, I insist, turns out to be a way meant to open possibilities, to stimulate our imagination, above all to encourage us to find ourselves in the Torah, and the Torah in ourselves.

The following extended passage illustrates a systematic and, in my mind, quite reasonable approach to explaining the book of Genesis. It requires us to ask, at each point, where we stand in the unfolding of the whole. Specifically, we place a given story into its larger narrative context. This we do by taking note of what comes first and what follows, how a given story relates to what has gone before.

LXXXV:II.

1. A. What is written prior to this passage?

B. "Meanwhile the Midianites had sold him in Egypt to Potiphar, an officer of Pharaoh, the captain of the guard" (Gen. 37:36), followed by: "It happened at that time that Judah went down from his brothers [and turned in to a certain Adullamite, whose name was Hirah. There Judah saw the daughter of a certain Canaanite, whose name was Shua; he married her and went in to her (Gen. 38:1)]."

C. The Scripture needed only to state, "And Joseph was brought down to Egypt" (Gen. 39:1).

D. R. Eleazar said, "It introduced this long digression about Judah so as to juxtapose a passage that deals with a fall from glory to another passage that deals with a fall from glory."

E. R. Yohanan, "The passage was introduced so as to juxtapose one statement concerning, 'discernment' to another such statement." [Cf. LXXXIV:XIX.3.B: Said R. Yohanan, "Said the Holy One, blessed be he, to Judah, 'You have said to your father, "...see now." By your life, you will hear the words, ""...see now, whose are these..." (Gen. 38:25).'"]

F. R. Samuel bar Nahman said, "So as to juxtapose the tale of Tamar to the tale of the wife of Potiphar. Just as the one was truly for the sake of Heaven, so the other was truly for the sake of Heaven."

G. For R. Joshua b. Levi said, "She foresaw through her horoscope that she was destined to produce a son with him, but she did not know whether it was from her or from her daughter. That is in line with this verse: 'Let now the monthly prognosticators stand up and save you from some of the things that will come upon you' (Is. 47:13)."

H. On this matter said R. Abin, "'From some...,' but not from all."

2 . A. Along these same lines: "And they were not ashamed" (Gen. 2A:25). "But the snake was more subtle [than any other wild creature that the Lord God had made]" (Gen. 3:1).

B. It would have been quite sufficient for Scripture to say: "And the Lord God made for the man and his wife garments of skin" (Gen. 3:21), [since this was done prior to the sin, and not afterward, so that statement should have appeared right after Gen. 2:25, rather than the verse that comes as Gen. 3:1, cited above].

C. Said R. Joshua b. Qorha, "It serves to let you know the sin that that wicked [creature] had got them to do. When he saw that they were having sexual relations, and he lusted after [the woman], [he tried to kill Adam by getting him to sin]."

D. Said R. Jacob of Kefar Hanan, "[The presentation of that detail] was postponed to that latter passage so as not to conclude the story of the creation of man with the matter of the snake. [So that detail was introduced only at the end of the narrative.]"

3 . A. Along these same lines: "And those who walk in pride he is able to abase" (Dan. 4:34), followed by, "Belshazzar, the king, made a great feast" (Dan. 5:1).

B. What happened to Evil-Merodach?

C. R. Eleazar said, "It was so as to juxtapose the story of one wicked person to the story of another wicked person, one destroyer with another, one man puffed up with pride with another."

D. R. Samuel bar Nahman said, "It is so as to juxtapose the conclusion of one dominion with the conclusion of another dominion."

4 . A. Along these same lines: "In that night Belshazzar, the Chaldean king, was slain" (Dan. 5:30). "And Darius the Mede received the kingdom" (Dan. 6:1).

B. What about, "In the third year of the reign of king Belshazzar" (Dan. 8:1)?

C. R. Huna in the name of R. Aha: "It was so that people should not say that the story was mere poetry, so that people should know that everything had been stated by the Holy Spirit."

D. Rabbis say, "It was so that the whole of the Book of Daniel would be treated as stated by the Holy Spirit."

5 . A. "It happened at that time that Judah went down from his brothers" (Gen. 38:1):

B. They said, "Come, let's scatter, for so long as we are gathered together, the bond of debt [for what we have done] is waiting to be collected."

C. Said the Holy One, blessed be he, to them, "If ten men are implicated in an act of theft, cannot one of them be seized in behalf of all of them?"

D. When they were found out in the matter of the silver cup, they said, "God has found out the iniquity of your servants" (Gen. 44:16).

E. Said R. Isaac, "The creditor has found the occasion to collect the bond of debt that is owing to him."

F. Said R. Levi, "It is comparable to one who overturns a barrel of wine, leaving only the lees." [Freedman, p. 790, n. 3: "God is punishing us to the last drop."]

6. A. ["It happened at that time that Judah went down from his brothers" (Gen. 38:1)]: They said, "Come, let's take charge of our own affairs [and find wives for ourselves].

B. "In the past, Jacob was obligated to marry us off to wives, but now that he is taken up with his sackcloth and fasting, it is not likely that he is going to find women for wives for us."

C. They said to Judah, "And is he not the head of us? Go and take care of yourself." Forthwith: "It happened at that time that Judah went down from his brothers" (Gen. 38:1).

No. 1 asks and answers a question we should now call "redaction-criticism." Why the stories are juxtaposed produces a number of interesting lessons, beginning with the moral comment on the descent of the brothers and of Judah, then the comparison of Tamar and Potiphar's wife, since Joseph married her daughter. Then at Nos. 2, 3, and 4 we have further examples of the same mode of thought. The entire construction then appeals to the passage before us as part of its larger rhetorical inquiry. Nos. 5, 6 introduce an interesting question. Why did Judah depart from his brothers? No. 5 gives one answer, No. 6 another. The former answer is that the brothers thought they could avoid punishment by scattering. The latter is more in consonance with the story to come. Both of them add a deep dimension to the text, by drawing together its fragments.

XCV:I.

1. A. "He sent Judah before him to Joseph, to appear before him in Goshen, and they came into the land of Goshen" (Gen. 46:28):

B. "The wolf and the lamb shall feed together" (Is. 65:25).

C. Come and see how every wound that the Holy One, blessed be he, inflicts in this world he heals in the age to come. [At issue is the following intersecting verse: "Then the eyes of the blind shall be opened, then shall the lame man leap as a hart, and the tongue of the dumb shall sing" (Is. 35:5).]

D. The blind are healed: "Then the eyes of the blind shall be opened."

E. The lame are healed: "...then shall the lame man leap as a hart."

F. The dumb are healed: "...and the tongue of the dumb shall sing."

G. All are healed, but just as a person goes out, so he comes back to life.

H. If he goes out blind, he comes back blind, if he goes out deaf, he comes back deaf, if he goes out dumb, he comes back dumb, if he goes out lame, he comes back lame.

I. Just as he is garbed when he goes out, so he is garbed when he comes back: "It is changed as clay under the seal, and they stand as in a garment" (Job 38:14).

J. From whom do you learn that lesson? It is from Samuel the Ramathite. When Saul brought him up, what did he say to the woman? "'What form is he of?' And she said, 'An old man comes up, and he is covered with a robe'" (1Sam. 28:14).

K. For that is what he had been wearing: "Moreover his mother made him a little robe" (1 Sam. 2:19).

L. And why is it the case that just as a person goes out, so he comes back to life?

M. It is so that the wicked of the world will not claim that, after they have died the Holy One, blessed be he, will heal them and afterward bring them back to life. It then would appear that these are not the ones who died, but others.

N. Accordingly, the Holy One, blessed be he, says, "If so, let them rise up out of the dust just as they went, and afterward I shall heal them."

O. Why so? "That you may know that...before me there was no God formed, neither shall any be after me" (Is. 43:10).

P. And afterward even the wild beasts are healed, as it is said, "The wolf and the lamb shall feed together." All are healed.

Q. But the one who brought [the ultimate] injury [of death] on all will not be healed: "And dust shall be the serpent's food" (Is. 45:28).

R. Why? Because he brought all of life down to the dust.

2. A. Another interpretation of the verse: "The wolf and the lamb shall feed together, the lion like the ox shall eat straw" (Is. 65:25):

B. "The wolf:" this refers to Benjamin: "Benjamin is a wolf that tears at prey" (Gen. 49:27).

C. "...and the lamb:" this speaks of the tribal fathers: "Israel is a scattered sheep" (Jer. 50:17).

D. "...shall feed together:" When is this the case? When Benjamin went down with them.

E. Jacob said to them, "My son shall not go down with you" (Gen. 42:38).

F. But when the time came and they went down, and Benjamin went down with them, they watched over him and kept good care of him.

G. So it says with regard to Joseph, "And he lifted up his eyes and saw his brother Benjamin...and said, 'God be gracious to you...'" (Gen. 43:29).

H. "...the lion:" this refers to Judah: "Judah is a lion's whelp" (Gen. 49:9).

I. "...like the ox:" "this speaks of Joseph: "And of Joseph he said..., 'His beauty is that of his firstling bullock'" (Deut. 33:13, 17).

J. They turned out to eat together: "And they sat before him, the firstborn according to his birthright and the youngest according to his youth...portions were taken to them..." (Gen. 43:33-34).

J. "and the lion like the ox shall eat straw:" therefore: "He sent Judah before him to Joseph, to appear before him in Goshen, and they came into the land of Goshen" (Gen. 46:28).

We note the persistence of a single question: how does this story relate to its larger context? But the question of context proves somewhat more complex than mere narrative considerations suggest. For the deeper foundations of all stories carry us into the profound question of salvation. The quest for context demands that we ask how a given story relates to the larger tale of how Israel is saved. So the rule at hand -- pay attention to what comes before and what follows afterward -- reflects a deep theology of Israel's history.

What makes this construction striking, therefore, is its focus on the eschatological meaning of the story at hand, which now gains yet a deeper dimension. If we start with No. 2, as the form requires us to do, we find that the intersecting verse, Is. 65:25, is made to refer to the tribal progenitors. Then the story at hand, involving the reunion and reconciliation of the tribes, finds its reference-point in the end of days. The message of No. 2 draws us back to No. 1, and here the vision of the eschatological moment comes to full expression. All will be healed, the blind, deaf, dumb, but all return as they had been. That point of emphasis in No. 1 imparts its sense on No. 2. In the coming age Israel will be restored to life as it had been before, but then God will heal Israel.

The art of the composition demands that the whole be read as a single statement, a single judgment upon Israel in the world to come: pretty much like Israel now, only to be healed. Then the theme, the reconciliation and unification of Israel, finds its moment of realization in the age to come, a rather wry comment on the present state of affairs. It would be difficult to find a better example of the rereading of the scriptural narrative through the prism of a deeper perspective.

4. The Founders as Paradigms

If I had to point to the single most important proposition of Genesis Rabbah, it is that, in the story of the beginnings of creation, humanity, and Israel, we find the message of the meaning and end of the life of the Jewish people. The deeds of the founders supply signals for the children about what is going to come in the future. So the biography of Abraham, Isaac, and Jacob also constitutes the history of Israel later on. If the sages could announce a single syllogism and argue it systematically, that is the proposition on which they would insist. The sages understood that stories about the progenitors, presented in the book of Genesis, define the human condition and proper conduct for their children, Israel in time to come. Accordingly, they systematically asked Scripture to tell them how they were supposed to conduct themselves at the critical turnings of life. One example of this commonplace pattern of interpretation -- the human and existential -- brings us to the way in which the founders of Israel taught the lesson of how to die, the human meaning of death.

XCVI:II.

1.   A.   "And when the time drew near that Israel must die, [he called his son Joseph and said to him, 'If now I have found favor in your sight, put your hand under my thigh and promise to deal loyally and truly with me. Do not bury me in Egypt, but let me lie with my fathers; carry me out of Egypt and bury me in their burying place.' He answered, I will do as you have said.' And he said, 'Swear to me.' And he swore to him. Then Israel bowed himself upon the head of his bed]" (Gen. 47:29-31):

B.   "For we are strangers before you and sojourners as all our fathers were, our days on the earth are as a shadow [and there is no hoping]" (1 Chr. 29:15).

C.   Would that it might be like the shadow of a wall or like the shadow of a tree, but it is like the shadow of a bird.

D. So it is written, "His days are as a shadow that passes away" (Ps. 144:4).

E. "...our days on the earth are as a shadow and there is no hoping" (1 Chr. 29:15):

F., No one can hope that he will not die. Everyone knows and states explicitly that they will die.

G. Abraham said, "Seeing that I go [from the world] childless" (Gen. 15:2).

H. Isaac: "That my soul may bless you before I die" (Gen. 27:"4).

I. Jacob: "...but let me lie with my fathers."

J. When did he say this? When he was going to die:

K. "And when the time drew near that Israel must die."

The intersecting verse simply underlines the reality of the situation and notes that all of the patriarchs recognized that they were going to die.

XCVI:III.

1. A. "And when the time drew near that Israel must die, [he called his son Joseph and said to him, 'If now I have found favor in your sight, put your hand under my thigh and promise to deal loyally and truly with me. Do not bury me in Egypt, but let me lie with my fathers; carry me out of Egypt and bury me in their burying place.' He answered, I will do as you have said.' And he said, 'Swear to me.' And he swore to him. Then Israel bowed himself upon the head of his bed]" (Gen. 47:29-31):

B. "There is no man that has power of the spirit...neither is there dominion in the day of death" (Qoh. 8:8).

C. Said R. Joshua of Sikhnin in the name of R. Levi, "As to the trumpets that Moses made in the wilderness, when Moses lay on the point of death, the Holy One, blessed be he, hid them away, so that he would not blow on them and summon the people to him.

D. "This was meant to fulfill this verse: '...neither is there dominion in the day of death' (Qoh. 8:8).

E. "When Zimri did his deed, what is written? 'And Phineas went after the man of Israel into the chamber' (Num. 25:8). So where was Moses, that Phineas should speak before he did?

F. "'...neither is there dominion in the day of death' (Qoh. 8:8).

G. "But the formulation expresses humiliation. Salvation was handed over to Phineas, [and Moses] abased himself.

H. "So too with David: 'How king David was old' (1 Kgs. 1:1). What is stated about him when he lay dying? 'Now the days of David drew near, that he should die' (1 Kgs. 21:1).

I. "What is said is not 'king David,' but merely 'David.'

J. "The same applies to Jacob, when he was on the point of death, he humbled himself to Joseph, saying to him, 'If now I have found favor in your sight.' [So he abased himself, since there is no dominion on the day of death.]

K. "When did this take place? As he drew near the end: 'And when the time drew near that Israel must die.'"

What strikes the exegete is the unprepossessing language used by Jacob in speaking to Joseph. The intersecting verse makes clear that, on the day of one's death, one no longer rules. Several examples of that fact are given, Moses, David, finally Jacob. So the syllogism about the loss of power on the occasion of death derives proof from a number of sources, and the passage has not been worked out to provide the exegesis of our base verse in particular. The exposition is all the more moving because the exegete focuses upon his proposition, rather than on the great personalities at hand. His message obviously is that even the greatest lose all dominion when they are going to die. In this way the deeds of the founders define the rule for the descendants.

5. The Genesis of Israel's Holy Way of Life

As a corollary to the view that the biography of the fathers prefigures the history of the descendants, sages maintained that the deeds of the children -- the holy way of life of Israel -- follow the model established by the founders long ago. So they looked in Genesis for the basis for the things they held to be God's will for Israel. And they found ample proof.

Sages invariably searched the stories of Genesis for evidence of the origins not only of creation and of Israel, but also of Israel's cosmic way of life, its understanding of how, in the passage of nature and the seasons, humanity worked out its relationship with God. The holy way of life that Israel lived through the seasons of nature therefore would make its mark upon the stories of the creation of the world and the beginning of Israel

Part of the reason sages pursued the interest at hand derived from polemic. From the first Christian century theologians of Christianity maintained that salvation did not depend upon keeping the laws of the torah. Abraham, after all, had been justified and he did not keep the Torah, which, in his day, had not yet been given. So sages time and again would maintain that Abraham indeed kept the entire Torah even before it had been revealed. They further attributed to Abraham, Isaac, and Jacob rules of the torah enunciated only later on, for example, the institution of prayer three times a day. But the passage before us bears a different charge. It is to Israel to see how deeply embedded in the rules of reality were the patterns governing God's relationship to Israel.   That relationship, one of human sin and atonement, divine punishment and forgiveness, expresses the most fundamental laws of human existence. Here is yet another rule that tells sages what to find in Scripture.

XCVIII:I.

1. A. "Then Jacob called his sons [and said, 'Gather yourselves together, that I may tell you what shall befall you in days to come. Assemble and hear, O sons of Jacob, and hearken to Israel, your father. Reuben, you are my first-born, my might and the first fruits of my strength, pre-eminent in pride and pre-eminent in power. Unstable as water, you shall not have pre-eminence, because you

went up to your father's bed, then you defiled it, you went up to my couch!']"
(Gen. 49:1-4):

  B. "I will cry to God Most High, [unto God who completes it for me]" (Ps.
57:3):

  C. "I will cry to God Most High:" on the New Year.

  D. "...unto God who completes it for me:" on the Day of Atonement.

  E. To find out which [goat] is for the Lord and which one is for an evil
decree.

2. A. Another matter:"I will cry to God Most High, [unto God who completes it
for me]" (Ps. 57:3):

  B "I will cry to God Most High:" refers to our father, Jacob.

  C. "...unto God who completes it for me:" for the Holy One, blessed be he,
concurred with him to give each of the sons a blessing in accord with his
character.

  D. "Then Jacob called his sons [and said, 'Gather yourselves together, that I
may tell you what shall befall you in days to come]."

The intersecting verse invites the comparison of the judgment of the Days
of Awe to the blessing of Jacob, and that presents a dimension of meaning that
the narrative would not otherwise reveal. Just as God decides which goat serves
what purpose, so God concurs in Jacob's judgment of which son/tribe deserves
what sort of blessing. So Jacob stands in the stead of God in this stunning
comparison of Jacob's blessing to the day of judgment. The link between
Jacob's biography and the holy life of Israel is fresh.

6. A Theology of Hope

What, then, tells sages how to identify the important and avoid the trivial?
The answer derives from the fundamental theological conviction that gives life to
their search of Scripture. It is that the task of Israel is to hope, and the message
of Genesis -- there for the sages to uncover and make explicit -- is always to
hope. For a Jew it is a sin to despair. This I think defines the iron law of
meaning, telling sages what matters and what does not, guiding their hands to
take up those verses that permit expression of hope -- that above all. Given the
definitive event of their day -- the conversion of the great empire of rome to
Christianity -- the task of hope proved not an easy assignment.

XCVIII:XIV.

4. A. "I hope for your salvation, O Lord" (Gen. 49:18):

  B. Said R. Isaac, "All things depend on hope, suffering depends on hope, the
sanctification of God's name depends on hope, the merit attained by the fathers
depends on hope, the lust for the age to come depends on hope.

  C. "That is in line with this verse: 'Yes, in the way of your judgments, O
Lord, we have hoped for you, to your name, and to your memorial, is the desire
of our soul' (Is. 26:8). The way of your judgments refers to suffering.

  D. "'...to your name:' this refers to the sanctification of the divine name.

E. "'...and to your memorial:' this refers to the merit of the fathers.

F. "'...is the desire of our soul:' this refers to the lust for the age to come.

G. "Grace depends on hope: 'O Lord, be gracious to us, we have hoped for you' (Is. 33:2).

H. "Forgiveness depends on hope: 'For with you is forgiveness' (Ps. 133:4), then: 'I hope for the Lord' (Ps. 130:5)."

The interesting unit is No. 4, which is explicit on the critical importance of hope in the salvific process, and which further links the exclamation to the setting in which it occurs. This seems to me to typify the strength of the exegesis at hand, with its twin-powers to link all details to a tight narrative and to link the narrative to the history of Israel.

7. Conclusion

We have travelled a long way from our original observation. We began by noting that sages heard much in little, took account of juxtapositions, introduced one verse to illuminate another. So at the outset we dealt with mainly literary matters. But as we proceeded, we realized that these traits of literary-critical character express both attitudes and convictions of a theological nature. So we could not remain entirely within the issue of method, narrowly defined as literary in character. Why not? Because method contains substance, contents dictate context, as much as method yields substance and context imparts meaning and significance to what is said. Still, we realize at the outset that, as we follow the exposition of the book of Genesis by the ancient sages of Judaism, the issue in no way rests on such simple matters as the technicalities of word-choice or of stylistic peculiarities. In other words, we deal with religious minds seeking religious truth. It is Judaism that lays down its judgment upon Genesis, and Genesis Rabbah declares in rich detail precisely the nature of that judgment.

Part One

THE JUDAISM OF GENESIS RABBAH:
A SYSTEMIC STATEMENT

Chapter One

The Judaism of Genesis Rabbah

The word "Judaism" would surely have presented a puzzle to the sages of Genesis Rabbah. But if we were to ask them to express, in some cogent way, the basic and systematic world-view and way of life that were theirs, they surely had suitable means for formulating their reply. And that would constitute their Judaism. What would they do? They would propose to see everything in some one thing. Specifically they would find the principal motifs and concerns of their world-view in a single passage. This mode of organizing and expressing ideas, so different from our own more abstract and philosophical one, served them well. Putting everything together in one thing allowed them to impute to Scripture, hence to God's revelation to Moses, all of the most important dimensions of their social world. Or, to turn matters around, if we survey the repertoire of issues and ideas they discovered in a given verse, we find, on an occasion such as the following, a quite systematic and well-composed statement of pretty much everything of consequence.

LXX:VIII.

2.   A.   "Then Jacob lifted up his eyes. As he looked, he saw a well in the field" (Gen. 29:1):

B.   R. Hama bar Hanina interpreted the verse in six ways [that is, he divides the verse into six clauses and systematically reads each of the clauses in light of the others and in line with an overriding theme, of which there are six in all]:

C.   "'As he looked, he saw a well in the field:' this refers to the well [of water in the wilderness, Num. 21:17].

D.   "'...and lo, three flocks of sheep lying beside it:' specifically, Moses, Aaron, and Miriam.

E.   "'...for out of that well the flocks were watered:' from from there each one drew water for his standard, tribe, and family."

F.   "And the stone upon the well's mouth was great:"

G.   Said R. Hanina, "It was only the size of a little sieve."

I.   [Reverting to Hama's statement:] "'...and put the stone back in its place upon the mouth of the well:' for the coming journeys. [Thus the first interpretation applies the passage at hand to the life of Israel in the wilderness.]

3.   A.   "'As he looked, he saw a well in the field:' refers to Zion.

B.   "'...and lo, three flocks of sheep lying beside it:' refers to the three festivals.

C. "'....for out of that well the flocks were watered:' from there they drank of the holy spirit.

D. "'...The stone on the well's mouth was large:' this refers to the rejoicing of the house of the water-drawing."

E. Said R. Hoshaiah, "Why is it called 'the house of the water drawing'? Because from there they drink of the Holy Spirit."

F. [Resuming Hama b. Hanina's discourse:] "'...and when all the flocks were gathered there:' coming from 'the entrance of Hamath to the brook of Egypt' (1 Kgs. 8:66).

G. "'...the shepherds would roll the stone from the mouth of the well and water the sheep:' for from there they would drink of the Holy Spirit.

H. "'...and put the stone back in its place upon the mouth of the well:' leaving it in place until the coming festival. [Thus the second interpretation reads the verse in light of the Temple celebration of the Festival of Tabernacles.]

4 . A. "'...As he looked, he saw a well in the field:' this refers to Zion.

B. "'...and lo, three flocks of sheep lying beside it:' this refers to the three courts, concerning which we have learned in the Mishnah: **There were three courts there, one at the gateway of the Temple mount, one at the gateway of the courtyard, and one in the chamber of the hewn stones [M. San. 11:2].**

C. "'...for out of that well the flocks were watered:' for from there they would hear the ruling.

D. "The stone on the well's mouth was large:' this refers to the high court that was in the chamber of the hewn stones.

E. "'...and when all the flocks were gathered there:' this refers to in the Land of Israel.

F. "'...the shepherds would roll the stone from the mouth of the well and water the sheep:' for from there they would hear the ruling.

G. "'...and put the stone back in its place upon the mouth of the well:' for they would give and take until they had produced the ruling in all the required clarity." [The third interpretation reads the verse in light of the Israelite institution of justice and administration.]

5 . A. "'As he looked, he saw a well in the field:' this refers to Zion.

B. "'...and lo, three flocks of sheep lying beside it:' this refers to the first three kingdoms [Babylonia, Media, Greece].

C. "'...for out of that well the flocks were watered:' for they enriched the treasures that were laid upon up in the chambers of the Temple.

D. "'...The stone on the well's mouth was large:' this refers to the merit attained by the patriarchs.

E. "'...and when all the flocks were gathered there:' this refers to the wicked kingdom, which collects troops through levies over all the nations of the world.

F. "'...the shepherds would roll the stone from the mouth of the well and water the sheep:' for they enriched the treasures that were laid upon up in the chambers of the Temple.

G. "'...and put the stone back in its place upon the mouth of the well:' in the age to come the merit attained by the patriarchs will stand [in defense of

Israel].' [So the fourth interpretation interweaves the themes of the Temple cult and the domination of the four monarchies.]

6. A. "'As he looked, he saw a well in the field:' this refers to the sanhedrin.

B. "'...and lo, three flocks of sheep lying beside it:' this alludes to the three rows of disciples of sages that would go into session in their presence.

C. "for out of that well the flocks were watered:' for from there they would listen to the ruling of the law.

D. "'...The stone on the well's mouth was large:' this refers to the most distinguished member of the court, who determines the law-decision.

E. "'...and when all the flocks were gathered there:' this refers to disciples of the sages in the Land of Israel.

F. "'...the shepherds would roll the stone from the mouth of the well and water the sheep:' for from there they would listen to the ruling of the law.

G. "'...and put the stone back in its place upon the mouth of the well:' for they would give and take until they had produced the ruling in all the required clarity." [The fifth interpretation again reads the verse in light of the Israelite institution of legal education and justice.]

7. A. "'As he looked, he saw a well in the field:' this refers to the synagogue.

B. "'...and lo, three flocks of sheep lying beside it:' this refers to the three who are called to the reading of the Torah on weekdays.

C. "'...for out of that well the flocks were watered:' for from there they hear the reading of the Torah.

D. "'...The stone on the well's mouth was large:' this refers to the impulse to do evil.

E. "'...and when all the flocks were gathered there:' this refers to the congregation.

F. "'...the shepherds would roll the stone from the mouth of the well and water the sheep:' for from there they hear the reading of the Torah.

G. "'...and put the stone back in its place upon the mouth of the well:' for once they go forth [from the hearing of the reading of the torah] the impulse to do evil reverts to its place." [The sixth and last interpretation turns to the twin themes of the reading of the Torah in the synagogue and the evil impulse, temporarily driven off through the hearing of the Torah.]

The six themes read in response to the verse cover (1) Israel in the wilderness, (2) the Temple cult on festivals with special reference to Tabernacles, (3) the judiciary and government, (4) the history of Israel under the four kingdoms, (5) the life of sages, and (6) the ordinary folk and the synagogue. The whole is an astonishing repertoire of fundamental themes of the life of the nation, Israel: at its origins in the wilderness, in its cult, in its institutions based on the cult, in the history of the nations, and, finally, in the twin social estates of sages and ordinary folk, matched by the institutions of the master-disciple circle and the synagogue. The vision of Jacob at the well thus encompassed the whole of the social reality of Jacob's people, Israel.

LXX:IX.

1. A. R. Yohanan interpreted the statement in terms of Sinai:

B. "'As he looked, he saw a well in the field:' this refers to Sinai.

C. "'...and lo, three flocks of sheep lying beside it:' these stand for the priests, Levites, and Israelites.

D. "'...for out of that well the flocks were watered:' for from there they heard the Ten Commandments.

E. "'...The stone on the well's mouth was large:' this refers to the Presence of God."

F. "...and when all the flocks were gathered there:"

G. R. Simeon b. Judah of Kefar Akum in the name of R. Simeon: "All of the flocks of Israel had to be present, for if any one of them had been lacking, they would not have been worthy of receiving the Torah."

H. [Returning to Yohanan's exposition:] "'...the shepherds would roll the stone from the mouth of the well and water the sheep:' for from there they heard the Ten Commandments.

I. "'...and put the stone back in its place upon the mouth of the well:' 'You yourselves have seen that I have talked with you from heaven' (Ex. 20:19)."

Yohanan's exposition adds what was left out, namely, reference to the revelation of the Torah at Sinai. In the passage before us, therefore, sages have succeeded in discovering in a rather homely image all of the deepest concerns of their world-view: Israel's history, institutions, beliefs, way of life -- everything in some one thing.

Chapter Two

The Doctrine of Merit

Sages opened the book of Genesis knowing as fact a number of propositions, which, they took for granted, affected the events and shaped the facts of the document at hand, as of all other components of the Torah. Among these, one unfamiliar, but exceedingly important fact was this. If something good happened to someone, the cause ordinarily derived from the merit that that person had attained, or that someone else, related to that person, had handed on. So if a woman became pregnant, always deemed the greatest blessing God could bestow, the immediate question is, on account of what sort of merit? or on account of whose merit? It could be her own or an ancestor's merit. But if something good happened, that demanded of the exegete an account of the cause. How then would one attain merit? That question finds its answer in stories explaining the matter of the source of merit, on the one side, and its beneficial result, on the other.

In the first example, Jacob reflects on the power that Esau's merit had gained for Esau. He had gained that merit by living in the land of Israel and also by paying honor and respect to Isaac. Jacob then feared that, because of the merit gained by Esau, he, Jacob, would not be able to overcome him. So merit worked on its own; it was a credit gained by proper action, which went to the credit of the person who had done that action.

LXXVI:II.

2. A. "Then Jacob was greatly afraid and distressed" (Gen. 32:7): [This is Jacob's soliloquy:] "Because of all those years that Esau was living in the Land of Israel, perhaps he may come against me with the power of the merit he has now attained by dwelling in the Land of Israel.

B. "Because of all those years of paying honor to his father, perhaps he may come against me with the power of the merit he attained by honoring his father.

C. "So he said: 'Let the days of mourning for my father be at hand, then I will slay my brother Jacob' (Gen. 27:41).

D. "Now the old man is dead."

E. Said R. Judah bar Simon, "This is what the Holy One, blessed he he, had said to him, 'Return to the land of your fathers and to your kindred' (Gen. 31:3). [Supplying a further soliloquy for Jacob:] 'Perhaps the stipulations [of protection by God] applied only up to this point [at which I enter the land].'"

Another important side of the conception of merit attributes to the ancestors that store of merit upon which the descendants draw. So the Israelites later on enjoy enormous merit through the deeds of the patriarchs and matriarchs. That conception comes to expression in what follows:

LXXVI:V.

2. A. "...for with only my staff I crossed this Jordan, and now I have become two companies:"

B. R. Judah bar Simon in the name of R. Yohanan: "In the Torah, in the Prophets, and in the Writings we find proof that the Israelites were able to cross the Jordan only on account of the merit achieved by Jacob:

C. "In the Torah: '...for with only my staff I crossed this Jordan, and now I have become two companies.'

D. "In the prophets: 'Then you shall let your children know, saying, "Israel came over this Jordan on dry land"' (Josh. 4:22), meaning our father, Israel.

E. "In the Writings: 'What ails you, O you sea, that you flee? You Jordan, that you burn backward? At the presence of the God of Jacob' (Ps. 114:5ff.)."

F. Said R. Levi, "There is a place, where [Freedman:] the Jordan falls with a roar into the hot springs of Tiberias.

G. "In his fear Jacob hid in there and locked Esau out. But the Holy One, blessed be he, dug a hole for him at another spot 'When you pass through the waters, I will be with you, and through the rivers, and they shall not overflow you, when you walk through the fire, you shall not be burned' (Is. 43:2)."

Merit deriving from the ancestors helped Jacob himself:

LXXVII:III.

3. A. "When the man saw that he did not prevail against Jacob, [he touched the hollow of his thigh, and Jacob's thigh was put out of joint as he wrestled with him]" (Gen. 32:25):

B. Said R. Hinena bar Isaac, "[God said to the angel,] 'He is coming against you with five "amulets" hung on his neck, that is, his own merit, the merit of his father and of his mother and of his grandfather and of his grandmother.

C. "'Check yourself out, can you stand up against even his own merit [let alone the merit of his parents and grandparents].'

D. "The matter may be compared to a king who had a savage dog and a tame lion. The king would take his son and sick him against the lion, and if the dog came to have a fight with the son, he would say to the dog, 'The lion cannot have a fight with him, are you going to make out in a fight with him?'

E. "So if the nations come to have a fight with Israel, the Holy One, blessed be he, says to them,. 'Your angelic prince could not stand up to Israel, and as to you, how much the more so!'"

Merit might project not only backward, deriving from an ancestor and serving a descendant, but forward as well. Thus Joseph accrued so much merit that the generations that came before him were credited with his merit:

LXXXIV:V.

2. **A.** "These are the generations of the family of Jacob. Joseph [being seventeen years old, was shepherding the flock with his brothers]" (Gen. 37:2):

B. These generations came along only on account of the merit of Joseph.

C. Did Jacob go to Laban for any reason other than for Rachel?

D. These generations thus waited until Joseph was born, in line with this verse: "And when Rachel had borne Joseph, Jacob said to Laban, 'Send me away'" (Gen. 30:215).

E. Who brought them down to Egypt? It was Joseph.

F. Who supported them in Egypt? It was Joseph.

G. The sea split open only on account of the merit of Joseph: "The waters saw you, O God" (Ps. 77:17). "You have with your arm redeemed your people, the sons of Jacob and Joseph" (Ps. 77:16).

H. R. Yudan said, "Also the Jordan was divided only on account of the merit of Joseph."

The passage at hand asks why only Joseph is mentioned as the family of Jacob. The inner polemic is that the merit of Jacob and Joseph would more than suffice to overcome Esau. Not only so, but Joseph survived because of the merit of his ancestors:

LXXXVII:VIII.

1. **A.** "She caught him by his garment....but he left his garment in her hand and fled and got out of the house. [And when she saw that he had left his garment in her hand and had fled out of the house, she called to the men of her household and said to them, 'See he has brought among us a Hebrew to insult us; he came in to me to lie with me, and I cried out with a loud voice, and when he heard that I lifted up my voice and cried, he left his garment with me and fled and got out of the house']" (Gen. 39:13-15):

B. He escaped through the merit of the fathers, in line with this verse: "And he brought him forth outside" (Gen. 15:5).

C. Simeon of Qitron said, "It was on account of bringing up the bones of Joseph that the sea was split: 'The sea saw it and fled' (Ps. 114:3), on the merit of this: '...and fled and got out.'"

How then do people acquire merit? It is through those acts of supererogatory grace they perform that the gain God's special love, for both themselves and their descendants. Here is a concrete example of how acts of worth or merit accrue to the benefit of the heirs of those that do them:

C:VI.

1. **A.** "When they came to the threshing floor of Atad, which is beyond the Jordan, they lamented there with a very great and sorrowful lamentation, and he made a mourning for his father seven days" (Gen. 50:10):

B. Said R. Samuel bar Nahman, "We have reviewed the entire Scripture and found no other place called Atad. And can there be a threshing floor for thorns [the Hebrew word for thorn being *atad*]?

C. "But this refers to the Canaanites. It teaches that they were worthy of being threshed like thorns. And on account of what merit were they saved? It was on account of the acts of kindness that they performed for our father, Jacob [on the occasion of the mourning for his death]."

D. And what were the acts of kindness that they performed for our father, Jacob?

E. R. Eleazar said, "[When the bier was brought up there,] they unloosened the girdle of their loins."

F. R. Simeon b. Laqish said, "They untied the shoulder-knots."

G. R. Judah b. R. Shalom said, "They pointed with their fingers and said, 'This is a grievous mourning to the Egyptians' (Gen. 50:11).

H. Rabbis said, "They stood upright."

I. Now is it not an argument *a fortiori* : now if these, who did not do a thing with their hands or feet, but only because they pointed their fingers, were saved from punishment, Israel, which performs an act of kindness [for the dead] with their adults and with their children, with their hands and with their feet, how much the more so [will they enjoy the merit of being saved from punishment]!

J. Said R. Abbahu, "Those seventy days that lapsed between the first letter and the second match the seventy days that the Egyptians paid respect to Jacob. [Seventy days elapsed from Haman's letter of destruction until Mordecai's letter announcing the repeal of the decree (cf. Est. 3:12, 8:9). The latter letter, which permitted the Jews to take vengeance on their would-be destroyers, should have come earlier, but it was delayed seventy days as a reward for the honor shown by the Egyptians to Jacob (Freedman, p. 992, n. 6).]"

The Egyptians gained merit by honoring Jacob in his death, so Abbahu. This same point then registers for the Canaanites. The connection is somewhat farfetched, that is, through the reference to the threshing floor, but the point is a strong one. Yet merit derives not only from exceptional deeds of a religious or moral character. People attain merit simply through hard work, through living up to their calling.

LXXIV:XII.

1. A. "If the God of my father, the God of Abraham and the Fear of Isaac, had not been on my side, surely now you would have sent me away empty-handed. God saw my affliction and the labor of my hand and rebuked you last night" (Gen. 31:41-42):

B. Zebedee b. Levi and R. Joshua b. Levi:

C. Zebedee said, "Every passage in which reference is made to 'if' tells of an appeal to the merit accrued by the patriarchs. [Freedman, p. 684, n. 2: It introduces a plea for or affirmation of protection received for the sake of the patriarchs.]"

D. Said to him R. Joshua, "But it is written, 'Except we had lingered' (Gen. 43:10) [a passage not related to the merit of the patriarchs]."

E. He said to him, "They themselves would not have come up except for the merit of the patriarchs, for it if it were not for the merit of the patriarchs, they never would have been able to go up from there in peace."

F. Said R. Tanhuma, "There are those who produce the matter in a different version." [It is given as follows:]

G. R. Joshua and Zebedee b. Levi:

H. R. Joshua said, ""Every passage in which reference is made to 'if' tells of an appeal to the merit accrued by the patriarchs except for the present case."

I. He said to him, "This case too falls under the category of an appeal to the merit of the patriarchs."

J. R. Yohanan said, "It was on account of the merit achieved through sanctification of the divine name."

K. R. Levi said, "It was on account of the merit achieved through faith and the merit achieved through Torah.

L. "The merit achieved through faith: 'If I had not believed...' (Ps. 27:13).

M. "The merit achieved through Torah: 'Unless your Torah had been my delight' (Ps. 119:92)."

2. A. " God saw my affliction and the labor of my hand and rebuked you last night" (Gen. 31:41-42):

B. Said R. Jeremiah b. Eleazar, "More beloved is hard labor than the merit achieved by the patriarchs, for the merit achieved by the patriarchs served to afford protection for property only, while the merit achieved by hard labor served to afford protection for lives.

C. "The merit achieved by the patriarchs served to afford protection for property only: 'If the God of my father, the God of Abraham and the Fear of Isaac, had not been on my side, surely now you would have sent me away empty-handed.'

D. "The merit achieved by hard labor served to afford protection for lives: 'God saw my affliction and the labor of my hand and rebuked you last night.'"

The main interest is in the theology of merit. No. 1 investigates the meaning of an expression used in the base-verse, among other passages. The exegesis is not particular to our base verse. No. 2 serves to prove a syllogism on the basis of the verses before us, standing closer to the formulation of the verses themselves. The issue of the merit of the patriarchs comes up in the reference to the God of the fathers, and that accounts for the selection of the theme at hand.

Chapter Three

Torah Study

The Judaism of the sages identified its doctrines with the Torah revealed to Moses by God at Mount Sinai. Sages therefore regarded study of the Torah as a principal religious action (one which, of course, would generate much merit). They moreover took for granted that the great and holy figures of the past, from the beginning with Abraham onward, also had studied the torah, Jacob, for example, undertaking studies with Shem. Study of the torah entailed more than merely acquiring information. It required discipleship, as a social action, and a certain mode of philosophical thought, on the intellectual side. Israel, moreover, found its strength in study of the Torah,. which meant, for one thing, the use of the mind to solve problems -- the mind and not the fist. The fist belonged to Esau, identified with Rome, and the intellect, to Israel, beginning with Jacob. Here is a clear statement of the character of mind of a master of the Torah.

LXV:XX.

2. A. "The voice is Jacob's voice:"
  B. Jacob rules only by his voice [through reasoned argument].
  C. "...but the hands are the hands of Esau:"
  D. and Esau rules only by the power of his hands [by force].
3. A. "The voice is Jacob's voice:"
  B. Said R. Phineas, "When the voice of Jacob is drawn mute, then: 'the hands are the hands of Esau.' He is called and comes."
4. A. "The voice is Jacob's voice, but the hands are the hands of Esau:"
  B. Said R. Berekhiah, "When Jacob uses his voice to express anger [against God], then the hands of Esau take control, but when his voice speaks clearly, then the hands of Esau do not take control."
5. A. Said R. Abba bar Kahana, "No philosophers in the world ever arose of the quality of Balaam ben Beor and Abnomos of Gadara. All of the nations of the world came to Abnomos of Gadara. They said to him, 'Do you maintain that we can make war against this nation?'
  B. "He said to them, 'Go and make the rounds of their synagogues and the study houses. If you find there children chirping out loud in their voices [and studying the Torah], then you cannot overcome them. If not, then you can conquer them, for so did their father promise them: "The voice is Jacob's voice," meaning that when Jacob's voice sounds forth in synagogues, Esau has no power.'"

Jacob rules through measured, calm, and reasoned discourse. Jacob rules through study of the Torah. The nations of the world have no power over Jacob when Jacob studies Torah. The voice of Jacob prevails but when Jacob does not speak up, then Esau prevails. This single message comes in a number of forms and versions. The union of Torah-study with merit proves commonplace. Here is one such example, specifying both the source of the merit and also the outcome.

LXVI:I.
1. A. "May God give you of the dew of heaven [and of the fatness of the earth, and plenty of grain and wine. Let peoples serve you and nations bow down to you. Be lord over your brothers and may your mother's sons bow down to you. Cursed be everyone who curses you, and blessed be every one who blesses you]" (Gen. 27:27-29):

B. "My root was spread out to the waters, and the dew lay all night on my branch" (Job 29:19).

C. Said Job, "It was because my doors were wide open that when everybody reaped dried ears, I reaped ears full of sap."

D. What is the scriptural basis for that statement?

E. "My root was spread out to the waters, and the dew lay all night on my branch" (Job 29:19).

F. Jacob said, "Because I engaged in study of the Torah, which is compared to water, I had the merit of being blessed with dew."

G. "May God give you of the dew of heaven."

The reference to dew in the intersecting verse accounts for its inclusion with the base verse, and then the two verses are drawn together in a solid link. The main point is to introduce the theme of Torah-study. A further effort to introduce the theme of Torah-study involves the relationships of Issachar and Zebulun, the one a tribe famed for its mastery of the Torah and its role in the government of the country, the other responsible for the support of the masters of Torah. This relationship finds a place in the story of the birth of the tribes:

LXXII:V.
3. A. Said R. Levi, "Come and see how suitable was the mediation of the mandrakes, for it was on account of the mandrakes that two great tribes arose in Israel, Issachar and Zebulun.

B. "Issachar was occupied in study of the Torah, while Zebulun set sail and came home and provided what his brother needed, so that the Torah became great in Israel.

C. "That is the meaning of this verse: 'The mandrakes give forth fragrance' (Song 7:15)."

4. A. "[And God hearkened to Leah and she conceived and bore Jacob a fifth son.] Leah said, 'God has given me my hire, because I gave my maid to my husband,' so she called his name Issachar" (Gen. 30:18):

B. Issachar was the nine in the order of the birth of the tribes, but he made his offerings second after the king:

C. "On the second day Nethanel, son of Zuar, prince of Issachar, offered" (Num. 7:18).

D. The reason is that he was learned in the Torah: "And of the children of Issachar, men that had understanding of the times; the heads of them were two hundred, and all their brethren were at their commandment" (1 Chr. 12:33).

E. What is the meaning of "the times"?

F. R. Tanhuma said, "The seasons."

G. Other say, "The rules of intercalation of the calendar."

H. "...the heads of them were two hundred," for two hundred heads of sanhedrins were produced by the tribe of Issachar.

I. "...and all their brethren were at their commandment" (1 Chr. 12:33): for all their brethren made the law accord with their instruction, and he provided for them rulings in accord with the law revealed to Moses at Sinai.

J. And how come all of this glory came to Issachar?

K. It was on account of Zebulun, for he would conduct business affairs and provide for Issachar, who was a master of Torah.

L. That is in line with this verse: "Zebulun will dwell at the shore of the sea" (Gen. 49:13).

M. Now when Moses came to bestow a blessing on Israel, he gave precedence to the blessing for Zebulun over the blessing for Issachar: "Rejoice, Zebulun, in your going out, and Issachar in your tents" (Deut. 33:18).

N. The meaning is this: Because of "Issachar in your tents," ["Rejoice, Zebulun, in your going out"].

O. And some say, "Issachar is in the tents of Zebulun."

No. 3 introduces the theme of the relationship of the two tribes born of the present transaction, Issachar and Zebulun. The repertoire of No. 4 scarcely refers to the base verse but simply presents a sizable set of verses and comments in which Issachar and Zebulun appear. The following goes over the same theme in a fresh way:

XCVIII:XII.

1. A. ["Issachar is a strong ass, crouching between the sheepfolds; he saw that a resting place was good, and that the land was pleasant; so he bowed his shoulder to bear, and became a slave at forced labor]" (Gen. 49:14-15).] "Issachar is a strong ass:" Just as in the case of an ass, its bones are visible, so the Torah-learning of Issachar was visible to him.

B. "...crouching between the sheepfolds:" This refers to the two rows of disciples of sages who are in session before them.

C. "...he saw that a resting place was good:" this refers to the Torah, as it is said, "For I have given you a good portion" (Prov. 4:2).

D. "...and that the land was pleasant:" this is the Torah: "The measure thereof is longer than the land" (Job 11:9).

E. "...so he bowed his shoulder to bear:" the yoke of the Torah.

F. "...and became a slave at forced labor:" these are the two hundred heads of sanhedrins who derived from the tribe of Issachar.

G. That is in line with the following verse: "And of the children of Issachar, men that had understanding of the times; the heads of them were two hundred, and all their brethren were at their commandment" (1 Chr. 12:33).

H. What is the meaning of "the times"?

I. R. Tanhuma said, "The seasons."

J. R. Yose bar Qisrai says, "The rules of intercalation of the calendar."

K. "...the heads of them were two hundred," for two hundred heads of sanhedrins were produced by the tribe of Issachar.

L. "...and all their brethren were at their commandment" (1 Chr. 12:33): for all their breathren made the law accord with their instruction, and he provided for them rulings in accord with the law revealed to Moses at Sinai.

M. And how come all of this glory came to Issachar?

N. It was on account of Zebulun, for he would conduct business affairs and provide for Issachar, who was a master of Torah.

O. That is in line with this verse: "Zebulun will dwell at the shore of the sea" (Gen. 49:13).

P. Now when Moses came to bestow a blessing on Israel, he gave precedence to the blessing for Zebulun over the blessing for Issachar: "Rejoice, Zebulun, in your going out, and Issachar in your tents" (Deut. 33:18).

Q. The meaning is this: Because of "Issachar in your tents," ["Rejoice, Zebulun, in your going out"].

R. And some say, "Issachar is in the tents of Zebulun."

The motif of Torah-study finds a place in a broad range of situations to which, in Scripture itself, it is remote. For example, wherever possible, heroic figures found schools for Torah-study:

XCV:III.

1. A. "He sent Judah before him to Joseph, to appear before him in Goshen, and they came into the land of Goshen" (Gen. 46:28):

B. What is the meaning of the word "to appear" [which is built on the root that means "to teach"]?

C. Said R. Nehemiah, "It was his task to set up a study-house there, so that he would teach Torah, in which the tribal fathers would recite the Torah.

D. "You may know that that is the case, for when Joseph went his way from him, Jacob knew that passage of the Torah that he was studying when he departed, and he had been reviewing it with him. When the brothers of Joseph came and told him, 'Joseph is still alive...his heart fainted, for he did not believe them' (Gen. 45:26), Jacob remembered from what passage Joseph had departed.

E. "So Jacob thought, 'I know that it was from studying the passage on the heifer whose neck is broken in the case of the finding of the neglected corpse that Joseph took his leave of me.'

F. "He said to them, 'He will give you some sign that indicates the passage of the Torah that he left off studying when he left me. Then I shall believe you.'

G. "And Joseph too remembered the passage that he had left off studying. What did Joseph do? He gave them wagons, as it is said, 'And Joseph gave them wagons' (Gen. 45:21) [and the word for 'wagon' and the word for 'heifer' use the same consonants].

H. "This serves to teach you that wherever he went, he engaged in study of the Torah, just as his fathers did, even though, up to that moment, the Torah had not yet been given.

2. A. Now lo, it is written with respect to Abraham, "Because Abraham hearkened to my voice and kept my torahs" (Gen. 26:5). Whence did Abraham study Torah?

B. Said R. Simeon b. Yohai, "[His father did not teach him, he never had a master. Whence did he learn Torah?] The Holy One, blessed be he, designated his two kidneys like two full jugs, and they flowed and taught him wisdom, in line with the following verse: 'I will bless the Lord, who has given me counsel, yes, in the night seasons my kidneys instruct me' (Ps. 16:7)."

C. R. Levi said, "He studied Torah on his own, as it is said, 'The dissembler in his heart shall have his fill from his own ways, and a good man shall be satisfied from himself' (Prov. 14:14)."

D. Said R. Samuel b. Nahman in the name of R. Jonathan: "Even the laws governing the commingling of domain in courtyards [for purposes of creating a single domain for carrying on the Sabbath] did Abraham know."

E. For it is said, "[I will multiply your descendants as the stars of heaven and will give to your descendants all these lands; and by your descendants all the nations of the earth shall bless themselves,] because Abraham obeyed my voice and kept my charge, my commandments, my statutes, and my laws" (Gen. 26:4-5).

F. How old was Abraham when he recognized his creator?

G. R. Hananiah said, He was one year old when he recognized his creator."

H. R. Levi in the name of R. Simeon b. Laqish: "He was three years old."

I. "How do we know? It is stated, 'because Abraham obeyed my voice and kept my charge,' that is, he listened to the voice of his creator and kept his charge [for the years numbered by the numerical value of the consonants in the word] 'because' and since he lived 175 years, and the letters of the word for 'because' bear the numerical value of 172, he was three years of age when he converted."

J. And he observed even the most minor details of the Torah and taught Torah to his sons, as it is said, "For I have known him to the end that he may command his children" (Gen. 18:19).

K. Said the Holy One, blessed be he, to him, "You have taught Torah to your son in this world. But in the world to come, I in my majesty will teach them the Torah, as it is said, 'And all your children shall be taught of the Lord' (Is. 54:13)."

Joseph sent a sign to Jacob that only Jacob would understand. Once more the eschatological dimension is probed, with No. 2 making the point explicit. So the settlement in the land of Goshen is treated as a foretaste of the end of days, and the Torah-study center that Jacob sent Judah to create is explicitly linked to what is to come.

Chapter Four

The Encounter With God

God in Genesis Rabbah, as in the book of Genesis, plays the part of passionate but tragic hero, everywhere engaged, always caring for what people do. The encounter with God for the sages at hand proves immediate, personal, and profound. No abstract concept, God intervenes, responds, rewards, punishes, and, in all, is everywhere the active partner in the unfolding drama of the creation of the world, the fall of the first man and woman, the degeneration of humanity, and the redemption brought about by Abraham, Isaac, Jacob, and their descendants, the children of Israel. In such a setting we should like in vain for theology. What we find in rich and rewarding abundance is an account of a deeply human encounter between God and humanity. God's interest, the sages who read Genesis insist, is in finding the good in humanity. Hence God does whatever can be done to give humanity the occasion for gaining God's grace:

LV:VII.

1. A. "And he said , 'Take, I pray you, your son, your only son, Isaac, whom you love, and go to the land of Moriah, and offer him there as a burnt offering upon one of the mountains of which I shall tell you'" (Gen. 22:3):

    B. He said to him, "Take, I pray you," meaning, "By your leave."

    C. "...your son."

    D. He said to him, "Which son?"

    E. He said to him, "...your only son."

    F. "This one is the only son of his mother, and that one is the only son of his mother."

    G. "...whom you love."

    H. "Where are the dividing walls within the womb? [I love them both.]"

    I. "Isaac."

    J. Why did he not tell him to begin with? It was so as to make Isaac still more precious in his view and so to give him a reward for each exchange.

    K. This accords with the view of R. Yohanan, for R. Yohanan said, "'Go from your country'(Gen. 12:1), refers to your hyparchy.

    B. "'From your birthplace' refers to your neighborhood.

    C. "'From your father's house' refers literally to the house of your father.

    D. "To the land that I will show you:" but why did he not inform him [in advance where that would be]?

E. "It was so as to make it still more precious in his view and to give him a reward for each step that he took [in perfect faith and reliance on God]."

F. Said R. Levi bar Haytah, , "'Go, go' (Gen. 12:1) is repeated twice [once in the present context, the other at Gen. 22:1, in going to offer up Isaac at Mount Moriah].

G. "We do not know which of them is more precious, the first or the second. On the basis of that which is written, 'And take yourself to the land of Moriah' (Gen. 22:2), I know that the second was more precious than the first. [Mount Moriah is the holiest place in the Land of Israel.]"

The main point is that God protracts the suspense to provide occasion for Abraham to distinguish himself all the more. God's particular metier, sages maintain is to carry out acts of love:

LVIII:IX.

1. A. "After this, Abraham buried [Sarah his wife in the cave of the field of Machpelah east of Mamre, that is Hebron, in the land of Canaan]" (Gen. 23:19):

B. "He who follows after righteousness and love finds life, prosperity, and honor" (Prov. 21:21).

C. "He who follows after righteousness" refers to Abraham, as it is said, "That they make keep the way of the Lord, to do righteousness and justice" (Gen. 18:19).

D. "...and love:" for he dealt lovingly with Sarah [in burying her].

E. "...finds life, [prosperity, and honor]" (Prov. 21:21): "And these are the days of the years of Abraham's life, which he lived, a hundred and seventy-five years" (Gen. 25:7).

F. "...prosperity, and honor:"

G. Said R. Samuel bar R. Isaac, "Said the Holy One, blessed be he, to him, 'My profession is to practice acts of love. Since you have taken over my profession, put on my cloak as well [as a fellow-craftsman, wearing the same signifying clothing]: 'And Abraham was old, well advanced in age' (Gen. 24:1)." [God dresses in the garment of old age, so Dan. 7:13 (Freedman, p. 515, n. 1)]."

The intersecting verse leads to a stunning climax at G. In redactional terms the framer has built a bridge from story to story, joining the burial of Sarah to the beginning of the next account, Gen. 24:1. In theological terms he has linked Abraham to God. In moral terms he has made the principal trait of God, hence of the human being like God, the practice of acts of lovingkindness, that is, those acts of *hesed*, translated here, "love," that God does as the divine profession. In a world in which humanity is made in God's image, humanity also serves, at its best, as the model for God's image.

Obviously, thoughtful people will want to raise the question of the source of human suffering: old age, disease, and death. The sages at hand, in line with their profoundly hopeful conception of existence, find God's benevolence in all three aspects of the human condition others might regard as tragic. These sages do not perceive the human condition as tragic but as ample testimony of God's love and only God's love. Whatever God metes out to humanity exhibits purpose and concern, including chronic sickness, old age, and death. Sages' radically affirmative view of creation and of the Creator required that they take exactly that position.

LXV:IX.

1. A. "When Isaac was old, and his eyes were dim, so that he could not see, he called Esau his older son, and said to him, 'My son,' and he answered, 'Here I am'" (Gen. 27:1):

B. Said R. Judah bar Simon, "Abraham sought [the physical traits of] old age [so that from one's appearance, people would know that he was old]. He said before him, 'Lord of all ages, when a man and his son come in somewhere, no one knows whom to honor. If you crown a man with the traits of old age, people will know whom to honor.'

C. "Said to him the Holy One, blessed be he, 'By your life, this is a good, thing that you have asked for, and it will begin with you.'

D. "From the beginning of the book of Genesis to this passage, there is no reference to old age. But when Abraham our father came along, the traits of old age were given to him, as it is said, 'And Abraham was old' (Gen. 24:1).'

E. "Isaac asked God for suffering. He said before him, 'Lord of the age, if someone dies without suffering, the measure of strict justice is stretched out against him. But if you bring suffering on him, the the measure of strict justice will not be stretched out against him. [Suffering will help counter the man's sins, and the measure of strict justice will be mitigated through suffering by the measure of mercy.]'

F. "Said to him the Holy One, blessed be he, 'By your life, this is a good, thing that you have asked for, and it will begin with you.'

G. "From the beginning of the book of Genesis to this passage, there is no reference to suffering. But when Isaac came along, suffering was given to him: his eyes were dim.'

H. "Jacob asked for sickness. He said before him, 'Lord of all ages, if a person dies without illness, he will not settle his affairs for his children. If he is sick for two or three days, he will settle his affairs with his children.'

I. "Said to him the Holy One, blessed be he, 'By your life, this is a good, thing that you have asked for, and it will begin with you.'

J. "That is in line with this verse: 'And someone said to Joseph, "Behold, your father is sick"' (Gen. 48:1)."

K. Said R. Levi, "Abraham introduced the innovation of old age, Isaac introduced the innovation of suffering, Jacob introduced the innovation of sickness.

L. "Hezekiah introduced the innovation of chronic illness. He said to him, 'You have kept a man in good condition until the day he dies. But if someone is sick and gets better, is sick and gets better, he will carry out a complete and sincere act of repentance for his sins.'

M. "Said to him the Holy One, blessed be he, 'By your life, this is a good, thing that you have asked for, and it will begin with you.'

N.   "'The writing of Hezekiah, king of Judah, when he had been sick and recovered of his sickness' (Is. 38:9)."

O.   Said R. Samuel b. Nahman, "On the basis of that verse we know that between one illness and another there was an illness more serious than either one."

The syllogism that the suffering, old age, sickness, and the like come to benefit humanity leads to the inclusion of the base verse. But obviously the syllogism makes no effort to clarify the present verse or its context. This same notion explains not only the human condition of illness and death but also specific ailments visited on holy persons:

LXV:X .

1 . A.   "[When Isaac was old, and his eyes were dim,] so that he could not see, [he called Esau his older son, and said to him, 'My son,' and he answered, 'Here I am']" (Gen. 27:1):

B.   R. Eleazar b. Azariah said, "'...see' the wickedness of the wicked person.

C.   "Said the Holy One, blessed be he, 'Should Isaac go out to the market and have people say, "Here is the father of that wicked man."

D.   "'It is better that I make his eyes dim, so he will stay home.'

E.   "So it is written, 'When the wicked rise, men hide themselves' (Prov. 28:28).

F.   "On the basis of this verse, they have said, 'Whoever raises a wicked son or a wicked disciple will have his eyes grow dim.

G.   "The case of the wicked disciple derives from Ahijah the Shilonite, who raised up Jeroboam, so his eyes grew dim: 'Now Ahijah could not see, for his eyes were set by reason of his old age' (1 Kgs. 14:4). It was because he had produced Jeroboam, the wicked disciple.

H.   "As for a wicked son, that is shown by the case of Isaac."

2 . A.   Another matter: "So that he could not see..."

B.   It was on account of that spectacle [at Moriah].

C.   Now at the moment at which our father, Abraham, bound Isaac his son, the ministering angels wept. That is in line with this verse: "Behold, their valiant ones cry outside" (Is. 33:7).

D.   The tears fell from their eyes into his and made a mark on them, so when he got old, his eyes dimmed: "When Isaac was old, and his eyes were dim, so that he could not see..."

3 . A.   Another matter: "So that he could not see..."

B.   It was on account of that spectacle.

C.   Now at the moment at which our father, Abraham, bound Isaac his son, he looked upward and gazed upon the Presence of God.

D.   They made a parable. The case may be compared to that of a king who was strolling in the gate of his palace, and he looked up and saw the son of his ally peeking in and gazing at him through a window. He said, "If I put him to death, I shall alienate my ally. But I shall give a degree that his windows be stopped up [so he will not do this again].

E. Now at the moment at which our father, Abraham, bound Isaac his son, he looked upward and gazed upon the Presence of God. Said the Holy One, blessed be he, "If I put him to death, I shall alienate Abraham, my ally. But I shall give a degree that his eyes should be stopped up [so he will not do this again]."

F. "When Isaac was old, and his eyes were dim, so that he could not see...."

No. 1 explains Isaac's blindness in the familiar framework; he tolerated Esau's wicked ways or at least had to be protected from them. Nos. 2, 3 then link the blindness to something he saw when he was bound on the altar. The parable is striking, since it presents the blindness as an act of mercy on God's part.

All forms of suffering, therefore, derive from God and bring a blessing of one kind or another. The following insists on that point:

XCII:I.

1. A. "May God almighty grant you mercy before the man, that he may send back your other brother and Benjamin. If I am bereaved of my children, I am bereaved" (Gen. 43:14):

B. R. Phineas in the name of R. Hanan of Sepphoris opened discourse by citing the following verse: "'Happy is the man whom you chasten, O Lord.' And if someone should come along to object, then: '...and whom you teach out of your Torah' (Ps. 94:12).

C. "What is written with respect to Abraham? 'And I will bless you and make your name great' (Gen. 12:2).

D. "But when he went forth, famine leaped upon him, but he did not complain or object.

E. "[Thus Jacob said to his sons,] 'So too you, if troubles come upon you, do not object or complain.'"

2. A. Said R. Alexandri, "You have no one without troubles. Happy is the person whose Torah bring about his sufferings [that is, because of his hard work in studying the Torah]."

B. Said R. Joshua b. Levi, "All sufferings that come upon a person and prevent him from his Torah-study constitute sufferings that serve to rebuke. But all forms of suffering that do not prevent a person from studying the Torah are sufferings that come out of love [that a person may suffer in this world and joy all the more the age to come]."

3. A. Rabbi saw a blind man who was laboring in Torah-study. He said to him, "Peace to you, free man."

B. He said to him, "Did you hear that I used to be a slave?"

C. He said to him, "No, but you will be a free man in the age to come."

4. A. Said R. Yudan, "It is written, 'And if he smite out his slave's tooth or his slavewoman's tooth, he shall let him go free for his tooth's sake' (Ex. 21:27).

B. "He upon whom troubles come, how much the more so!"

5. A. R. Phineas in the name of R. Hoshaia: "'Happy is the man whom you chasten, O Lord.' The word 'Lord' is not written out in the four-lettered name of God, but only with the two letters, YH. The matter may be compared to one who is judged before the court and said, 'May it be so.' [Freedman, p. 848, n.

3: *Yah* is by a play on words interpreted as a shortened form of *yehi*, 'let it be so, but no more.' Thus even the man who is happy in God's chastisement yet prays to be spared further suffering.]

B. "So it was with our father, Abraham: 'He who in the future is destined to say to suffering, "Enough," may he say to my suffering now, "Enough."'

C. "'And God Almighty give you mercy' (Gen. 43:14). [The word for 'Almighty,' *shaddai*, contains letters, *dai*, that, read by themselves, mean, 'Enough.']"

The sustained exposition of the problem of suffering deals with a number of distinct themes. It is therefore a composite. Then the point at which the intersecting verse returns us to the base verse, No. 5, reaches back to No. 1, without attention to the intervening units. These take up the matter of suffering brought on by God's love as distinct from suffering aimed at chastisement. The melange can have been omitted without affecting the main point, which is to impute to Jacob both acceptance of divine punishment and the prayer that that will be enough. The message to Israel -- patience but hope -- requires no comment.

What individual men and women do, whether blessing or cursing, derives from God and indicates a measure of God's participation. At the crucial turnings in Israel's supernatural life, when a blessing is bestowed, God plays a part:

LXVII:I.

1. A. "Then Isaac trembled violently [and said, 'Who was it then that hunted game and brought it to me, and I ate it all before you came, and I have blessed him? yes, and he shall be blessed]'" (Gen. 27:33):

B. "The trembling on account of man brings a snare, but whoever puts his trust in the Lord shall be set up on high" (Prov. 29:25):

C. The trembling that Ruth caused to Boaz, as it is said, "And the man trembled and turned himself" (Ruth 3:8).

D. "...brings a snare:" for he could have cursed her. [He might have done the wrong thing, but he avoided the trap.]

E. "...but whoever puts his trust in the Lord shall be set up on high:" for [God] put in his heart [the impulse to bless her] and he blessed her: "Blessed are you of the Lord, my daughter" (Ruth 3:10).

F. Along these same lines, the trembling that Jacob caused Isaac was such that he could have cursed him,

G. "...but whoever puts his trust in the Lord shall be set up on high," for [God] put in his heart [the impulse to bless him] and he blessed him: "...yes, and he shall be blessed."

The intersecting verse is chosen because of its reference to trembling, with the further reference to the passage in Ruth allowing for the introduction of the notion of a blessing. Here again it is impossible to know whether this complex composition, with its deft reversion to our base verse, has been made up all at once or brought into being piece by piece. The net effect is very powerful, since it introduces God's action into Isaac's blessing of Jacob. It further links the story at hand to the coming of the Messiah through Ruth and Boaz. God made the men make the right choice, so he had a part in the blessing.

LXVII:III.

1. A. ["Then Isaac trembled violently and said, 'Who was it then that hunted game and brought it to me, and I ate it all before you came, and I have blessed him? yes, and he shall be blessed'" (Gen. 27:33):] Said R. Eleazar, "The validation of a writ is effected only through the confirmation of the signatures of the witnesses.

   B. "So, if you might imagine that, had Jacob not deceived his father, he would not have taken the blessings, Scripture states explicitly, '...yes, and he shall be blessed.'"

2. A. Said R. Isaac, "He was coming to curse him. Said the Holy One, blessed be he, to him, 'Be careful, for if you curse him, you curse yourself.

   B. "For lo, you have said to him, 'Those who curse you will be cursed, and those who bless you will be blessed' (Gen. 27:29)."

3. A. Said R. Levi,"There are six things that serve a person, over three of which a person is in charge, and over three of which a person is not in charge.

   B. "Over the eye, ear, and nose, a person is not in charge, for a person sees, hears, and smells what one does not necessarily want to see, hear or smell.

   C. "Over the mouth, hand, and foot a person is in charge. As to the mouth, if someone wants, the person will study the Torah, and if someone wants, the person will slander others or blaspheme or revile.

   D. "As to the hand, if someone wants he may give out charity, and if someone wants, he may rob or murder.

   E. "As to the feet, if someone wants, he may walk to theaters or circuses, and if someone wants, he may walk to synagogues or houses of study.

   F. "But in a moment at which a potential victim has sufficient merit, the Holy One, blessed be he, takes those limbs of which a person is in charge and removes them from his power.

   G. "As to the hand: 'And his hand, which he put forth against him, dried up' (1 Kgs. 13:45).

   H. "As to the mouth: 'Yes, and he shall be blessed.'

   I. "As to the feet: 'My son, do not walk in the way with them, for their feet run to evil' (Prov. 1:15)."

No. 1 makes an important point about the interpolation at Gen. 27:33. No. 2 adds an interesting point of its own, now revising the view of Isaac. The syllogism of No. 3 rests on the notion that if the victim of a person's mouth, hand, or foot has sufficient merit, God will not permit a wicked person free use of his mouth, hand, or foot. The syllogism draws on our base verse, which is why the passage is inserted here.

Knowledge of God derives from the encounter with God. Humanity knows about God only what can be learned from its relationship with God, in particular in the record of the Torah. At the same time a measure of speculation on more abstract questions does make an appearance:

LXVIII:IX.

1. A. "And he lighted upon a certain place and stayed there that night, because the sun had set" (Gen. 28:11):

    B. R. Huna in the name of R. Ammi, "[Since the word 'place' stands for God as the Omnipresent, the verse is understood to mean that Jacob encountered God as Omnipresent. So we ask:] Why is the name of the Holy One, blessed be he, changed and represented as "the Place'? Because he is the place in which his world exists."

    C. Said R. Yose bar Halpata, "We do not know whether the Holy One, blessed be he, is the place in which his world exists, or whether his world is the place in which he exists. On the basis of this statement, 'Behold, there is a place with me' (Ex. 33:21), it follows that the Holy One, blessed be he, is the place in which his world exists,and the world is not the place in which he exists."

    D. Said R. Isaac, "It is written, 'The eternal God is a dwelling place' (Deut. 33:27). We do not know whether the Holy One, blessed be he, is the dwelling place in which his world exists, or whether his world is the dwelling place in which he exists. On the basis of this statement, 'Lord, you have been our dwelling place' (Ps. 90:1), it follows that the Holy One, blessed be he, is the dwelling place in which his world exists,and the world is not the dwelling place in which he exists."

    E. Said R. Abba bar Yudan, "The matter may be compared to the case of a hero riding on a horse, with his robes flowing down both sides of the horse. The horse is secondary to the rider, and the rider is not secondary to the horse. That is in line with this verse: 'You ride upon your horses, upon your chariots of victory' (Hab. 3:8)."

2. A. "And he lighted upon...:" (Gen. 28:11):

    B. [The word for "lighted upon," also bears the sense of praying, hence:] he prayed.

3. A. Said R. Joshua b. Levi, "The first patriarchs ordained the recitation of the Prayer three times a day.

    B. "Abraham ordained the recitation of the Prayer at dawn, as it says, 'And Abraham God up early in the morning to the place where he had stood before the Lord' (Gen. 19:27), and the word 'standing' speaks of prayer: 'Then Phineas stood up and prayed' (Ps. 106:30).

    C. "Isaac ordained the recitation of the Prayer at eventide, as it is said, 'And Isaac went out to meditate in the field toward evening' (Gen. 24:63), and the word for 'meditate' refers to prayer: 'I pour out my meditation before him' (Ps. 142:3).

    D. "Jacob ordained the recitation of the Prayer in the evening: '"And he lighted upon' (Gen. 28:11).

    E. "The word for 'lighted upon' bears the sense of praying, in the following verse: 'Neither lift up cry nor prayer for them, nor make intercession [using the same verb] to me' (Jer. 7:16)."

    F. Said R. Samuel bar Nahman, "The recitation of the Prayer three times a day corresponds to the three times a day that the day changes in character. In the evening it is necessary to recite, 'May it please you, O Lord my God, that you bring me forth from darkness to light.'

G. "At dawn it is necessary to say, 'I thank you, O Lord my God, that you have brought me forth from darkness to light.'

H. "At eventide it is necessary to so, 'May it be pleasing to you, O Lord my God, that just as you have given me the merit of seeing the sun at its rising, so you will give me the merit of seeing it at its setting.'"

I. Rabbis say, "The recitation of the Prayer three times a day corresponds to the daily whole offerings. The recitation of the Prayer at dawn corresponds to the daily whole offering of the morning. The recitation of the Prayer at eventide corresponds to the daily whole-offering brought at dusk. And as to the recitation of the Prayer in the evening, it is not subject to a fixed rule."

J. Said R. Tanhuma, "Also the recitation of the Prayer in the evening is subject to a fixed rule. It corresponds to the limbs and innards of the animal offerings which were consumed in the altar fires throughout the night."

No. 1 presents an elaborate theological speculation. It is attached because the word "place" bears dual meanings, as explained. No. 2 proceeds along the same theme, now having Jacob say prayers. This leads directly to No. 3. None of these three items serves a narrow exegetical purpose Including them here is for syllogistic and thematic reasons, which is to say the compositors of the document wished to introduce themes such as those at hand, reworking the narrative in a more profound dimension.

Israel wants of God not merely the blessing of daily and individual life. Israel is in a difficult condition, lacking control over its own national destiny. From God Israel as a nation requires an act of redemption. When will this come, and, of greater importance, how will people know that it will come? These are the questions addressed in what follows:

LXXVIII:I.

1. A. "Then he said, 'Let me go, for the day is breaking'" (Gen. 32:26):

B. "They are new every morning, great is your faithfulness" (Lam. 3:23):

C. Said R. Simeon bar Abbah, "Since you renew us morning by morning, we know for certain that your faithfulness is great to redeem us."

D. Said R. Alexandri, "Since you renew us morning by morning, we know for certain that your faithfulness is great to resurrect the dead."

The cited verse makes a point about God's reliability. God can redeem Israel or raise the dead, and the coming of the dawn indicates that certainty. The act of redemption depends upon God's love. Sages draw the contrast between God's love and human love, showing that while they share the same fundamental quality, God's love is different:

LXXX:VII.

1. A. "But Hamor spoke with them, saying, ['The soul of my son Shechem longs for your daughter; I pray you give her to him in marriage. Make marriages with us; give your daughters to us, and take our daughters for yourselves. You shall dwell with us; and the land shall be open to you; dwell and trade in it; and get property in it']" (Gen. 34:8-10):

B. Said R. Simeon b. Laqish, "There are three expressions of love that the Holy One, blessed be he, used to express his affection for Israel: cleaving, loving, delighting in [and these expressions occur in three distinct verses]:

C. "...cleaving: 'But you who cleaved to the Lord your God' (Deut. 4:4).

D. "...loving: 'The Lord did not set his love upon you...because you were more in number than any people' (Deut. 7:7).

E. "...delighting in: 'And all nations shall call you happy, for you are a delightful land' (Mal. 3:12).

F. "But in the passage at hand, concerning a wicked person, we are able in a single verse to derive all of them:

G. "...cleaving: 'And his soul cleaved' (Gen. 34:4).

H. "...loving: 'The soul of my son Shechem loves for your daughter' (Gen. 34:8).

I. "...delighting in: 'Because he had delight in Jacob's daughter' (Gen. 34:19)."

J. R. Abba b. Elishib adds yet two more, "Love and speech.

K. "Love: 'I have loved you' (Mal. 1:2).

L. "...and speech: 'Speak to the heart of Jerusalem' (Is. 40:12).

M. "But in the passage at hand, concerning a wicked person, we derive all of them:

N. "Love: 'And he loved the girl' (Gen. 34:3).

O. "Speech: 'And he spoke to the heart of the girl' (Gen. 34:3)."

No. 1 cites the verses at hand in a substantial syllogism, but, it is clear, the purpose is to make use of the philological point to link the story at hand to the history of Israel. Specifically, the compositor wishes to contrast the love of a carnal nature, at which the nations are adept, with love of a theological character, which God bestows upon Israel. So the story at hand serves a much more profound purpose of supplying an analogy by means of contrast between God's love for Israel and Shechem's love of Dinah. It is a stunning and daring contrast -- yet commonplace.

Part Two

ISRAEL AND CREATION

Chapter Five

The Anti-Gnostic Polemic

We proceed to a sequence of compositions which, as a set conduct a sustained and powerful polemic against positions commonly espoused by Gnostic writers in the period from the second century onward. We shall discover the substance of those positions inductively. When we find out the views against which sages argue, we also may construct a picture of the views of their opponents within Jewry or otherwise. Let us start with an explicit statement of whom sages regard as the opposition:

VIII:VIII.

1. A. R. Samuel bar Nahman in the name of R. Jonathan: "When Moses was writing out the Torah, he wrote up the work of each day [in sequence]. When he came to the verse, 'And God said, "Let us make man...,"' (Gen. 1:26), he said, 'Lord of the age, in saying this you give an opening to heretics [to claim that there are two dominions in heaven, so the creator-God had to consult with others in making the world, because he was not alone and all-powerful].'

   B. "He said to him, 'Write it anyhow, and if someone wants to err, let him err.'

   C. "The Holy One, blessed be he, said to him, 'Moses, as to this man whom I am going to create, will I not bring forth both great and unimportant descendants from him?

   D. "It is so that, if a great man has to get permission from a lesser person and says, 'Why in the world should I have to get permission from an unimportant person,' people will say to him, 'Learn a lesson from your creator, who created the creatures of the upper world and the creatures of the lower world, but when he came to create man, went and took counsel with the ministering angels.'"

2. A. Said R. Layyah [Hila], "There is no taking counsel here. Rather the matter may be compared to the case of a king who was walking about at the door of his palace and saw a clod tossed [on the ground]. He said, 'What should we do with it?'

   B. "Some say, 'Use it for public baths,' and others, 'For private baths.'

   C. "The king said, 'I shall make a statue [of myself] with it, and who is going to stand in my way?'"

No. 1 answers the pressing question by supplying a context in which people notice the use of the plural, "we." The usage indicates how one should conduct himself, and has no theological meaning whatsoever. This answer then matches that of No. 2: even though the king   out of courtesy may consult lesser authorities, in the end he does just what he wishes, and that without regard to the advice others may give him. The point then underlines that the king makes no sort of bath whatsoever. Why then does the author of the parable select, in particular, a statue? It is hardly random, in light of the statement, later on, that man is made in God's image. So the answer is decisive and stunning. After consulting the angels, God did what he wished, and what was that? It was to make another God, that is, man in God's image. That represents a stunning rejection of the angels and affirmation of man.

VIII:X.
1. **A.** Said R. Hoshiah, "When the Holy One, blessed be he, came to create the first man, the ministering angels mistook him [for God, since man was in God's image,] and wanted to say before him, 'Holy, [holy, holy is the Lord of hosts].'

   B. "To what may the matter be compared? To the case of a king and a governor who were set in a chariot, and the provincials wanted to greet the king, "Sovereign!' But they did not know which one of them was which. What did the king do? He turned the governor out and put him away from the chariot, so that people would know who was king.

   C. "So too when the Holy One, blessed be he, created the first man, the angels mistook him [for God]. What did the Holy One, blessed be he, do? He put him to sleep, so everyone knew that he was a mere man.

   D. "That is in line with the following verse of Scripture: 'Cease you from man, in whose nostrils is a breath, for how little is he to be accounted' (Is. 2:22)."

This is simply a stunning follow-up to the foregoing. Since man is in God's image, the angels did not know man from God. Only that man sleeps distinguishes man from God. I cannot imagine a more daring affirmation of humanity. The theme derives from the verse that states, "...in our image, after our likeness" (Gen., 1:26), but this passage is not cited in the present construction. Clearly VIII:X simply carries forward the concluding entry of VIII:IX, in which the relevant verse is cited. We have, then, no mere anthology on the cited verse. We have a profoundly polemical statement about the true character and condition of man. Moreover, even at VIII:IX.2.E the cited verse plays no substantial role. It is as if the framer did not wish to give emphasis to Gen. 1:26 and chose rather to submerge that verse, while making such observations as proved needful. Accordingly, "In our image" yields the view that the complete image of man is attained in a divine union between man and woman, and, further, the syllogism that what makes man different from God is that man sleeps, and God does not sleep. Given the premise of the base verse and the issues inherent in the allegation that man is in God's image, the treatment here proves extraordinary.

VIII:XI.

2. A. R. Joshua b. R. Nehemiah in the name of R. Hinena bar Isaac and rabbis in the name of R. Eleazar: "He created in him four traits applicable to beings of the upper world and four of the lower world.

B. "As to traits applicable to creatures of the upper world, he stands up straight like ministering angels, he speaks as do ministering angels, he has the power of understanding as do ministering angels, and he sees as do ministering angels."

C. But does a beast not see?

D. [That indeed is the case,] but a man sees from the side.

E. "As to traits applicable to creatures of the lower world, he eats and drinks like a beast, he has sexual relations like a beast, he defecates like a beast, and he dies like a beast."

3. A. R. Tipdai in the name of R. Aha: "The creatures of the upper world were created in the image and likeness [of God] and do not engage in sexual relations, while the creatures of the lower world engage in sexual relations and were not created in the image and likeness [of God].

B. "Said the Holy One, blessed be he, 'Lo, I shall create him in the image and likeness [of God], like the creatures of the upper world, but he will engage in sexual relations, like creatures of the lower world."

C. R. Tipdai in the name of R. Aha: "The Holy One, blessed be he, said, 'If I create him solely with traits of creatures of the upper world, he will live and never die, and if I do so solely with traits of creatures of the lower world, he will die and not live. Instead, I shall create him with traits of creatures of the upper world and with traits of creatures of the lower world.

D. "'If he sins, he will die, and if not, he will live.'"

Sin now makes the difference. Man has traits of angels and traits of beasts. When he is righteous, his angelic and heavenly traits mark him as in God's image, and when he sins, he is not in the likeness and the image of God. No. 1 takes up the cited verse. Nos. 2 and 3 go over the same matter, which in no way intersects with the verse at hand but pursues an interest of its own, namely, the divine and human traits of man. What is interesting is that the appropriate "base-verse" is once more "In our image, after our likeness" (Gen. 1:26). Why so? The question that is answered is what traits of human beings are divine, in line with the verse at hand, and what traits are not. Perhaps in a better edition VIII:XI.2, 3 would be located together with VIII:X. But the really interesting question remains the one we addressed just now, namely, why has the framer not cited Gen. 1:26's reference to man in God's image as a principal point of exegesis and subjected it to the sort of treatment he has lavished on Gen. 1:26's reference to "*Let us* make...."

One available theory is that the allusion to man in God's image may have appeared to exegetes too close to the Christians' claim of Jesus as God incarnate, an issue the exegetes before us do not appear to have wished to confront in connection with the "base-verse" at hand. It is as if the principal threat came from "heretics" who sought proof for the belief in two dominions, e.g., Gnostic convictions about a creator God and another, unknown God as well. But a different sort of "heretic," maintaining that God had been incarnate as man in the form of Jesus, who, in the period in which the document came into its final form, triumphed as Christ, ruler of the world, does not appear to have received his appropriate reply in the present context. That view is treated as though no one held it.

IX:I.

1. A. "And God saw everything that he had made, and behold, it was very good" (Gen. 1:31):

B. R. Levi in the name of R. Hama bar Hanina commenced [discourse by citing the following verse of Scripture]: "It is the glory of God to conceal a thing, but the glory of kings is to search out a matter" (Prov. 25:2).

C. R. Levi in the name of R. Hama bar Hanina: "From the beginning of the book [of Genesis] to this point: 'it is the glory of God to conceal a thing,' but from this point forward: 'the glory of kings is to search out a matter.'

D. "The reference to 'glory' applies to words of Torah, which are compared to kings, as it is said, 'By me kings rule' (Prov. 8:15).

E. "'To search out a matter' [amplifies the verse,] 'And God saw everything that he had made, and behold it was very good' (Gen. 1:31)."

The fact that the verse has God examine -- hence, search out -- the results of six days of creation evidently draws attention to the intersecting verse. Up to this point the works of creation have been kept a secret, but from this point onward the king, the ruler, takes over and investigates the character of what is going on. So from here on "one may search out the matter" [Freedman, p. 64, n. 1]. There is no hidden God, or God who has absconded. All things are public and open: in the Torah.

IX:II.

1. A. R. Tanhuma opened [discourse by citing the following verse of Scripture]: "He has made every thing beautiful in its time" (Qoh. 3:11).

B. Said R. Tanhuma, "The world was created at the proper time. The world was not ready to be created prior to this time." [God admired the works of creation because the world was brought into being when it was ripe. Hence what has attracted the exegete's attention, once again, is the question, what is it about the world that God found to be very good? The answer here is that the world was "beautiful in its time," the right one for God to create.]

2. A. Said R. Abbahu, "On the basis of the cited verse, we learn that the Holy One, blessed be he, had created worlds and destroyed them [as unsuccessful], until he created this world. He said, 'This one pleases me, the others did not please me.'"

B. Said R. Phineas, "The scriptural verse that supports R. Abbahu's view is this: 'And God saw all that he had made...' (Gen. 1:31)."

Both exercises make a single point. Tanhuma's takes the form of the citation of an intersecting verse; the compositor obviously relies on IX:I.1.A. for the base verse, so whatever he used he has revised to accord with the requirements of the present context. Abbahu does not have an intersecting verse, but the base-verse supplies a proof-text for his syllogism.

We see two modes of making the same point, the one through the intersecting verse and the base verse, which we may call exegetical, the other syllogistic, joined with facts supplied by Scripture to prove the syllogism. The editor has joined the materials and set them here for good reason. We cannot say that he has created a mere anthology of materials relevant to Gen. :131. Prior to the work of composition the compositor had clearly defined what point he wished to make. It is the perfection of creation, the best of all creations, completed at just the right moment.

IX:III.

1. A. ["And God saw all that he had made, and behold, it was very good" (Gen. 1:31):] R. Yohanan and R. Simeon b. Laqish:

B. R. Yohanan said, "A mortal king builds a palace, then examining the upper floors in one inspection and the lower ones in another, but the Holy One, blessed be he, could take in both the upper floors and the lower floors in a single look." [Freedman, p. 65, n. 1: Interpreting "And God saw *everything* that he had made" -- in a single glance.]

C. Said R. Simeon b. Laqish, ""'Lo, it was very good' refers to this world. '*And* lo, it was very good' [with the addition of *and*] encompasses the world to come. The Holy One, blessed be he, encompassed both of them with a single look."

2. A. R. Simeon b. Laqish in the name of R. Eleazar b. Azariah: "'Ah, Lord God, behold, you have made the heaven and the earth' (Jer. 32:17). From that moment: 'There is nothing too hard for you.' (Jer. 32:17)."

B. R. Haggai in the name of R. Isaac, "'And you, Solomon, my son, know the God of your father and serve him with a whole heart and with a willing mind, for the Lord searches all hearts and understands all the imaginations of the thoughts' (1 Chr. 28:9). [Taking the root of the word for 'imaginations,' YSR, which serves also as the root for the word, 'form' or 'create,' we interpret as follows:] Before thought is formed in the heart of man, it already is revealed before you."

C. R. Yudan in the name of R. Isaac: "Before a creature is actually created, his thought is already revealed before you."

D. Said R. Yudan in his own name, "'For there is not a word in my tongue but lo, O Lord, you know it altogether' (Ps. 139:4). Before my tongue forms speech, already 'lo, O Lord, you know it altogether.'"

No. 1 interprets the reference to God's seeing, making noteworthy what in the text is a dormant detail. No. 2 seems to me to answer the question, Did God not know, prior to creation, whether what he would make would be any good? Is that why he had to look at it and declare it very good? The answer of course is that God knows before human creation precisely what mortals will go and do, all the more so before his own act of creation does he know the outcome of all things.

If we look back at the sequence of propositions from IX:I onward, what do we find? First, the mystery of creation is sealed and not to be revealed. Second, it is true that God made worlds before this one. But the reason is that only with the creation of this world did God know that the world he created was very good. God fully inspected this world and found it very good. God knew full well what he was doing from the beginning. If people maintained that the creator-god was an evil bungler, the present sequence would present a systematic reply. God not only did not bungle creation but knew precisely what he was doing from beginning to end. The reference to God's inspecting creation and finding it very good, then, contains no implication that God did not know what he was doing, since he knew full well from before creation precisely what he was doing. That accounts for IX:II's emphasis on God's power to see it all, all at once, providing a restatement of the same notion. IX:III spells out it. So we have to read the three paragraphs as a continuous statement of a sizable syllogism.

Obviously, were we to reconstruct the argument against which the authorship of the document directs its counter-argument, we should once more find ourselves in the midst of a gaggle of gnostics. But that observation seems altogether too general, for "gnostic" stands for many positions sharing few indicative traits. All we can identify are the most general, hence commonplace, propositions. Without a theory on the particular sort of gnostic position against which argument flows, we cannot materially advance the large-scale interpretation of our document. Shortly we shall have reason to identify the holders of the position contrary to the one advanced by the present authorship.

IX:VI.

1. A. Said R. Simeon b. Eleazar, "'And behold, it was very good' (Gen. 1:31) means: 'And behold, sleep is good.'

    B. "But is sleep *very* good [under all circumstances]? Have we not learned in the Mishnah: **Wine and sleep are a pleasure for them** [the wicked] **and also a pleasure for the world** [M. San. 8:5] [but sleep is not a pleasure for the world when the righteous go to sleep, since the world is then deprived of their righteous deeds. Accordingly, sleep is not invariably *very* good.]

    C. "[Sleep is very good because] a person sleeps a bit and then gets up and works hard in Torah-study [accomplishing more than he would if he had not slept for a little while]."

The anthology continues, now taking up new themes deemed relevant to the words, "very good." We move from death to sleep, which is compared to death. We recall, moreover, that it is what distinguishes man from God, who never sleeps.

IX:VII.

1. A. Nahman in the name of R. Samuel: "'Behold, it was very good' refers to the impulse to do good. '*And* behold, it was very good' encompasses also the impulse to do evil.

B. "And is the impulse to do evil '*very* good'?

C. "[Indeed so, for] if it were not for the impulse to do evil, a man would not build a house, marry a wife, and produce children. So does Solomon say, 'Again I considered all labor and all excelling in work, that is rivalry with his neighbor' (Qoh. 4:4)."

The anthology now moves along to a new topic. Rivalry is deemed an aspect of the impulse to do evil which produces good results.

IX:VIII.

1. A. Said R. Huna, "'Behold, it was very good' refers to the measure that metes out good [things to people', while, '*And* behold, it was very good' refers to the measure that metes out suffering as well.

B. "And can anyone say that the measure of suffering is 'very good'?

C. "Rather, on account of that measure people reach the life of the world to come, and so does Solomon say, 'And reproofs of chastisement are the way to [eternal] life' (Prov. 6:23).

D. "You may say: Go forth and see what is the path that brings a man to the life of the world to come. You have to conclude, it is the measure of suffering."

The impulse to do evil draws in its wake the suffering that people undergo. Is this too very good? Indeed so, for the reason that is given: it is what brings people to the world to come.

IX:IX.

1. A. Said R. Zeirah, "'Behold, it was very good' refers to the Garden of Eden.' '*And* behold, it was very good' encompasses Gehenna.

B. "And can anyone say that Gehenna is '*very* good'?

C. "Rather, the matter may be compared to a king who had an orchard and brought workers into it, building a paymaster's hut at the gate. He said, 'Whoever shows himself worthy through hard work in the orchard may go into the paymaster's hut [and collect his wages], and whoever does not show himself worthy in the labor of the orchard may not go into the paymaster's hut.

D. "So for whoever stores up a treasury of merit through performing religious duties and supererogatory good deeds, lo, there is the Garden of Eden, and for whoever does not store up for himself a treasury merit through the performance of religious duties and good deeds, lo, there is Gehenna."

That is why Gehenna is very good, in line with the foregoing. Just as the suffering of people prepares them for the life of the age to come, so the promise of Gehenna makes them wish to avoid failures in performing religious deeds.

IX:X.

1. A. Said R. Samuel bar R. Isaac, "'Lo, it was very good' refers to the angel of life. '*And* lo, it was very good' refers to the angel of death.

B. "And can anyone say that the angel of death is 'very good'?

C. "Rather, the matter may be compared to the case of a king who made a banquet and invited guests and set before them a spread of every good thing. He said, 'Whoever eats and says a blessing for the king may eat and enjoy himself, but whoever eats and does not say a blessing for the king will have his head cut off with a sword.'

D. "So here, for whoever stores up a treasury of merit attained through performance of religious duties and good deeds, lo there is the angel of life. And for whoever does not store up a treasury of merit attained through performance of religious duties and good deeds, lo, there is the angel of death."

From suffering and Gehenna we move on to the angel of death, also encompassed in the perfection of creation.

IX:XI.

1. A. Said R. Simeon bar Abbah, "'Behold, it was very good' refers to the measure that metes out good things to people. '*And* behold, it was very good' refers to the measure that metes out punishment to people.

B. "And can anyone say that the measure that metes out punishment is '*very* good'?

C. "What it means is that God reflected long on how to impose [the measure of punishment]."

2. A. R. Simon in the name of R. Simeon bar Abba, "All of the measures [of reward and punishment] have ceased, but the principle of measure for measure has not ceased."

B. R. Huna in the name of R. Yose, "From the very beginning of the creation of the world, the Holy One, blessed be he, foresaw: By the measure that a person metes out to others, so by that measure is [his fate] meted out [M. Sot. 1:7].

C. "Therefore Scripture has said, 'And behold, it was very good,' meaning, 'and behold, the measure is good' [a play on the word for 'very,' M'D and 'measure,' MDH.]"

Obviously, IX:VI-IX:XI.1 follow a single formal pattern. The repetition of a single form serves to make a single point through unifying numerous examples. The rhetorical formalization serves to construct a cogent list of proofs for one syllogism. That syllogism, presented through illustration and then made explicit at the very end, is that the world is "very good" because there is an exact justice in what happens in the world. "Measure for measure" marks creation and its rules. While some maintain that the world presents marks of imperfection and of the creator's incompetence of malicious spirit, the contrary is the case.

For at issue throughout is the simple question, How can creation be "very good" if there is evil in the world? So we systematically review the challenges to the view that creation is "very good." These encompass death, IX:V.,1 sleep, IX:VI, the impulse to do evil, IX:VII, suffering, IX:VIII, Gehenna, IX:IX, the angel of death, IX:X, and the measure of punishment, IX:XI. All of these negative aspects of creation mar the goodness of the work of the creator-God and point to the conclusion that the creator was evil, not good. By repeating the matter in a protracted catalogue and in a single form, the compositor makes his point. Everything people think mars creation in fact marks its perfection.

Death is good because it prevents the wicked from getting what they have not earned, hence, death insures justice in creation. Sleep is good because it permits the sage to study Torah all the more effectively when he awakes. The evil impulse produces good results. Suffering is the route to eternal life. Gehenna likewise insures justice for those who have earned a reward, by preventing those who have not earned a reward from getting one. The angel of death takes up the same task. And as to punishment? It is inflicted only with justice. So in the end, there is a mete punishment for those who deserve it and a proper reward for those who earn it, so IX:XI.2.

If I had to guess against whom the compositors of this striking composition argue, I should find my clue at IX:VI. That pericope clearly addresses sages. Who else cares about why sleep is a disadvantage and finds compensation in improved alertness in learning? The troubling questions at hand prove urgent in particular to sages and their disciples. So the polemic looks to be addressed to within.

IX:XII.

1. A. All rabbis say the following in the name of R. Haninah, R. Phineas, R. Hilqiah in the name of R. Simon: "'The word 'very' and the word for man are written with the same consonants [M'D, 'DM, respectively]. The letters for both are the same.

B. "The meaning then is as follows: 'And God saw everything that he had made, and behold, it was very good' (Gen. 1:31) -- and behold, man is good.'"

Now comes the climax. The crown of creation is man, and when God praises creation, the intent focuses in the end upon humanity. We cannot treat as distinct from the foregoing the present, stunning conclusion. Rather, the passage that breaks the established form also presents the point of the antecedent catalogue. The purpose of the whole then leads us to conclude that the human being is "very good." Commonly, when the Mishnah presents a sustained, formal list, making a point through a shift in the established rhetorical pattern, the framers will take on a further item, not entirely consonant in subject-matter or purpose, with what has come before. That is what follows in context.

Chapter Six

Israel and Creation

Sages read the narrative of creation and the fall of Adam to testify to the redemption and the salvation of Israel. Let me begin with a single example of the syllogism at hand and then offer a more general statement of it. The following passage provides a stunning example of the basic theory of sages on how the stories of creation are to be read:

XXIX:III.

1. A. "And Noah found grace" (Gen. 6:8):

B. Said R. Simon, "There were three acts of finding on the part of the Holy One, blessed be he:

C. "'And you found [Abraham's] heart faithful before you' (Neh. 9:8).

D. "'I have found David my servant' (Ps. 89:21).

E. "'I found Israel like grapes in the wilderness' (Hos. 9:10)."

F. His fellows said to R. Simon, "And is it not written, 'Noah found grace in the eyes of the Lord' (Gen. 6:8)?"

G. He said them, "He found it, but the Holy One, blessed be he, did not find it."

H. Said R. Simon, "'He found grace in the wilderness' (Jer. 31:1) on account of the merit of the generation of the Wilderness."

The proposition draws on the verse at hand, but makes its own point. It is that the grace shown to Noah derived from Israel. Noah on his own -- that is, humanity -- enjoyed salvation only because of Israel's merit. The proposition is striking and daring. God "found," that is, made an accidental discovery of a treasure, only three: Abraham, David, and Israel, that is, the beginning, the end, and the holy people that started with Abraham and found redemption through David. As if to underline this point, we refer, H, to the generation of the Wilderness and its faith, which merited gaining the Land.

XXX:VIII.

1. A. "[Noah was righteous...] blameless [in his generation]" (Gen. 6:9):

B. Bar Hotah said, "Whoever is described as 'blameless' lived out his years to the full limit of a septennate. [Freedman, p. 236, n. 1: He lived a multiple of seven years after this epithet was applied to him. Thus Noah lived 350 years after the Flood.]"

2. A. R. Yohanan said, "Whoever is described with the verb to be,[as in 'Noah was...,'] remained just as he was, beginning to end."

B. The following objection was raised: "And lo, it is written, 'Abraham was one, and he inherited the earth' (Ez. 33:24). On the basis of the use of the word 'one' do we know that he was one, beginning to end? [Surely he changed in the course of his life.]"

C. He said to him, "Indeed, this item does not contradict my proposition." [We shall now carry forward this statement.]

D. R. Yohanan and R. Hanina both said, "At the age of forty-eight, Abraham came to recognize his creator. Then how in his regard can one understand the use of the word 'was,' [since he was not the same, beginning and end, but vastly changed in his life]? He was designated to lead the entire world to repentence."

E. [Continuing the former proposition:] "The use of the word 'was' in the case of 'Man was...,' (Gen. 3:22) means that the first man was designated for death.

F. "The use of the word 'was' in the case of the snake (Gen. 3:1) means that the snake was designated as the vehicle of punishment.

G. "The use of the word 'was' in the case of Cain (Gen. 4:2) means that Cain was designated to go into exile.

H. "The use of the word 'was' in the case of Job ["Job was...," (Job 1:1)] means that Job was designated for suffering.

I. "The use of the word 'was' in the case of Noah means that Noah was designated for the performance of a miracle.

J. "The use of the word 'was' in the case of Moses [at Ex. 3:1] means that Moses was designated to serve as the redeemer.

K. "The use of the word 'was' in the case of Mordecai [Est. 2:5] means that he was designated for redemption."

3. A. R. Levi said, "Any figure of whom the word 'was' is used will see a new age."

B. Said R. Samuel bar Nahman, "And they are five."

C. As to Noah: to begin with, Scripture says, "The waters wear the stones" (Job 14:19).

D. For R. Levi said in the name of R. Yohanan, "Even the lower millstone was dissolved by the water."

E. And now Scripture says of him, "The sons of Noah that came forth" (Gen. 9:18). This proves that he saw a new age.

F. As to Joseph: to begin with, Scripture says, "His feet they hurt with chains." (Ps. 104:18).

G. And now Scripture says of him, "And Joseph ruled over the entire earth" (Gen. 42:6). This proves that he saw a new age.

H. As to Moses: to begin with, he fled from Pharaoh, and now he drowned him in the sea. This proves that he saw a new age.

I. As to Job: to begin with, Scripture says, "He pours out my gall upon the ground" (Job 16:13).

J. And now, Scripture says of him, "And the Lord gave Job twice as much as he had before" (Job 42:10). This proves that he saw a new age.

K. As to Mordecai: to begin with, he was ready for crucifixion, and now he crucified his crucifier. This proves that he saw a new age.

4. A. Rabbis say, "Any figure of whom the word 'was' is used fed and sustained others."

B. Noah fed and sustained those with him for twelve full months, as it is said, "And take for yourself of all food that is edible" (Gen. 6:21).

C. Joseph fed and sustained the whole world, as it is said, "And Joseph sustained" (Gen. 47:12).

D. Moses fed and sustained Israel in the wilderness for the entire period of forty years.

E. Job fed and sustained others: "Or have I eaten food myself alone" (Job 31:17). "Did not orphans eat with me."

F. But did Mordecai feed and sustain others?

G. R. Yudan said, "Mordecai approached all the wet-nurses and found no one to breastfeed Esther, so he breastfed her himself.

H. R. Berekhiah, R. Abbahu in the name of R. Eleazar, "Milk came to him so he could breastfeed her."

I. R. Abbahu gave this interpretation in the community and the community ridiculed it.

J. He said to them, But is it not an explicit statement of the Mishnah: Milk of a male is insusceptible to uncleanness [M. Makh. 6:7]?"

The intricate composition, certainly the work, in the end, of a single hand, is introduced because of the exegetical task of explaining the use of the verb *to be* in the base verse. No. 2 takes up that question, and everything else follows. The composition works it sway through villains and then heroes. At No. 2 we deal with three of the one, an intermediate figure, then three of the others, thus Adam, the snake, Cain, then Job, then Noah, Moses, and Mordecai. At Nos. 3, 4 we have Noah, Joseph, Moses, Job, Mordecai, and then Noah, Joseph, Moses, and Mordecai. What is important is that the figure of Noah remains among the saints, once more linking Noah to the righteous, and, by the way, Israel's sacred history to Noah. The exegetical purpose begins with the philological task, showing by a succession of historical facts what a given usage signals. But the possibilities of the construction focus not upon Noah but upon Mordecai, and, if I had to choose, I would select Mordecai as the center of discourse. Then the facts of history are so selected and arranged as to highlight the truly unusual character of Mordecai in line with the earlier saints and heroes. None of this, of course, has been worked out for the purposes of the exposition of the book of Genesis.

A cogent and uniform world-view accompanied the sages at hand when they approached the text of Genesis. This world-view they systematically joined to that text, fusing the tale at hand with that larger context of imagination in which the tale was received and read. Accordingly, when we follow the sages' mode of interpreting the text, we find our way deep into their imaginative life. Scripture becomes the set of facts that demonstrate the truth of the syllogisms that encompassed and described the world, as sages saw it. My demonstration of the systematic and deeply polemical reading will take the simple form of successive illustration of the basic thesis. That thes:5 is that Israel's salvific history informs and infuses the creation of the world. That story takes on its true meaning from what happened to Israel, and it follows that Israel's future history accounts for the creation of the world.

XX:I.

1. A. "Then the Lord God said to the serpent, 'Because you have done this, cursed are you above all cattle and above all wild animals'" (Gen. 3:14):

   B. "A slanderer shall not be established in the earth; the violent and wicked man shall be hunted with thrust upon thrust" (Ps. 140:12).

   C. Said R. Levi, "In the world to come the Holy One, blessed be he, will take the nations of the world and bring them down to Gehenna. He will say to them, 'Why did you impose fines upon my children.' They will say to him, 'Some of them slandered others among them. The Holy One, blessed be he, will then take these [Israelite slanderers] and those and bring them down to Gehenna."

2. A. Another interpretation: "A slanderer" refers to the snake, who slandered his creator.

   B. "Will not be established [standing upright] on earth:" "Upon your belly you shall go" (Gen. 3:14).

   C. "The violent and wicked man shall be hunted:" What is written is not "with a thrust" but "with thrust after thrust," [since not only the serpent was cursed]. What is written is "thrust after thrust," for man was cursed, woman was cursed, and the snake was cursed.

   D. "And the Lord God said to the serpent...."

We have an exegesis of a base verse and intersecting verse, that is in that "classic" form in which the intersecting verse is fully worked out and only then drawn to meet the base verse. No. 1 treats the intersecting verse as a statement on its own, and then No. 2 reads the verse in line with Gen. 3:14. But the intersecting verse is hardly chosen at random, since it speaks of slander in general, and then at No. 2 the act of slander of the snake is explicitly read into the intersecting verse. So the intersection is not only thematic, not by any means. The upshot of the exercise links Israel's history to the history of humanity in the garden of Eden. No. 1 focuses upon the sacred history of Israel, making the point that slanderers in Israel cause the nation's downfall, just as the snake caused the downfall of humanity, the point

XIX:VII.

1. A. "And they heard the sound of the Lord God walking in the garden in the cool of the day" (Gen. 3:8):

   B. Said R. Hilpai, "We understand from the verse at hand that a sound may move [since the verse refers to the 'sound moving in the garden'], but we have not heard that fire moves.

   C. "And how on the basis of Scripture do we know that fire moves? It is in the following verse: 'And the fire travelled down upon the earth' (Ex. 9:23)."

2. A. Said R. Abba bar Kahana, "The word is not written, 'move,' but rather, 'walk,' bearing the sense that [the Presence of God] leapt about and jumped upward.

B. "[The point is that God's presence leapt upward from the earth on account of the events in the garden, as will now be explained:] The principal location of the Presence of God was [meant to be] among the creatures down here. When the first man sinned, the Presence of God moved up to the first firmament. When Cain sinned, it went up to the second firmament. When the generation of Enosh sinned, it went up to the third firmament. When the generation of the Flood sinned, it went up to the fourth firmament. When the generation of the dispersion [at the tower of Babel] sinned, it went up to the fifth. On account of the Sodomites it went up to the sixth, and on account of the Egyptians in the time of Abraham it went up to the seventh.

C. "But, as a counterpart, there were seven righteous men who rose up: Abraham, Isaac, Jacob , Levi, Kahath, Amram, and Moses. They brought the Presence of God [by stages] down to earth.

D. "Abraham brought it from the seventh to the sixth, Isaac brought it from the sixth to the fifth, Jacob brought it from the fifth to the fourth, Levi brought it down from the forth to the third, Kahath brought it down from the third to the second, Amram brought it down from the second to the first. Moses brought it down to earth."

E. Said R. Isaac, "It is written, 'The righteous will inherit the land and dwell therein forever' (Ps. 37:29). Now what will the wicked do? Are they going to fly in the air? But that the wicked did not make it possible for the Presence of God to take up residence on earth [is what the verse wishes to say]."

Both entries explain the word "walk," the one removing the corporeal sense of the verse by saying that the verb refers not to God but to the sound or voice, the other by giving the verb an altogether spiritual meaning. What is striking is the claim that while the wicked (gentiles) drove God out of the world, the righteous (Israelites) brought God back into the world. This theme, linking the story of the fall of man to the history of Israel, with Israel serving as the counterpart and fulfillment of the fall at creation.

XIX:IX.

1. A. "And the Lord God called to the man and said to him, 'Where are you?'" (Gen. 3:9):

B. [The word for "where are you" yields consonants that bear the meaning,] "How has this happened to you?"

C. [God speaks:] "Yesterday it was in accord with my plan, and now it is in accord with the plan of the snake. Yesterday it was from one end of the world to the other [that you filled the earth], and now: 'Among the trees of the garden' (Gen. 3:8) [you hide out]."

2. A. R. Abbahu in the name of R. Yose bar Haninah: "It is written, 'But they are like a man [Adam], they have transgressed the covenant' (Hos. 6:7).

B. "'They are like a man,' specifically, like the first man. [We shall now compare the story of the first man in Eden with the story of Israel in its land.]

C. "'In the case of the first man, I brought him into the garden of Eden, I commanded him, he violated my commandment, I judged him to be sent away and driven out, but I mourned for him, saying "How..."'[which begins the book of Lamentations, hence stands for a lament, but which, as we just saw, also is written with the consonants that also yield, 'Where are you'].

D. "'I brought him into the garden of Eden,' as it is written, 'And the Lord God took the man and put him into the garden of Eden' (Gen. 2:15).

E. "'I commanded him,' as it is written, 'And the Lord God commanded...' (Gen. 2:16).

F. "'And he violated my commandment,' as it is written, 'Did you eat from the tree concerning which I commanded you' (Gen. 3:11).

G. "'I judged him to be sent away,' as it is written, "And the Lord God sent him from the garden of Eden' (Gen. 3:23).

H. "'And I judged him to be driven out.' 'And he drove out the man' (Gen. 3:24).

I. "'But I mourned for him, saying, "How...".' 'And he said to him, "Where are you"' (Gen. 3:9), and the word for 'where are you' is written, 'How....'

J. "'So too in the case of his descendants, [God continues to speak,] I brought them into the Land of Israel, I commanded them, they violated my commandment, I judged them to be sent out and driven away but I mourned for them, saying, "How...."'

K. "'I brought them into the Land of Israel.' 'And I brought you into the land of Carmel' (Jer. 2:7).

L. "'I commanded them.' 'And you, command the children of Israel' (Ex. 27:20). 'Command the children of Israel' (Lev. 24:2).

M. "'They violated my commandment.' 'And all Israel have violated your Torah' (Dan. 9:11).

N. "'I judged them to be sent out.' 'Send them away, out of my sight and let them go forth' (Jer 15:1).

O. "'....and driven away.' 'From my house I shall drive them' (Hos. 9:15).

P. "'But I mourned for them, saying, "How...."' 'How has the city sat solitary, that was full of people' (Lam. 1:1)."

I find deeply moving both treatments of Gen. 3:9. No. 1 simply contrasts one day with the next, a stunning and stark statement, lacking all decoration. No. 1 certainly sets the stage for No. 2 and the whole must be regarded as a thoughtful composition. The other, No. 2, equally simply compares the story of man in the Garden of Eden with the tale of Israel in its Land. Every detail is in place, the articulation is perfect, and the result, completely convincing as an essay in interpretation. All of this rests on the simple fact that the word for "where are you" may be expressed as "How...," which, as is clear, invokes the opening words of the book of Lamentations. So Israel's history serves as a paradigm for human history, and vice versa.

XIX:XI.

1. A. "The man said, 'The woman whom you gave to be with me gave me fruit of the tree, and I ate'" (Gen. 3:12):

B. There are four on whose pots the Holy One, blessed be he, knocked, only to find them filled with piss, and these are they: Adam, Cain, the wicked Balaam, and Hezekiah.

C. Adam: "The man said, 'The woman whom you gave to be with me gave me fruit of the tree and I ate" (Gen. 3:12).

D. Cain: "And the Lord said to Cain, 'Where is Abel, your brother?" (Gen. 4:9).

E. The wicked Balaam: "And God came to Balaam and said, 'What men are these with you?'" (Num. 22:9)

F. Hezekiah: "Then came Isaiah the prophet to king Hezekiah and said to him, 'What did these men say?'" (2 Kgs. 20:14).

G. But Ezekiel turned out to be far more adept than any of these: "'Son of man, can these bones live?' And I said, 'O Lord God, you know'" (Ez. 37:3).

H. Said R., Hinena bar Pappa, "The matter may be compared to the case of a bird that was caught by a hunter. The hunter met someone who asked him, 'Is this bird alive or dead?'

I. "He said to him, 'If you want, it is alive, but if you prefer, it is dead.' So: "'Will these bones live?" And he said, "Lord God, you know.'""

The colloquy once more serves to find in Israel's history a counterpart to the incident at hand. Only Ezekiel knew how to deal with a question that bore with it the answer: God will do as he likes, God knows the answer. That is, the sole appropriate response is one of humility and acceptance of God's will

XX:V.

1. A. "Upon your belly you shall go" (Gen. 3:14):

B. When the Holy One, blessed be he, said to him, "Upon your belly you shall go," the ministering angels came down and cut off his hands and feet. His roar went forth from one end of the world to the other.

C. The destruction of the snake serves to teach a lesson concerning the fall of Babylonia and turns out to derive a lesson from that event: "Its cry is like that of the snake" (Jer. 46:22).

2. A. R. Yudan and R. Huna:

B. One of them said, "You are the one who caused my creatures to walk along bent over [in grief caused by the advent into the world of death], so you too: 'Upon your belly you shall go' (Gen. 3:14)."

C. Said R. Eleazar, "Even the curse of the Holy One, blessed be he, contains a blessing. If God had not said to him, 'On your belly you shall go' (Gen. 3:14), how could the snake flee to the wall to find refuge, or to a hole to be saved?"

3. A. "And dust you shall eat [all the days of your life]" (Gen. 3:14):

B. Said R. Hilpai, "It is not any sort of dirt, but the snake digs down until it reaches rock or virgin soil, and he takes up the sinews of the earth and eats."

4. A. Said R. Levi, "In the age to come every creature will find its remedy, except for the snake and the Gibeonites.

B. "The snake: 'And earth shall be the snake's food' (Is. 65:25).

C. "The Gibeonites: 'And they that serve the city out of all the tribes of Israel shall till it' (Ez. 48:19). The sense is that all of the tribes of Israel will force them to till it."

5. A. R. Isi and R. Hoshaia in the name of R. Hiyya the Elder said, "There are four things [on the basis of Gen. 3:14, which the Holy One said to the snake]: "Said the Holy One, blessed be he, to him, 'I made you to be king over all domesticated and wild beasts, but you did not want it: "Cursed are you above all cattle and above all wild animals" (Gen. 3:14).

B. "'I made you to walk upright like a man, but you did not want it: "Upon your belly you shall go" (Gen. 3:14).

C. "'I made you to eat the sort of food humans eat, but you did not want it: "And you shall eat dirt" (Gen. 3:14).

D. "'You wanted to kill man and marry his wife: "I will put enmity between you and the woman, and between your seed and her seed" Gen. 3:15).'

E. "So what turns out is that what he wanted was not given to him, and what he had was taken away from him.

F. "And so we find in the case of Cain, Korach, Balaam, Doeg, Gihazi, Ahitophel, Absalom, Adonijah, Uzziah, and Haman: what they wanted was not given to them, and what they had was taken away from them."

If we had to specify the repertoire of exegetical initiatives available to the authors, we could not do better than to follow the program before us. We find here five entirely familiar themes or polemics. First comes the inquiry into the relationship between the tale at hand and the paradigm of Israel's history. Second, we are asked to find, even in God's curse, a blessing. Third, we attend to the plain facts of philosophy, here, natural philosophy, of interest to the exegetes as shown in their observations about the gestation period of beasts and the like. Fourth, we turn to the coming or future age. Finally, we validate divine justice, showing its exactness. The order of entries before us indicates no clear logic, but the repertoire of interests surely encompasses types of points repeatedly made in the unfolding exegesis of the story of the world.

XXI:I.

1. A. "Then the Lord God said, 'Behold, the man has become like one of us, [knowing good and evil, and now, lest he put forth his hand and take also of the tree of life and eat and live forever]'" (Gen. 3:22):

B. "It is written, "Then I heard a holy one speaking, and another holy one said to that certain one who spoke" (Dan. 8:13).

C. "The one" refers to the Holy One, blessed be he: "The Lord, our God, the Lord is One" (Deut. 6:4).

D. "Holy," for everyone says before him, "Holy...."

E. "Speaking" means "issuing harsh decrees against his creatures."

F. [For example,] "Thorns and thistles it shall bring forth to you" (Gen. 3:18).

G. "And another holy one said to that certain one who spoke:"

H. R. Huna said, "It was to Mr. So-and-so."

I. Aqilas translated the passage, "It was to one who was within that he spoke, meaning the first man, whose presence lay within [and closer to God than] that of the serving angels [since he stood closer to God than they did]." [The remainder of the exegesis flows from Aqilas's view of the locus of discourse.]

J. "How long shall be the vision concerning the continual burnt offering?" (Dan. 8:13);

K. "Will the decree that has been issued against the first man go on forever?"

L. "And the transgression that causes desolation" (Deut. 8:13):

M. "So too will his transgression desolate him even in the grave?"

N. "To give both the sanctuary and the host to be trampled underfoot" (Dan. 8:13):

O. "Will he and his descendants be made into chaff before the angel of death?"

P. "And he said to me, 'Until evening, morning two thousand and three hundred, then shall the sanctuary be victorious'" (Dan. 8:14):

Q. R. Azariah, R. Jonathan b., Haggai in the name of R. Isaac: "In any case in which it is evening, it is not morning, and in any case in which it is morning, it surely is not evening. [So what is the sense of this passage?] But when it is morning for the nations of the world, it is evening for Israel, and as to 'morning,' at that time [at which it is morning for Israel],' then 'shall the sanctuary be victorious,' for at that time I shall declare him justified of that decree: 'Behold, let the man become like one of us' (Gen. 3:22)."

The fully exploited intersection of the intersecting and base verses turns the statement of Gen. 3:22 into a powerful promise. Man will indeed become like the One, at the time that the gentiles reach their evening, and Israel, morning. So once more the condition of Israel serves as a paradigm for the human situation, but this in a most concrete and specific way. The nations of the world embody the curse of God to man, and Israel, the promised future blessing. The framer of the passage carefully avoids speculation on the meaning of the numbers used in Daniel's passage, so the apocalyptic power of Daniel's vision serves the rather generalized messianic expectations of sages, without provoking dangerous speculation on the here and now.

XXI:VII.

3. A. Judah b. Padaiah interpreted, "Who will remove the dust from between your eyes, O first man! For you could not abide in the commandment that applied to you for even a single hour, and lo, your children can wait for three years to observe the prohibition of the use of the fruit of a tree for the first three years after it is planted: 'Three years shall it be as forbidden to you, it shall not be eaten' (Lev. 19:23)."

B. Said R. Huna, "When Bar Qappara heard this, he said, 'Well have you expounded matters, Judah, son of my sister!'"

No. 3 then compares the character of Israel to the character of the first man, calling Israel "descendants of the first man" and pointing out that they can observe a commandment for a long time. The example is apt, since Israel observes the prohibition involving the fruit of a newly planted tree, and does so for three years, while the first man could not keep his hands off a fruit tree for even an hour. This of course states with enormous power the fact that Israel's history forms the counterpart to the history of humanity. But while the first man could not do what God demanded, Israel can and does do God's will.

XXXIV:IX.

1.   A.   "Then Noah built an altar to the Lord" (Gen. 8:20):

B.   What is written is "he understood" [that is, the word is so spelled out that it can be read as "understood" rather than "built"], with the implication that he thought matters out in this way: "What is the reason that the Holy One, blessed be he, ordered more clean than unclean animals?

C.   "Is it not that he wanted me to offer up animals of the clean classification?"

D.   Forthwith: "And he took of every clean animal" (Gen. 8:20).

2.   A.   "And offered up burnt offerings on the altar" (Gen. 8:20):

B.   R. Eliezer b. Jacob said, "It was on the great altar in Jerusalem, the same place at which the first man made his offering: 'And it shall please the Lord better than a bullock that has horns and hoofs' (Ps. 69:32)."

3.   A.   "And when the Lord smelled the pleasing odor" (Gen. 8:21):

B.   R. Eleazar and R. Yose bar Hanina:

C.   R. Eleazar says, "The children of Noah [when they made offerings] offered their sacrifices in the status of peace-offerings. [They kept portions of the sacrificial beast, e.g., the hide, and burned up on the fire only the minimal sacrificial parts.]"

D.   R. Yose bar Hanina said, "They prepared them in the status of whole-offerings [burning up the entire animal and not keeping any portions for the sacrificer and sacrifier (he who benefits from the offering)]."

E.   R. Eleazar objected to the view of R. Yose bar Hanina, "And is it not written, 'And of their fat portions' (Gen. 4:4)? It was an offering in the status of one, the fat portions of which are burned up on the altar [and not eaten by the sacrificer]."

F.   How does R. Yose bar Hanina treat this passage? He interprets it to refer to the fat animals [and not to the portions of those that were offered up, but only to "the best of the flock"].

G.   R. Eleazar objected to the view of R. Yose bar Hanina, "And lo, it is written: 'And he sent the young men of the children of Israel, who offered burnt offerings and sacrificed peace offerings of oxen unto the Lord' (Ex. 24:5)? [This was before revelation, and hence would indicate that the children of Noah, into the category of which the Israelites fell at that time, prior to the giving of the Torah, offered not only whole offerings but also peace offerings, just as Eleazar maintains]."

H.   How does R. Yose bar Hanina treat this verse? He interprets the reference to "peace-offerings" to mean that they offered up the beasts with their hides, without flaying them and cutting them into pieces. [So even though the verse refers to peace offerings, in fact the animals were offered up as whole offerings, hide and all.]

I. R. Eleazar objected to R. Yose bar Hanina, "And is it not written, 'And Jethro, Moses' father-in-law, took a burnt-offering and sacrifices' (Ex. 18:12)? [The reference to a burnt offering would suffice, so the inclusion of the further reference to "sacrifices" indicates that there was an offering made in a different classification, hence, peace-offerings.]"

J. How does R. Yose bar Hanina deal with this verse? He accords with the view of him who said that Jethro came to Moses after the giving of the Torah, [at which point Jethro was in the status of an Israelite. Hence the type of offering Jethro gave would indicate only what Israelites did when they made their sacrifices and would not testify to how children of Noah in general offered up their animals.]

K. [We shall now deal with the point at which Jethro rejoined Moses.] Said R. Huna, "R. Yannai and R. Hiyya the Elder differed on this matter."

L. R. Yannai said, "It was prior to the giving of the Torah that Jethro came."

M. R. Hiyya the Elder said, "It was after the giving of the Torah that Jethro came."

N. Said R,. Hanina, "They did not in fact differ. The one who said that it was prior to the giving of the Torah that Jethro came holds that the children of Noah offered peace-offerings [in addition to offerings in accord with the rules governing the classification of whole-offerings]. The one who maintains that it was after the giving of the Torah that Jethro came takes the position that the children of Noah offered up animals only in the status of whole-offerings."

O. The following verse supports the view of R. Yose bar Hanina, "Awake, O north wind" (Song 4:16) refers to the whole offering, which was slaughtered at the north side of the altar. What is the sense of "awake"? It speaks of something that was asleep and now wakes up.

P. "And come, you south" (Song 4:16) speaks of peace-offerings, which were slaughtered [even] at the south side of the altar. And what is the sense of "come"? It speaks of a new and unprecedented practice. [Hence the rules governing peace-offerings constituted an innovation. Freedman, p. 184, n. 1: Thus it was only now, after the giving of the Torah, that the practice of sacrificing peace-offerings was introduced.]

Q. R. Joshua of Sikhnin in the name of R. Levi: "Also the following verse supports the view of R. Yose bar Hanina: 'This is the torah governing the preparation of the whole-offering, that is the whole-offering [of which people already are informed]' (Lev. 6:2) meaning, that whole-offering that the children of Noah used to offer up.

R. "When by contrast the passage speaks of peace-offerings, it states, 'And this is the law of the sacrifice of peace-offerings' (Lev. 7:11), but it is not written, 'which they offered up,' but rather, 'which they will offer up' (Lev. 7:11), meaning, only in the future. [Hence peace-offerings' rules, allowing the sacrificer and sacrifier a share in the animal that is offered up, represented an innovation, not formerly applicable, in support of the view of R. Yose bar Hanina that such offerings' rules constituted an innovation.]"

4. A. "And when the Lord smelled the pleasing odor,[the Lord said in his heart, 'I will never again curse the ground because of man, for the imagination of man's heart is evil from his youth']" (Gen. 8:21):

B. He smelled the fragrance of the flesh of Abraham, our father, coming up from the heated furnace.

C. He smelled the fragrance of the flesh of Hananiah, Mishael, and Azariah, coming up from the heated furnace.

D. The matter may be compared to the case of a king, whose courtier brought him a valuable present. It was a fine piece of meat on a lovely plate [following Freedman].

E. His son came along and brought him nothing. His grandson came along and brought him a present. He said to him, "The gift you brought is like the gift your grandfather brought."

F. So God smelled the fragrance of the sacrifice of the generation of persecution.

5. A. R. Shillum in the name of R. Menahama bar R. Zira: "The matter may be compared to the case of a king who wanted to build a palace by the sea, but did not know where to build it. He came across a flask of perfume and followed its scent and built the palace on that spot.

B. "That is in line with this verse: 'For he has founded it upon the seas' (Ps. 24:2). On whose account? On account of those of whom the following speaks: 'Such is the generation of those that seek after him, that seek your face, even Jacob, Selah (Ps. 24:6)."

No. 1 completes the discourse on Noah's preparation of the sacrifice;this will not dominate what follows. No. 2 opens with the explicit link between the site of Noah's sacrifice and the altar at Jerusalem. At issue now is the relationship between the sacrifices of humanity at large and those of Israel. That accounts for the introduction of No. 3, a familiar item better situation (if it belongs at all) with the story of Abel's sacrifice, at which it is at least tangentially relevant. No. 3 goes its own way, taking up an issue to which the exegesis of the cited passage is peripheral. The discourse is fully spelled out, but in no way adds to the interpretation of the present passage. But the relevance to Gen. 8:21 cannot be missed, since at issue is whether God prefers a sacrifice in which the entire beast is burned up or one in which part of the beast is shared by the priest and the sacrifier. Nos. 4, 5 now take up the important link between the sacrifice of Noah and the cult of Israel. The true sacrifices to God come from those who give their lives for his name. Now in context we address those who accepted death by burning, equivalent to the burning up of the animals that produces the sweet smell God likes. So the blood-sacrifice is turned into a symbol for Israel's sacrifice of itself in God's name.

The effect of the composition exceeds the contribution of the several discrete parts, for the point of the compositor is, first, Israel's sacrifices, offered at Jerusalem, succeed those of Noah, and, second, those sacrifices really derive from the flesh and blood of the children of Israel, who offer themselves for God's name. The intersection of Israel's cultic history with the sacrifice of Noah so proves the main point to be read at the present passage, a substantial and important proposition indeed. But the proposition concerns not the cult in times past but the sacrifice of Israel in the present, as is made explicit at Nos. 4, 5.

We come at the end to a simple and clear statement of the main point of it all:

LXXXIII:V.
1. A. Wheat, straw, and stubble had a fight.

    B. Wheat said, "It was on my account that the field was sown."

    C. Stubble said, "It was on my account that the field was sown."

    D. Wheat said, "The day will come and you will see."

    E. When the harvest time came, the householder began to take the stubble and burn it, and the straw and spread it, but the wheat he made into heaps.

    F. Everyone began to kiss the wheat. [I assume this is a reference to the messianic passage, "Kiss the son" which is also to be translated, "Kiss the wheat" (Ps. 2:12).]

    G. So too Israel and the nations of the world have a fight.

    H. These say, "It was on our account that the world was created," and those say, "It was on our account that the world was created."

    I. Israel says, "The day will come and you will see."

    J. In the age to come: "You shall fan them and the wind will carry them away" (Is. 41:16).

    K. As to Israel: "And you shall rejoice in the Lord, you shall glory in the Holy One of Israel" (Is. 41:16).

Here at the end sages make explicit their basic view. The world was created for Israel, and not for the nations of the world. At the end of days everyone will see what only Israel now knows.

Chapter Seven

The Temple and the Celebration of Creation

Not only does creation point to the sanctity of Israel. The biographies of the patriarchs and matriarchs repeatedly adumbrate the Temple and its cult. We recall that the sages at hand find in the stories of creation and Noah reason to celebrate Israel's life and hope for Israel's salvation. They also are able to find in the stories of those same lives numerous references to the Temple, its cult and its future destruction and restoration. So the stories of Genesis in yet another way are made to testify to the hope of Israel. The case that follows shows how Jacob devoted himself to the sanctity of the cult. His entire concern for the birthright, which would give him the status of firstborn, was to protect the cult from the presence of Esau, who, we must recall, always stood for Rome.

LXIII:XIII.

4. A. "Jacob said, 'Swear to me first.' So he swore to him and sold his birthright to Jacob" (Gen. 25:33):

B. Why did Jacob risk his life for the right of the firstborn?

C. For we have learned in the Mishnah: **Before the tabernacle was set up, the high places were permitted, and the rite of offering was carried out by the first born. Once the tabernacle was set up, the high places were forbidden, and the rite of offering was carried out by the priests**[M. Zebahim 14:4].

D. He said, "Should that wicked man stand and make offerings?" Therefore Jacob risked his life for the right of the firstborn.

5. A. That is in line with the following verse: "I will prepare you for blood, and blood shall pursue you, surely you have hated blood, therefore shall blood pursue you" (Ez. 35:6).

B. But did Esau hate blood?

C. R. Levi in the name of R. Hama bar Hanina: "This is the blood of circumcision [which Esau did hate]."

D. R. Levi in the name of R. Samuel b. Nahman,"This refers to the blood of the offerings by the firstborn."

E. Rabbis say, "You have hated the blood of man when it is in his body, in line with this verse: 'Yes, he loved cursing and it came to him and he did not delight in blessing' (Ps. 109:17)."

F. R. Levi in the name of R. Hama bar Hanina, "He did not take pleasure in the birthright."

G. R. Huna said, "This refers to the blood of the offerings, which are called a blessing, in line with this verse: 'An altar of earth you shall make for me...I will come to you and bless you' (Ex. 20:21)."

What was at stake was a considerable issue. Esau had no right to make offerings, he had no respect for the Temple and its cult. The same motif recurs in much more detail. Now the entire exchange between Isaac and Jacob points to the coming Temple of Jerusalem.

LXV:XXIII.

1. A. ["See the smell of my son is as the smell of a field which the Lord has blessed" (Gen. 27:27):] Another matter: this teaches that the Holy One, blessed be he, showed him the house of the sanctuary as it was built, wiped out, and built once more.

B. "See the smell of my. son:" This refers to the Temple in all its beauty, in line with this verse: "A sweet smell to me shall you observe" (Num. 28:2).

C. "...is as the smell of a field:" This refers to the Temple as it was wiped out, thus: "Zion shall be ploughed as a field" (Mic. 3:12).

D. "...which the Lord has blessed:" This speaks of the Temple as it was restored once more in the age to come, as it is said, "For there the Lord commanded the blessing, even life for ever" (Ps. 133:3).

The conclusion explicitly links the blessing of Jacob to the Temple throughout its history. The concluding proof-text presumably justifies the entire identification of the blessing at hand with what was to come.

LXVI:III.

1. A. May God give you [of the dew of heaven and of the fatness of the earth, and plenty of grain and wine] (Gen. 27:28):

B. "May he give you and go and give you again.

C. "May he give you blessings and may he give you [Freedman:] the means of holding them.

D. "May he give you what belongs to you and may he give you what belongs to your father.

E. "May he give you what belongs to you and may he give you what belongs to your brother."

F. R. Aha: "May he give you what belongs to you and may he give you [Freedman:] of his own divine strength.

G. "When? When you need it, in line with this verse, 'And Samson called to the Lord and said, "O Lord, remember me, I pray you, and strengthen me, I pray you, only this once, O God" (Judges 16:28).'

H. "He said, 'Lord of the age, Remember in my behalf the blessing with which my ancestor blessed me, "May he give you [Freedman:] of his own divine strength."'"

2. A. "of the dew of heaven:"

B. This refers to mana: "Then said the Lord to Moses, Behold I will cause to rain bread from heaven for you" (Ex. 216:4).

3. A. "and of the fatness of the earth:"

   B. This refers to the well, which produced diverse fat fish.

4. A. "and plenty of grain" refers to young men: "Grain shall make the young men flourish" (Zech. 9:17).

   B. "and wine:" refers to maidens: "And new wine for the maids" (Zech. 9:17).

5. A. Another interpretation: "May God give you of the dew of heaven:" speaks of Zion: "Like the dew of Hermon that comes down on the mountains of Zion" (Ps. 133:3).

   B. "and of the fatness of the earth:" speaks of the offerings.

   C. "and plenty of grain:" alludes to firstfruits.

   D. " and wine:" these are the drink offerings.

6. A. Another interpretation: "May God give you of the dew of heaven:" this is Scripture.

   B. "and of the fatness of the earth:" this is Mishnah.

   C. "and plenty of grain :" this is Talmud.

   D. "and wine:" this is lore.

No. 1 works out the first clause, on giving. No. 2 proceeds to the dew, No. 3, 4, 5 to the other parts of the composition. We proceed in the concluding units to rework the same matter in a more figurative way, ending, of course, with the imputation of the symbols critical to the sages' own world. Nos. 5, 6 draw the recurrent parallel between Temple offerings and Torah-study. Jacob's dream of the ladder with angels ascending and descending produced for him a vision of the Temple to come:

LXVIII:XII.

3. A. "And he dreamed a dream" (Gen. 28:12): Bar Qappara taught on Tannaite authority, "There is no dream without a proper interpretation.

   B. "'That there was a ladder:'refers to the ramp to the altar.

   C. "'...set up on the earth:' that is the altar, 'An altar of dirt you will make for me' (Ex. 20:24).

   D. "'...and the top of it reached to heaven:' these are the offerings, for their fragrance goes up to heaven.

   E. "'...and behold, the angels of God:' these are the high priests.

   F. "'...were ascending and descending on it:' for they go up and go down on the ramp.

   G. "'And behold, the Lord stood above it:' 'I saw the Lord standing by the altar' (Amos 9:1)."

4. A. Rabbis interpreted the matter to prefigure Sinai: "'And he dreamed:

   B. "'...that there was a ladder:' this refers to Sinai.

   C. "'...set up on the earth:' 'And they stood at the lower part of the mountain' (Ex. 19:17).

   D. "'...and the top of it reached to heaven:' 'And the mountain burned with fire into the heart of heaven' (Deut. 4:11).

   E. "'...and behold, the angels of God:' these are Moses and Aaron.

   F. "'...were ascending:' 'And Moses went up to God' (Ex. 19:3).

G. "'...and descending on it:' "And Moses went down from the mount' (Ex. 19:14).

F. "'...And behold, the Lord stood above it:' 'And the Lord came down upon Mount Sinai' (Ex. 19:20)."

No. 3 reads the dream in terms of the Temple cult, and No. 4 in terms of the revelation of the Torah at Sinai, and No. 5 has the dream refer to the patriarchs.

LXVIII:XIII.

1. A. [Resuming the discourse of LXVIII:XII.3-4,] R. Joshua b. Levi interpreted the verse at hand to speak of the Exiles of Israel [symbolized in Jacob's exile from the Land]:

B. "'And Jacob went out from Beer Sheba:' 'Cast them out of my sight and let them go forth' (Jer. 15:1).

C. "'...and went toward Haran:' 'Wherewith the Lord has afflicted me in the day of his fierce anger' (Lam. 1:1) ["anger" using letters shared with the word for Haran].

D. "'And he lighted on a certain place:' 'Til there be no place' (Is. 5:8).

E. "'...and stayed there that night because the sun had set:' 'She who has borne seven languishes, her spirit droops, her sun has set' (Jer. 15:9).

F. "'...Taking one of the stones of the place:' 'The hallowed stones are poured out at the head of every street' (Lam. 4:1).

G. "'...he put it under his head:' 'For your headties are come down' (Jer. 13:18).

H. "'...and lay down in that place to sleep:' 'Let us lie down in our shame and let our confusion cover us' (Jer. 3:25).

I. "'And he dreamed:' this alludes to the dream of Nebuchadnezzer.

J. "'...that there was a ladder:' this alludes to Nebuchadnezzar's image, for the word for image shares the same letters as the word for ladder.

K. "'...set up on the earth:' 'He set it up in the plain of Dura' (Dan. 3:1).

L. "'...and the top of it reached to heaven:' 'Whose height was three score cubits' (Dan. 3:1).

M. "'...and behold, the angels of God:' Hananiah, Mishael, and Azariah.

N. "'...were ascending and descending on it:' they were raising him up and dragging him down, dancing on him, leaping on him, abusing him: 'Be it known to you, O king, that we will not serve your gods' (Dan. 3:18).

O. "'And behold, the Lord stood beside him and said:' 'You servants of God, most high, come forth and come hither' (Dan. 3:26)."

2. A. Another interpretation: "And behold the angels of God..." refers to Daniel.

B. "...ascending and descending on it:" he went up and brought forth what it had swallowed from its mouth.

C. That is in line with this verse: "And I will punish Bel in Babylonia and I will bring forth out of his mouth that which he has swallowed up" (Jer. 51:44).

D. "And behold the Lord stood beside him" (Gen. 28:13): "O Daniel, servant of the living God" (Dan. 6:21).

The exegesis of the story of Jacob's dream in terms of Israel's history is worked out yet once more. The sources of interpretation are the Temple, Sinai, the lives of the patriarchs, and the Exile. It would be difficult to point to a more complete symbolic repertoire to evoke Israel's salvific life than one which encompasses Israel's cult, revelation, and salvation on the other side of the Exile, that is, creation, celebrated in the cult, revelation, then redemption. The tripartite categories fully work themselves out in a rather complex structure. The following carries through the same idea.

LXIX:VII.

1. A. "Then Jacob awoke [from his sleep and said, 'Surely the Lord is in this place, and I did not know it']" (Gen. 28:16):

B. Said R. Yohanan, "He awoke from his repetition of Mishnah-traditions" [a play on the words for "sleep" and "Mishnah," which share consonants].

2. A. "'...Surely the Lord is in this place, and I did not know it'" (Gen. 28:16):

B. [Since the word for "surely" and the word for "where" share the same consonants, we interpret:] "Where does the Presence of God dwell? It is 'in this place, and I did not know it.'"

3. A. "And he was afraid and said, 'How awesome is this place! [This is none other than the house of God, and this is the gate of heaven']" (Gen. 28:17):

B. R. Eleazar in the name of R. Yose b. Zimra, "The ladder is set in Beer Sheba and its slopes over the Temple.

C. "What verse of Scripture indicates it? 'Jacob left Beer Sheba' (Gen. 28:10). 'And he was afraid and said, "How awesome is this place! [This is none other than the house of God, and this is the gate of heaven."'"

D. Said R. Judah bar Simon, "The ladder stood in the sanctuary and its sloped to Beth El.

E. "What verse of Scripture indicates it? 'And he was afraid and said, "How awesome is this place! [This is none other than the house of God, and this is the gate of heaven].'" 'And he called the name of that place Beth El' (Gen. 28:19)."

4. A. "And he was afraid and said, 'How awesome is this place! This is none other than the house of God, 'And he was afraid and said, "How awesome is this place! [This is none other than the house of God, and this is the gate of heaven."'"

B. Said R. Aha, "'This particular gate is destined to be opened for many righteous like you.'"

5. A. Said R. Simeon b. Yohai, "The sanctuary above is only eighteen *mil* s higher than that down below. What is the verse of Scripture that proves it?

B. "'This is none other than the house of God, *and this is* the gate of heaven.' Now the numerical value of the word for *'and this'* is eighteen."

6. A. Another matter: It teaches that the Holy One, blessed be he, showed him the house of the sanctuary built, destroyed, and rebuilt.

B. "And he was afraid and said, 'How awesome is this place!'" refers to the sanctuary as it was built: "Awful is God out of your holy places" (Ps. 68:36).

C. "*This* is none other" speaks of the Temple when it was destroyed: "For *this* our heart is faint" (Lam. 5:17).

D. "...than (KY)the house of God, and this is the gate of heaven:" refers to the Temple as it will be rebuilt and made permanent in the age to come: "For (KY) he has made strong the bars of your gates" (Ps. 147:13).

Nos. 1, 2 work on the amplification of the meanings of words. No. 3 takes up the relationships among the holy places at Beer Sheba, Jerusalem, and Beth El, relating all three to the present narrative. No. 4 and No. 5 continue this same motif, now relating the Temple in Jerusalem to its counterpart in heaven. No. 6 then brings us to the necessary conclusion, the history of the sanctuary, built, destroyed, but destined to be rebuilt.

The focus on Jacob in particular derives from the fact that Jacob built an altar. His action then finds its counterpart in the building of the Temple.

LXXXII:II.

1. A. R. Isaac commenced discourse by citing this verse: "'An altar of earth you shall me for me...in every place where I cause my name to be mentioned I will come to you and bless you' (Ex. 20:24):

    B. "[God says,] 'Now if upon the one who builds an altar to my name, lo, I come and bestow a blessing, Jacob, whose face is incised on my throne, how much the more so shall I appear to him and bless him.'

    C. "That is in line with this verse: 'God appeared to Jacob again, when he came from Paddan-aram, and blessed him.'"

2. A. R. Levi opened discourse by citing this verse: "'And an ox and a ram for peace-offerings...for today the Lord appears to you' (Lev. 9:4).

    B. "He said, 'If to this one, who offered up an ox and a ram for my name, lo, I reveal myself to him and bless him, Jacob, whose face is incised on my throne, how much the more so shall I appear to him and bless him.'

    C. "That is in line with this verse: 'God appeared to Jacob again, when he came from Paddan-aram, and blessed him.'"

3. A. "Blessed are you when you come in and blessed are you when you go out" (Deut. 28:6):

    B. When Jacob came to the house of his father-in-law to be, he was bearing blessings, and when he left his father-in-law's house, he was bearing blessings.

    C. When he came to his father-in-law's house he was bearing blessings: "And God Almighty bless you" (Gen. 28:4).

    D. And when he left his father-in-law's house, he was bearing blessings: "God appeared to Jacob again, when he came from Paddan-aram, and blessed him."

4. A. R. Berekhiah began by citing this verse: "'You shall also decree a thing and it shall be established for you, and light will shine upon your ways' (Job 22:28).

    B. "'You shall also decree a thing and it shall be established for you' refers to Jacob.

    C. "'...and light will shine upon your ways' refers to two journeys in which light will come forth [once when Jacob went to Laban, the second when he came home].

D. "When Jacob came to the house of his father-in-law to be, he was bearing blessings, and when he left his father-in-law's house, he was bearing blessings.

E. "When he came to his father-in-law's house he was bearing blessings: 'And God Almighty bless you' (Gen. 28:4).

F. "And when he left his father-in-law's house, he was bearing blessings: 'God appeared to Jacob again, when he came from Paddan-aram, and blessed him.'"

5. A. "I am the Lord...who confirms the word of his servant and performs the counsel of his angels" (Is. 44:26ff.):

B. R. Berekhiah in the name of R. Levi: "Since he confirms the word of his servant, do we not know that he also will perform the counsel of his angels?

C. "But an angel appeared to Jacob and said to him, 'He is destined to reveal himself to you in Beth El and to change your name, and I shall be standing there.'

D. "That is why it is written, 'At Beth El he would find him, and there he would speak with *us* ' (Hos. 12:5). 'With you' is not what is written, but rather, 'with us' [that is, the angel and Jacob].

E. "So the Holy One, blessed be he, appeared to him in order to carry out the statements of that angel.

F. "And as to Jerusalem, since all of the prophets prophesied about it, how much the more so [will God's words be confirmed]: 'God appeared to Jacob again, when he came from Paddan-aram, and blessed him.'"

The point of interest at No. 1 is in the reference in the base verse to God's appearing to and blessing Jacob. Now we are looking for the context in which to explain that action, and it is in the building of the promised altar, as Jacob was instructed at Gen. 35:1. So once more the effect of the exegesis is to draw together the strands of the narrative, on the one side, and to link the entire composition to a pressing concern of Israel's life, on the other. That is why the resort to the Temple as the center of both imagery and argument proves critical to the intent of the exegetes. The building of each of the altars prefigures the Temple to come. The Temple to come for its part prefigures the redemption that lies beyond. No. 2 occurs with reference to Abraham, as does No. 1, and both go over the same matter, namely, the basis for God's favor to the patriarchs. They then guarantee that God will also bless and appear to those who, later on, do the sorts of deeds done by the patriarchs and matriarchs. No. 3 draws the parallel between Jacob's going out and his coming back, underlining the somewhat odd nature of the narrative, since Jacob's return has already found full and complete portrayal. No. 4 goes over the same ground. No. 5 links the revelation to Jacob and the confirmation of the prophet's prophesies about the future of Jerusalem, so once more linking the life of the patriarch to the history of the cult and the nation.

Part Three

DEEDS OF THE FOUNDERS, LESSONS FOR THE CHILDREN

Chapter Eight

Abraham

The systematic reading of Genesis by the framers of Genesis Rabbah yields two dominant propositions. One is that what the patriarchs and matriarchs of the book of Genesis did in their day gives the signal to the generations to come of what Israel is to do. The other is that the lives of the patriarchs and matriarchs foretell the sacred history of Israel. So the deeds of the founders teach lessons on how the children should live, and the biographies of the founders tell how the children how Israel is to endure. The one message addresses the individual and the family, the other, the nation and the peoples. In this part we take up the lessons for individual life, in the next, the tale of national redemption.

Abraham had no teacher, and the Torah had not yet been given. So how did he know what he should do? He followed God's example, and God responded to Abraham's wisdom. The single stunning claim concerning Abraham is that he took up the profession of God, which was and is to practice deeds of lovingkindness. This view begins our picture of sages' revisioning of Abraham.

LVIII:IX.

1. A. "After this, Abraham buried [Sarah his wife in the cave of the field of Machpelah east of Mamre, that is Hebron, in the land of Canaan]" (Gen. 23:19):

   B. "He who follows after righteousness and love finds life, prosperity, and honor" (Prov. 21:21).

   C. "He who follows after righteousness" refers to Abraham, as it is said, "That they make keep the way of the Lord, to do righteousness and justice" (Gen. 18:19).

   D. "...and love:" for he dealt lovingly with Sarah [in burying her].

   E. "...finds life, [prosperity, and honor]" (Prov. 21:21): "And these are the days of the years of Abraham's life, which he lived, a hundred and seventy-five years" (Gen. 25:7).

   F. "...prosperity, and honor:"

   G. Said R. Samuel bar R. Isaac, "Said the Holy One, blessed be he, to him, 'My profession is to practice acts of love. Since you have taken over my profession, put on my cloak as well [as a fellow-craftsman, wearing the same signifying clothing]: 'And Abraham was old, well advanced in age' (Gen. 24:1)." [God dresses in the garment of old age, so Dan. 7:13 (Freedman, p. 515, n. 1)]."

The intersecting verse leads to a stunning climax at G. In redactional terms the framer has built a bridge from story to story, joining the burial of Sarah to the beginning of the next account, Gen. 24:1. In theological terms he has linked Abraham to God. In moral terms he has made the principal trait of God, hence of the human being like God, the practice of acts of lovingkindness, that is, those acts of *hesed*, translated here, "love," that God does as the divine profession.

Stated in its classic formulation, the basic approach holds that the deeds of the founders are a sign to the children. What in practical terms that means we already know. What Abraham did produced merit for him, so if we follow his example, we too shall gain merit, as in the following:

XXXIX:III.

1. A. R. Berekhiah commenced discourse by citing the following verse of Scripture]: "'We have a little sister' (Song 8:8). This passage speaks of Abraham, who united the entire world for us. [At hand is a play on the word for 'sister,' the consonants of which can yield the word for 'unite.']"

B. Bar Qappara: "The matter may be compared to someone who sews up a tear [a play on the same two words]."

C. "Little" (Song 8:8): For while he was yet small, he built up a treasury of merit for the religious duties and acts of goodness that he carried out.

D. "And she does not have breasts" (Song 8:8): No breasts gave him suck, neither in acts of religious duty or of goodness [since he had no example from whom to learn].

E. "What shall we do for our sister on the day when she shall be spoken for?" (Song 8:8): On the day on which the wicked Nimrod threw him down in the heated furnace.

F. "If she is a wall, we will build upon her" (Song 8:9): If he stands up against Nimrod like a wall, [God] will build upon him.

G. "If she is a door, we will enclose her with boards of cedar" (Song 8:9): If he is poor in merit accruing for doing acts of religious duty and good deeds [a play on the words for door and poor, both of which use the letters DL],

H. "we will enclose her with boards of cedar" (Song 8:9): and just as a drawing lasts only for a moment, so I shall sustain him only for a time. [The play now is on the words for "enclose" and "drawing."] [Freedman, p. 314, n. 4: A drawing is easily rubbed off. He translates: We will treat her like a drawing.]

I. He said before him, "Lord of the ages, 'I am a wall' (Song 8:10). I stand up as firmly as a wall.

J. "'And my breasts are like the towers of the wall' (Song 8:10). My sons are Hananiah, Mishael, and Azariah."

K. "Then I was in his eyes as one who found wholeness [peace]" (Song 8:10). He entered whole and came out whole.

L. "Now the Lord said to Abram, 'Go from your country'" (Gen. 12:1).

The systematic reading of Song 8:8-10 in line with Abram works quite well, linking the story of Abram in Nimrod's furnace to Hananiah, Mishael, and

Azariah in later times. The power of the identification, of course, lies in linking the story in Daniel, which took place in Babylonia, to the story of Abraham, leaving his family in the same region and going to the Holy Land. H is somewhat jarring; it makes Abram plead with God to stand by him. Then the appeal to Hananiah, Mishael, and Azariah, I-J, and the further reference at K to the shared experience in the fiery furnace, serve as Abram's case for God's continuing support. Another case of showing how Abraham attained merit is as follows:

LIX:I.
1. A. "Now Abraham was old, well advanced in years; and the Lord had blessed Abraham in all things" (Gen. 24:1):

B. "The hoary head is a crown of glory, it is found in the way of righteousness" (Prov. 16:31).

C. R. Meir went to Mamala. He saw that everyone there had black hair [so there were no old people]. He said to them, "What family do you come from? Could it be that you come from the family of Eli, concerning whom it is written, 'And all the increase of your house shall die as young men' (1 Sam. 2:33)?"

D. They said to him, "Rabbi, pray for us."

E. He said to them, "Go and carry out works of righteousness [charity], and you will gain the merit of enjoying old age.

F. "What is the biblical verse that indicates it? 'The hoary head is a crown of glory, it is found in the way of righteousness' (Prov. 16:31).

G. "From whom do you learn that lesson? It is from Abraham. Because concerning him it is written, 'To do righteous deeds' (Gen. 18:19), he had the merit of attaining old age: 'Now Abraham was old, well advanced in years.'"

The intersecting verse is brought into relationship to the life of Abraham, which itself is clarified. Abraham had the merit of reaching a ripe old age because of the acts of righteousness (charity) that he had performed. What exactly are people to learn from the example of Abraham? The first lesson is to make proselytes to the service of the one God, the second, to live in the holy land (for the sages before us all lived in the land of Israel).

XXXIX:VIII.
1. A. "Go, go" (Gen. 12:1) [the consonants for "Get you" may be read to mean the word, "Go," repeated twice:]

B. R. Judah said, "'Go, go,' two times, indicates that one time he was told to go out of Aram Naharim, and the other time to go out of Aram Nahor."

C. R. Nehemiah said, "'Go, go,' two times, indicates that once he was told to go out of Aram Naharim, and once to fly from 'the covenant between the pieces' [Gen. 15], bringing him to Haran."

2. A. That [base verse] is in line with the following verse of Scripture: "Your people offer themselves willingly on the day of your warfare" (Ps. 110:3).

B. [Since the letters for "your people" may be read "with you," we interpret the verse as follows:] "I was with you when you willingly offered yourself for my Name, going down into the heated furnace."

C. "On the day of your warfare" (Ps. 110:3): [since the letters for "your warfare" may be read "your retinue," we interpret the verse as follows]: "When you gathered for me all of those great populations [to my service].

D. "In the mountains of holiness" (Ps. 110:3): "From the mountain of the world I sanctified you."

E. "From the womb of the dawn" (Ps. 110:3): "From the womb of the world I sought you for myself" [the word "dawn" and "sought" share the same consonants].

F. "Yours is the dew of youth" (Ps. 110:3): Our father Abraham was concerned, saying, "Is it possible that I am responsible for some sort of transgression, for I worshipped idolatry during all of those years!" Said the Holy One, blessed be he, to him, "'Yours is the dew of youth.' Just as dew evaporates, so your sins will evaporate. Just as dew is a sign of blessing for the world, so you are a sign of blessing for the world."

3. A. [The base verse is in line with the following intersecting verse:] "And I said, 'O that I had wings like a dove, then I would fly away and be at rest'"(Ps. 55:7):

B. Why like a dove?

C. R. Azariah in the name of R. Yudan b. R. Simon: "It is because when all other birds tire, they rest on a rock or a tree, but when a dove tires, it draws in one of its wings and limps along with the other of its wings."

D. "Then I would wander far off" (Ps. 55:8): wandering after wandering, move after move.

E. "I would lodge in the wilderness. Selah" (Ps. 55:8): It is better to abide in the wilderness areas of the Land of Israel than in the palaces abroad. [That applies in particular to Abram's wanderings in the land.]

F. And if you should say, had Abram not hesitated but delighted [to migrate to the Land of Israel], then why did he not go forth sooner than he did? It was because he had not yet received permission.

G. But as soon as he got permission, "So Abram went as the Lord had told him, and Lot went with him" (Gen. 12:4).

4. A. Said R. Levi, "When Abraham was traveling through Aram Naharim and Aram Nahor, he saw the people eating and drinking and having a good time. He said, 'I hope my portion will not be here!'

B. "When he got to the Ladder of Tyre, he saw the people at work, weeding in weeding time and hoeing in hoeing time. He said, 'I hope that my portion will be in this land.'

C. "Said the Holy One, blessed be he, to him, 'And to your seed I shall give this land' (Gen. 15:18)."

Once we have dealt with the peculiarity of the base-verse, No. ,1 we move directly to two intersecting verses, Ps. 110:3, at No. 2, and Ps. 55:7, at No. 3. Why someone should have found that Abraham's life called for a rereading of these verses in particular I cannot say. But both of them serve very well. Ps. 110:3 once more forms a link to the exegetical interest of the earlier passage on

Abraham in the fiery furnace of the Chaldaeans. No. 3 then joins Abraham's life to the history of Israel, with its movement from place to place. That seems to me the likely implication of the passage, first, because in the literature before us Israel commonly is compared to the dove, and, second, there is a specific warrant for the suggestion. It is the wry comment on the fact that Abraham abandoned the advantageous life of Ur for the labor-wracked life of the Land of Israel. That is the stunning stress of No. 3-4. So the whole leads us to the center-piece of the base-verse, which is "to the land that I will show you." That is the fact, even though that component of the base-verse does not appear to be subject to inquiry. If this interpretation of the composition proves sound, then the compositors show considerable subtlety. Abraham's lessons derive from both what he did and also what he said. That means that the exegetes found themselves free to listen to Abraham's statements in their own distinctive and fresh setting.

XL:VI.

1. A. "And for her sake he dealt well with Abram" (Gen. 12:16):

B. "And Pharaoh gave men orders concerning him, [and they set him on the way, with his wife and all that he had]" (Gen. 12:20).

C. R. Phineas in the name of R. Hoshaiah said, "The Holy One, blessed be he, said to our father, Abraham, 'Go and pave a way before your children.' [Set an example for them, so that whatever you do now, they will do later on.] [We shall now see how each statement about Abram at Gen. 12:10-20 finds a counterpart in the later history of Israel, whether Jacob or the children of Jacob.]

C. "You find that whatever is written in regard to our father, Abraham, is written also with regard to his children.

D. "With regard to Abraham it is written, 'And there was a famine in the land' (Gen. 12:10) In connection with Israel: 'For these two years has the famine been in the land'" (Gen. 45:6).

E. "With regard to Abraham: 'And Abram went down into Egypt' (Gen. 12:10).

F. "With regard to Israel: 'And our fathers went down into Egypt' (Num. 20:15).

G. "With regard to Abraham: 'To sojourn there' (Gen. 12:10).

H. "With regard to Israel: 'To sojourn in the land we have come' (Gen. 47:4).

I. "With regard to Abraham: 'For the famine is heavy in the land' (Gen. 12:10).

J. "With regard to Israel: 'And the famine was heavy in the land' (Gen. 43:1).

K. "With regard to Abraham: 'And it came to pass, when he drew near to enter into Egypt' (Gen. 12:11: 'When he was about to enter Egypt').

L. "With regard to Israel: 'And when Pharaoh drew near' (Ex. 14:10).

M. "With regard to Abraham: 'And they will kill me but you will they keep alive' (Gen. 12:12).

N. "With regard to Israel: 'Every son that is born you shall cast into the river, and every daughter you shall save alive' (Ex. 1:22).

O. "With regard to Abraham: 'Say you are my sister, that it may go well with me because of you' (Gen. 12:13).

P. "With regard to Israel: 'And God dealt well with the midwives' (Ex. 1:20).

Q. "With regard to Abraham: 'And when Abram had entered Egypt' (Gen. 12:14).

R. "Israel: 'Now these are the names of the sons of Israel, who came into Egypt' (Ex. 1:1).

S. "With regard to Abraham: 'And Abram was very rich in cattle, in silver, and in gold' (Gen. 13:23).

T. "With regard to Israel: 'And he brought them forth with silver and gold' (Ps. 105:37).

U. "With regard to Abraham: And Pharoah gave men orders concerning him and they set him on the way' (Gen. 12:20).

V. "Israel: 'And the Egyptians were urgent upon the people to send them out' (Ex. 12:33).

W. "With regard to Abraham: 'And he went on his journeys' (Gen. 13:3).

X. "With regard to Israel: 'These are the journeys of the children of Israel' (Num. 33:1)."

This powerful litany carefully links the story of Abram to the history of Israel, showing how the Israelites later on point by point relived the life of Abram. Any claim, therefore, that there were children of Abraham other than Israel ("after the flesh") finds refutation in this statement. The passage forms a striking conclusion to Gen. 12:10-20, because it treats the whole and not merely its segments, one by one, and the cogent statement draws out a message that relates to the entire composition. It would be hard to find a more careful effort to conclude a sustained discussion (whether what has gone before in fact was or was not a sustained discussion). Abraham's relationships to the kingdoms in the land prefigures, also, Israel's life later on. Gentiles pay back good by doing evil.

XLI:III.

1. A. ""Now Abram was very rich in cattle, in silver, and in gold" (Gen. 13:2):

B. That is in line with this verse: "And he brought them forth with silver and with gold, and there was none that stumbled among his tribes" (Ps. 105:37).

2. A. "And he journeyed on [from the Negeb as far as Bethel, to the place where his tent had been at the beginning, between Bethel and Ai]" (Gen. 13:3):

B. He journeyed on in those same routes that he had originally traveled.

C. Said R. Eleazar, "He went to collect what was owing to him."

3. A. "And Lot, who went with Abram, also had flocks and herds and tents" (Gen. 13:5):

B. Four advantages did Lot enjoy owing to Abraham.

C. "And Lot went with him" (Gen. 12:4).

D. "And Lot...also..." (Gen. 13:5).

E. "And he also brought back his brother Lot and his goods" (Gen. 14:16).

F. "And it came to pass, when God destroyed the cities of the plain, that God remembered Abraham and sent Lot out of the midst of the overthrow" (Gen. 19:29).

G. Now corresponding to these matters Lot's descendants [the Ammonites and Moabites] ought to have paid us back with acts of decency. And it was not enough for them not to pay us back with acts of decency, but they did deeds of evil to us.

H. That is in line with these verses of Scripture:

I. "And he sent messengers to Balaam...Come now, therefore, I pray you, curse this people" (Num. 22:5).

J. "And he gathered to him the children of Ammon and Amalek, and he went and smote Israel" (Judges 3:13).

K. "And it came to pass after this that...the children of Ammon and with them some of the Ammonites came against Jehoshaphat to battle" (2 Chr. 20:1).

L. "The adversary has spread out his hand upon all her treasures" (Lam. 1:10).

N. Sin pertaining to them is then recorded in four passages:

O. "An Ammonite or a Moabite shall not enter into the assembly of the Lord...because they met you not with bread and water in the way" (Deut. 23:4).

P. "Because they did not meet the children of Israel with bread and water" (Neh. 13:2).'

Q. "My people, remember now what Balak, king of Moab, devised" (Mic. 6:5).

R. Four prophets moreover came and pronounced doom against them, Isaiah, Jeremiah, Ezekiel, and Zephaniah.

S. Isaiah: "The burden of Moab" (Is. 15:1).

T. Jeremiah: "Then I will cause an alarm of war to be heard against Rabbah of the children of Ammon" (Jer. 49:2).

U. Ezekiel: "I will open the flank of Moab...together with the children of Ammon, to the children of the east...and I will execute judgments upon Moab" (25:9).

V. Zephaniah: "Surely Moab shall be as Sodom and the children of Amon as Gomorrah" (Zeph. 2:9).

For its part Israel's road lies through the way of submission and humility. The strength of the weak lies in their capacity to submit and accept.

XLI:IX.

1. A. "I will make your descendants as the dust of the earth" (Gen. 13:16):

B. Just as the dust of the earth is from one end of the world to the other, so your children will be from one end of the world to the other.

C. Just as the dust of the earth is blessed only with water, so your children will be blessed only through the merit attained by study of the Torah, which is compared to water [hence: through water].

D. Just as the dust of the earth wears out metal utensils and yet endures forever, so Israel endures while the nations of the world come to an end.

E. Just as the dust of the world is treated as something on which to trample, so your children are treated as something to be trampled upon by the government.

F. That is in line with this verse: "And I will put it into the hand of them that afflict you" (Is. 51:23), that is to say, those who make your wounds flow [Freedman].

G. Nonetheless, it is for your good that they do so, for they cleanse you of guilt, in line with this verse: "You make her soft with showers" (Ps. 65:11). [Freedman, p. 339, n. 33: "Words of the same root are used for 'make soft' and 'who afflict you.' The passage understands the former in the sense of making the rain flow and hence the latter too -- to make the wounds flow."]

H. "That have said to your soul, 'Bow down, that we may go over'" (Is. 51:23):

I. What did they do to them? They made them lie down in the streets and drew ploughs over them."

J. R. Azariah in the name of R. Aha: "That is a good sign. Just as the street wears out those who pass over it and endures forever, so your children will wear out all the nations of the world and will live forever."

The metaphor of "dust of the earth" yields quite a fresh meaning for the exegetes. Now it is not a mark that Israel will be numerous, but that Israel will survive the rule of the nations of the world. However humble its condition, Israel in the end will outlast its enemies. Israel's humility therefore testifies to its ultimate triumph. All of this emerges from the lesson of God to the patriarch, once more prefiguring Israel's life later on.

XLII:II.

1. A. R. Samuel commenced [discourse by citing the following verse]: "And this also is a grievous evil, that in all points as he came so shall he go" (Qoh. 5:15).

B. Said R. Samuel, "Just as he came, namely, with slops, so shall he leave [the world], namely, with slops."

2. A. Said R. Abin, "Just as [Israel's history] began with the encounter with four kingdoms, so [Israel's history] will conclude with the encounter with the four kingdoms.

B. "'Chedorlaomer, king of Elam, Tidal, king of Goiim, Amraphel, king of Shinar, and Arioch, king of Ellasar, four kings against five' (Gen. 14:9).

C. "So [Israel's history] will conclude with the encounter with the four kingdoms: the kingdom of Babylonia, the kingdom of Medea, the kingdom of Greece, and the kingdom of Edom."

3. A. R. Phineas said in the name of R. Abun, "'But they do not know the thoughts of the Lord, nor do they understand his counsel, for he has gathered them as the sheaves to the threshing floor' (Mic. 4:12).

B. "Why did 'all these join forces' (Gen. 14:3)? So that they might come and fall by the hand of Abraham: 'And it came to pass in the days of Amraphel' (Gen. 14:1)."

Just as Israel's history began with Abraham's encounter with the four kings, so it will end with a similar encounter. Accordingly, the fourth monarchy, namely Rome, marks the end. No. 3 presents a distinct and fresh point, that people do not know why God does things, or why they do them at God's initiative. But there is a solid reason. The message of the reading, all together, is that Israel may not know the meaning of its history, but God does know and have a plan, and things will work out in the end. The upshot is that Israel's later history finds its counterpart in the initial event in the public life of Abram, so, once more, the powerful motif of finding a counterpart between the life of Israel and the lives of the patriarchs makes its impact.

XLIII:III.

1. A.   "And the night was divided against them" (Gen. 14:15) [following Freedman's translation of the verse, which, in RSV, reads, "And he divided his forces against them by night"]:

   B.   R. Benjamin b. Japheth in the name of R. Yohanan: "The night divided on its own."

   C.   And rabbis say, "Its creator divided it.

   D.   "Said the Holy One, blessed be he, 'Abraham worked with me at midnight [in going to rescue the captives], so I shall work with him at midnight.'

   E.   "When did this take place? In Egypt, as it is said, 'And it came to pass at midnight' (Ex. 12:29)."

   F.   Said R. Tanhuma, "There are those who produce the statement in another formulation.

   G.   "Said the Holy One, blessed be he, 'Their father went forth at midnight, so I shall go forth with his children at midnight, as it is said, 'Thus says the Lord, "At about midnight I will go forth"' (Ex. 11:4)."

2. A.   "He routed them and pursued them to Hobah, north of Damascus" (Gen. 14:15):

   B.   Does someone pursue those who have already been killed?

   C.   Said R. Phineas, "Those who had pursued our father, Abraham, were [regarded as though they had been] killed, as it is said, 'For they pursue him whom you have smitten' (Ps. 69:27)."

3. A.   It is written, "Who has raised up one from the east, Righteousness calling him to his feet" (Is. 41:2):

   B.   It is the Life of the Ages who gave light for him in every place in which he walked. [Freedman, p. 354, n. 3: By a play on the words to awaken, raise up, is connected the word for to illumine.]

   C.   Said R. Berekhiah, "It was the star Righteousness [Jupiter] that gave light for him."

   D.   Said R. Reuben, "Righteousness cried out and said, 'If Abraham does not carry out what I represent, there will be no one who ever will carry out what I represent." [Freedman, p. 354, n. 5: Rendering: Righteousness personified summoned him to his feet, that is, to do it.]

4. A.   It is written, "He gives nations before him and makes him rule over kings, his sword makes them as the dust, his bow as the driven stubble" (Is. 41:2):

B. R. Judah and R. Nehemiah:

C. One of them said, "Abraham threw dust at them and it turned into swords, he threw straw and it turned into arrows."

D. The other said, "What is written is not 'he makes dust' but 'he makes *them* as the dust.' They threw swords at Abraham, but the swords turned into dust, and arrow, which turned into straw."

5. A. It is written, "He pursues them and passes on safely" (Is. 41:3):

B. R. Levi and R. Eleazar in the name of R. Yose: "Each footstep taken by Abraham was three *mil* s in length." [Freedman, p. 354, n. 6: The word for "safely" is read as an abbreviation of "three mils."]

C. R. Judah bar Simon said, "It was one *mil*, as it is said, 'The way with his feet he treads not' (Is. 41:3)."

No. 1 links the story of Abraham to the later history of Israel, an important motif throughout. No. 2 clarifies the language of the cited verse. Then Nos. 3, 4, and 5 work on the intersecting verse of Is. 41:23-3, which is read to speak of Abraham's war. The work is systematic and, within the system at hand, persuasive. Each gesture of Abraham likewise prefigures an aspect of Israel's life of godly service.

XLIII:IX.

1. A. "And the king of Sodom said to Abram, 'Give me the persons, but take the goods for yourself.' But Abram said to the king of Sodom, 'I have raised up my hand [RSV: sworn] [to the Lord God Most High, maker of heaven and earth, that I would not take a thread or a sandal-thong or anything that is yours, lest you should say, "I have made Abram rich"']" (Gen. 14:22-23):

B. [The reference of raising up the hand is now explained.] R. Judah said, "He had raised up heave-offering [out of the spoil], in line with this verse: 'Then you shall raise up part of it as a heave-offering gift to the Lord' (Num. 18:26)."

C. R. Nehemiah said, "He had taken an oath, in line with this verse: 'And he lifted up his right hand and his left hand to heaven and swore' (Den. 12:7)."

D. And rabbis say, "He sang a song on account of it, in line with this verse: 'My father's God, and I will raise him up' (Ex. 15:2)."

E. R. Berekhiah in the name of R. Eleazar: "Moses said, 'Using the same language that father did, when he said, 'I have raised up,' I shall sing my song" 'My father's God and I will raise him up' (Ex. 15:2)."

2. A. "...that I would not take a thread or a sandal-thong [or anything that is yours, lest you should say, "I have made Abram rich"']" (Gen. 14:22-23):

B. Said R. Abba bar Mammel, "Said the Holy One, blessed be he, to him, 'You have said, "a thread..." By your life, I shall give your descendants the religious duty of putting fringes on their garments, in line with this verse: "And that they put with the fringe of each corner a thread of blue" (Num. 15:38), that is, a thread of blue wool.

C. "[God continues,] '"or a sandal-thong..." By your life, I shall give your descendants the religious duty of the rite of the deceased childless brother's widow, involving as it does the sandal-thong, in line with this verse: "Then shall she loose his shoe from his his foot" (Deut. 25:9).'"

3. **A.** Another matter [interpreting the verse: "...that I would not take a thread or a sandal-thong [or anything that is yours, lest you should say, "I have made Abram rich""" (Gen. 14:22-23)]:

B. "A thread" refers to the altar, which is ornamented with blue and purple wool.

C. "Nor a sandal thong" refers to the badger skins.

4. **A.** Another matter [interpreting the verse: "...that I would not take a thread or a sandal-thong [or anything that is yours, lest you should say, "I have made Abram rich""" (Gen. 14:22-23)]:

B. "A thread" refers to the sacrifices, in line with what we have learned in the Mishnah: A thread of scarlet ran around the altar at the middle (M. Middot 3:1).

C. "Or a sandal thong" refers to the feet of the pilgrims, in line with this verse: "How beautiful are your steps in sandals" (Song 7:2).

5. **A.** "I will take nothing but what the young men have eaten and the share of the men who went with me; [in addition, even those who did not go with me should have a share, specifically] let Aner, Eshcol, and Mamre take their share" (Gen. 14:24):

B. "Then answered all the wicked men and base fellows, of those who went with David, and said, 'Because they did not go with us, we shall not give them any of the spoil.' Then said David, 'You shall not do this, my brothers. For as is the share of him who goes down to battle, so shall be the share of him who waits by the baggage; they shall all share alike.' And so it was from that day and above, that he made it a statute' (1 Sam. 30:22-25)."

C. Said R. Judah, "What is written is not 'onward,' but, 'from that day and above,' for from whom did David learn the rule? It was from Abraham, his forefather, who had said, 'I will take nothing but what the young men have eaten and the share of the men who went with me; [in addition, even those who did not go with me should have a share, specifically] let Aner, Eshcol, and Mamre take their share" (Gen. 14:24)."

No. 1 deals with the language of the statement, "raise up my hand." The first two treatments of the matter, Judah's and Nehemiah's, focus on the simple sense of the verse, while rabbis as before take an interest in the linkage of the events in the life of Abraham to the history of Israel later on. No. 2 does a still better job of linking the matter at hand with Israel's history. What is important is the effort to demonstrate a link between Abram and the religious duties revealed only later on in the Torah. So it can be shown that Abram kept the rules of the Torah even before the Torah was revealed, an important point of contention. So Abraham kept the Torah before it was given. Nos. 3, 4 revert to the matter of the altar, in line with the view that at hand is Jerusalem and its cult. No. 5 establish yet another link, this time drawing a parallel between Abram's conduct here and David's rule later on. Abraham also learned the rules of the cult, another proof, in the sages' mind, that Abraham received and kept the whole Torah before it was given.

XLIV:XIV.

1. A. "But he said, 'O Lord God, how am I to know that I shall possess it?'" (Gen. 15:8):

   B. R. Hama bar Haninah said, "It was not as though he were complaining, but he said to him, 'On account of what merit [shall I know it? That is, how have I the honor of being so informed?]'

   C. "He said to him, 'It is on account of the merit of the sacrifice of atonement that I shall hand over to your descendants.'"

2. A. "And he said to him, 'Bring me a heifer three years old, a she-goat three years old, a ram three years old, a turtledove and a young pigeon'" (Gen. 15:9):

   B. He showed him three kinds of bullocks, three kinds of goats, and three kinds of rams.

   C. Three kinds of bullocks, the bullock of the day of atonement, the bullock that is brought on account of the inadvertent violation of any of the religious duties, and the heifer whose neck is to be broken.

   D. He further showed him three kinds of goats, the goats to be offered on the festivals, the goats to be offered on the occasion of the new moons, and the goat to be offered for an individual.

   E. He further showed him three kinds of rams, the one for the guilt offering that is brought in a case of certainty [that one is liable to such an offering], the one that is to be brought as a suspensive guilt offering, and the lamb that is brought by an individual,.

   F "...a turtledove and a young pigeon" (Gen. 15:9): that is as is stated, a turtle dove and a young pigeon [stated in Aramaic].

3. A. "And he brought him all these" (Gen. 15:10):

   B. R. Simeon b. Yohai says, "All the forms of atonement did the Holy One, blessed be he, show to Abraham, but the tenth-*ephah* of fine flour he did not show to him [since it is omitted in the cited verse]."

   C. Rabbis say, "He even showed him the atonement-rite involving the tenth-*ephah* of fine flour. [How do we know it?] Here it is stated, 'All *these* ' and elsewhere: 'And you shall bring the meal-offering that is made of these *things* ' (Lev. 2:8). [The word *these* occurs in both passages, and the latter refers to the tenth-*ephah* of fine flour.]"

4. A. "But he did not cut the birds in two" (Gen. 15:10):

   B. The Holy One, blessed be he, showed him that an act of division of the carcass is carried on out in the case of the burnt-offering made of a bird, while an act of division is not carried out in the case of the sin-offering made of a bird.

Any implication that Abram's conversation with God was captious now is removed at No. 1. Nos 2-4 make the point that God showed Abram the rules of the cult, when he made his sacrifice at Jerusalem. So the origin of the cult is assigned to Abram and the story serves to explain why Jerusalem is the cult-center of Israel.

XLIV:XV.

1. A. Another matter: "Bring me a heifer three years old, [a she-goat three years old, a ram three years old, a turtledove, and a young pigeon]" (Gen. 15:9):

B. "Bring me a heifer three years old" refers to Babylonia, that produced three [kings important in Israel's history], Nebuchadnezzar, Evil Merodach, and Balshazzar.

C. "...a she-goat three years old" refers to Media, that also produced three kings, Cyrus, Darius, and Ahasuerus.

D. "...a ram three years old" refers to Greece.

E. R. Eleazar and R. Yohanan:

F. R. Eleazar said, "Greece conquered every point on the compass except for the east."

G. R. Yohanan said to him, "And indeed so, for is it not written, 'I saw the ram pushing westward and northward and southward, and no beasts could stand before him' (Dan. 8:4)?"

H. That indeed is the view of R. Eleazar, for the verse at hand does not refer to the east.

I. " a turtledove, and a young pigeon" (Gen. 15:9) refers to Edom. It was a turtle-dove that would rob.

2. A. "And he brought him all these" (Gen. 15:10):

B. R. Judah said, "He showed him the princes of the nations."

C. R. Nehemiah said, "It was the princes of Israel that he showed him."

D. In the view of R. Judah, [the statement, "He laid each half over against the other" indicates that] he set the throne of one opposite the throne of another. [Freedman, p. 371, n. 2: He showed him the hostility of the nations toward each other, in contrast with which the bird, symbolizing Israel, was not to be divided but united.]

E. In the view of R. Nehemiah, [laying each half over against the other symbolized the fact that] there, [in Jerusalem] the great sanhedrin of Israel [seated in semi-circles, so each half could see the other] was in session and laying down the laws of Israel.

3. A. "But he did not cut the birds in two" (Gen. 15:10):

B. R. Abba bar Kahana in the name of R. Levi: "The Holy One, blessed be he, showed him that whoever stands against the wave is swept away by the wave, and whoever does not stand against the wave is not swept away by the wave."

No. 1 links the sacrifices to the particular stages in Israel's history with the nations. So the dual link, one with the cult, the other with Israel's history, is forged. No. 2 takes up the same task. No. 3 then draws out the important lesson, which is that Israel, symbolized by the bird, has to ride out the waves of history (Freedman, p. 371, n. 5).

XLIV:XXI.

1. A. "When the sun had gone down and it was dark, [behold a smoking fire pot and a flaming torch passed between these pieces]" (Gen. 15:17):

B. That was intense darkness [in Aramaic].

2. A. "...behold a smoking fire pot and a flaming torch passed between these pieces" (Gen. 15:17):

B.   Simeon bar Abba in the name of R. Yohanan: "He showed him four things, Gehenna, the [four] kingdoms, the giving of the Torah, and the sanctuary.   He said to him, 'So long as your descendants are occupied with these latter two, they will be saved from the former two.   If they abandon two of them, they will be judged by the other two.'

C.   "He said to him, 'What is your preference?   Do you want your children to go down into Gehenna or to be subjugated to the four kingdoms?'"

D.   R. Hinena bar Pappa said, "Abraham chose for himself the subjugation to the four kingdoms."

E.   R. Yudan and R. Idi and R. Hama bar Hanina: "Abraham chose for himself Gehenna, but the Holy One, blessed be he, chose the subjugation to the four kingdoms for him."

F.   That [statement of Hinena b Papa] is in line with the following: "How should one chase a thousand and two put ten thousand to flight, except their rock had given them over'" (Deut. 32:30).   That statement refers to Abraham.

G.   "But the Lord delivered them up" (Deut. 32:30) teaches that God then approved what he had chosen.

3.   A.   R. Huna in the name of R. Aha: "Now Abraham sat and puzzled all that day, saying, 'Which should I choose?'

B.   "Said the Holy One, blessed be he, to him, 'Choose without delay.'   That is in line with this verse: 'On that day the Lord made a covenant with Abram' (Gen. 15:18)."

C.   This brings us to the dispute of R. Hinena bar Pappa with R. Yudan and R. Idi and R. Hama bar Haninah.

D.   R. Hinena bar Pappa said, "Abraham chose for himself the subjugation to the four kingdoms."

E.   R. Yudan and R. Idi and R. Hama bar Haninah said in the name of a single sage in the name of Rabbi: "The Holy One, blessed be he, chose the subjugation to the four kingdoms for him, in line with the following verse of Scripture: 'You have caused men to ride over our heads' (Ps. 66:12).   That is to say, you have made ride over our heads various nations, and it is as though 'we went through fire and through water' (Ps. 66:21)."

F.   R. Joshua said, "Also the splitting of the Red Sea he showed him, as it is written, 'That passed between these pieces' (Gen. 15:17), along the lines of the verse, 'O give thanks to him who divided the Red Sea in two' [in which the same word, the letters for pieces, occurs as 'in two'] (Ps. 86:13)."

The main interest at Nos. 2 and 3 is in linking the history of Israel to the passage at hand.   That exegesis surely is invited by the substance of the cited verses.   But the special interest of the exegetes is in Israel's suffering later on, with the particular stress on God's choosing subjugation to the nations as the appropriate penalty for Israel's failures to come.   In fact Abraham is made party to the entire future history of Israel, even choosing, in dealing with God, the penalty for their sin and their mode of atonement.

XLVII:VII.

1.   A.   "Then Abraham took Ishmael his son and all the slaves born in his house [or bought for his money, every male among the men of Abraham's house, and

he circumcised the flesh of their foreskins that very day, as God had said to him]" (Gen. 17:23):

B. Said R. Aibu, "When Abraham circumcised those who were born of his house, he made a mountain of foreskins, and the sun shone on them, and they putrefied. The stench rose to heaven before the Holy One, blessed be he, like the scent of incense.

C. "Said the Holy One, blessed be he, 'When my children will come into bad deeds, I shall remember in their behalf that scent and will be filled with mercy for them."

Israel enjoys the merit of Abraham's actions in the present narrative, a familiar theme. The acts of Abraham bear sacerdotal meaning and prefigure the Temple's sweet savor, rising to heaven. In the following we find a much more complex union of diverse themes, all of them having to do with Abraham as the paradigm of Israel, both the Israelite individual and the nation as a whole:

XLVIII:VI.
1. A. "Sinners in Zion are afraid" (Is. 33:14):

B. Said R. Jeremiah b. Eleazar, "The matter may be compared to the case of two children who ran away from school. While the one was being thrashed, the other trembled."

C. Said R. Jonathan, "Whenever there is a reference in Scripture to faithlessness, the passage speaks of heretics. The generative case for all of them is in this verse: 'The sinners in Zion are afraid, trembling has seized the ungodly' (Is. 33:14)."

D. Said R. Judah bar Simon, "The matter may be compared to the case of a bandit chief who rebelled against the king. The king said, 'To whoever arrests him I shall give a bounty.' Someone went and arrested him. The king said, 'Hold the two of them over until morning.' The one was trembling about what sort of bounty the king would give to him, and the other was afraid about what sort of judgment the king would mete out to him.

E. "So in the age to come Israel will be afraid: 'And they shall come in fear to the Lord and to his goodness' (Hos. 3:5).

F. "And the gentiles also will be afraid: 'Sinners in Zion are afraid' (Is. 33:14)."
2. A. Said R. Judah, "Why does the prophet refer to them as 'Everlasting burnings' (Is. 33:14)?

B. "For if he gave the nations the power to do so, they would commit the entire world to conflagration."
3. A. "He who walks righteously" (Is. 33:15) refers to Abraham: "To the end that he may command his children that they may keep the way of the Lord to do righteousness and justice" (Gen. 18:19).

B. "And speaks uprightly" (Is. 33:15): "The upright ones love you" (Song 1:4).

C. "He who despises the gain of oppressions" (Is. 33:15): "I will not take a thread or a shoe latchet" (Gen. 14:23).

D. "Who shakes his hands from the holding of bribes" (Is. 33:15): "I have lifted up my hand to the Lord, God Most High" (Gen. 14:22).

4. A.. "He shall dwell on high" (Is. 33:16):

B. R. Judah b. R. Simon in the name of R. Yohanan: "'He brought him above the vault of heaven. That is in line with the statement, 'Look toward heaven and number the stars,'and the meaning of the word 'look' is only 'from above to below.' [Hence he looked downward from above the vault of heaven.]"

5. A. "His place of defense shall be the munitions of rocks" (Is. 33:16) speaks of clouds of glory.

B. "His bread shall be given" (Is. 33:16): "While I fetch a morsel of bread" (Gen. 18:5).

C. "His waters shall be sure" (Is. 33:6): "Let a little water be brought and wash your feet" (Gen. 18:4).

D. "Your eyes shall see the king in his beauty" (Is. 33:17):

E. "'And the Lord appeared to him" (Gen. 18:1).

This classic rendition of the exegetical form in which an intersecting verse is systematically and thoroughly worked out, applied to a number of settings or contexts, and only at the end brought into contact with the base verse, has not commonly appeared to us in earlier passages. What we see is a sustained and successful exposition of Is. 33:14-17. Since the points of the successive clauses are worked out in their own terms, and not in terms of Abraham, one might regard the composition as a whole as having been completed prior to its use for the present purpose. When, at the end, the present case is reached, the intersection is not general but quite specific, with reference to the bread and water of Gen. 18:4-5 validating the climactic conclusion with Gen. l8:1. But a second glance at the two principal components, Nos. 1-2 and 3, 5 provides a different perspective. Nos. 1, 2 speak of the nations of the world and their fear of judgment at the same moment at which Israel looks forward to its final reward. Nos. 3, 5 then speak of Abraham and treat as a prefiguring of the future and fulfillment of the cited verses, Is. 33:15-17, the things that he did in the narrative of Gen. 18:1-5. So viewed from a distance, the two components -- that is, the two approaches to the exegesis of the intersecting verse -- match one another. We speak first of the nations and Israel, then of Abraham and God, making the single point that Abraham prefigures Israel's future vision of God and salvation. If this reading of the composite is sound, then the composite in fact forms a single, pointed and sustained composition, even though bits and pieces clearly have taken shape before the whole formed a single aggregate. The basic doctrine is that Abraham saved creation and set the standard for humanity. To the exegetes he is the single hero of Genesis:

XLVIII:VIII.

1. A. "At the door of his tent in the heat of the day" (Gen. 18:1):

B. {God stated to Abraham,] "You indeed opened a good door for passersby. You opened a good door for proselytes.

C. "For if it were not for you, I should not have created heaven and earth: 'He spreads them out as a tent to dwell in' (Is. 40:22).

D. "If it were not for you, I should not have created the orb of the sun: 'In them has he set a tent for the sun' (Ps. 119:5).

E. "If it were not for you, I should not have created the moon: 'Behold, even for the moon he does not set a tent' (Job 25:5)."

2. A. Said R. Levi, "In the age to come Abraham will sit at the gate of Gehenna, and he will not permit a circumcised Israelite to go down there. Then what will he do for those who sinned too much? He will remove the foreskin from infants who died before they were circumcised and will place it over [Israelite sinners] and then lower them into Gehenna [protected by the skin].

B. "That is in line with this verse: 'He has sent forth his hands to those that whole. He has profaned his covenant' (Ps. 55:21)."

3. A. "In the heat of the day" (Gen. 18:1):

B. R. Ishmael taught on Tannaite authority: "'And as the sun waxed hot, it [the mana] melted' (Ex. 16:21). That was at the fourth hour. You say it was at the fourth hour, but perhaps it was only at the sixth? When Scripture says, 'In the heat of the day' (Gen. 18:1), it must speak of the sixth hour.

C. "But perhaps matters are exactly the opposite? [No, for] at the fourth hour, it is cool in the shade and warm in the sun, but at the sixth hour, the sun and the shade are equally hot." [Freedman, p. 410, n. 5: "In the heat of the day" implies that it was hot everywhere, that condition is fulfilled at noon. But "and as the sun waxed hot" indicates that it was hot only in the sun but not in the shade.]

4. A. Said R. Yannai, "A hole was made in Gehenna [through which heat escaped so that] for a while the whole world was boiling for all of its inhabitants. Said the Holy One, blessed be he, 'My righteous man is suffering pain and should the world be comfortable?' [Surely not. So:]

B. "'In the heat of the day' (Gen. 18:1). [God made it warm so that everyone would be uncomfortable when Abraham was.]

5. A. ["In the heat of the day" (Gen. 18:1)]:

B. On the basis of the cited verse, we know that hot water is good for the wound.

The reference to "tent" calls for No. 1 in its wake a set of verses in which the word "tent" appears. These verses all have to do with creation, yielding the effort to draw a parallel between the life of Abraham and the creation of the world. What must follow is that the world was created for the sake of Israel. But that position is not announced, merely implicit. No. 2 takes up the theme of Abraham's guarding the door, now with a completely original message. Again, Israel's life is prefigured in Abraham's action, now with reference to the individual, not the nation and its history. No. 3 alludes to the verse at hand in the inquiry into its own syllogism. No. 4 makes its own point, extending the sense of "the heat of the day." No. 5 is tacked on. Since Abraham occupied so central a role in the history of humanity, it is no wonder that sages repeatedly insist he kept every detail of the law of the Torah.

XLIX:II.

6. A. R. Aha in the name of R. Alexandri, R. Samuel b. Nahman in the name of R. Jonathan: "Even the laws governing the commingling of domain in courtyards [for purposes of creating a single domain for carrying on the Sabbath] did Abraham know."

B. R. Phineas, R. Hilqiah, R. Simon in the name of R. Samuel: "Even the new name that the Holy One, blessed be he, is destined to assign to Jerusalem: 'On that day they will call Jerusalem "the throne of God"' (Jer. 3:17) Abraham knew."

C. R. Berekhiah, R. Hiyya, the rabbis of the other place [Babylonia] in the name of R. Judah: "There is not a single day on which the Holy One, blessed be he, does not create a new law in the court above. What is the scriptural verse that shows it? 'Hear attentively the noise of his voice and the meditation that goes out of his mouth' (Job 37:2). The word meditation speaks only of the Torah, as it is said, 'But you shall meditate therein day and night' (Joshua 1:8). Even those new laws Abraham knew."

No. 1 sets the stage for the articulation of God's thinking in the base verse by proving the God reveals his secret to persons of Abraham's category. That explains the self-evidence of God's question, cited at the end. It is a persuasive exercise. No. 2 is equally effective in expanding the account of God's reasoning in the rhetorical question at hand. No. 3 presents a powerful explanation for the special favor shown to Abraham, underlining how different was his relationship to God from that of Adam and Noah. No. 4 makes the same point in a different way. No. 5 shifts the ground of argument, reverting to Abraham in particular. No. 6 then expands on the theme of how much God revealed to Abraham. This is the point at which the narrative crosses the distinctive history of Israel. Abraham now knows the name of Jerusalem, the new laws of the heavenly academy, and the rules of the commingling of courtyards, that is, a matter quite distinctive to the rabbis and their tradition, at least, as they portray that particular matter. So in all the climax has Abraham know particularly Israelite matters. Abraham's errors, not only his merit, affected the future history of his descendants.

LIV:IV.

1. A. "Abraham set seven ewe lambs of the flock apart" (Gen. 21:28):

B. Said the Holy One, blessed be he, to him, "You have given him seven ewe lambs. By your life I shall postpone the joy of your descendants for seven generations.

C. "You have given him seven ewe lambs. By your life matching them his descendants [the Philistines] will kill seven righteous men among your descendants, and these are they: Hofni, Phineas, Samson, Saul and his three sons.

D. "You have given him seven ewe lambs. By your life, matching them the seven sanctuaries of your descendants will be destroyed, namely, the tent of meeting, the altars at Gilgal, Nob, Gibeon, Shiloh, and the two eternal houses of the sanctuary.

E. "You have given him seven ewe lambs. [By your life, matching them] my ark will spend seven months in the fields of the Philistines."

2. A. R. Jeremiah in the name of R. Samuel bar R. Isaac: "If the mere chicken of one of them had been lost, would he not have gone looking for it by knocking on doors, so as to get it back, but my ark spent seven months in the field and you pay not mind to it. I on my own will take care of it: 'His right hand and his holy arm have wrought salvation for him' (Ps. 98:1).

B. "That is in line with this verse: 'And the kine took the straight way' (1 Sam. 6:12). They went straight forward, turning their faces to the ark and [since the word for 'straight forward' contains the consonants for the word for 'song'] singing."

C. And what song did they sing?

D. R. Meir said, " 'The song of the sea. Here it is said, 'They went along...lowing as they went' (1 Sam. 6:12), and in that connection: 'For he is highly exalted' (Ex. 15:1). [The word for 'lowing' and the word for 'exalted' share the same consonants.]"

E. R. Yohanan said, "'O sing to the Lord a new song' (Ps. 98:1)."

F. R. Eleazar said, "'O Give thanks to the Lord, call upon his name' (Ps. 105:1)."

G. Rabbis said, "'The Lord reigns, let the earth rejoice' (Ps. 97:1)."

H. R. Jeremiah said, "The three: 'O sing to the Lord a new song, sing to the Lord, all the earth' (Ps. 96:1). 'The Lord reigns, let the peoples tremble' (Ps. 99:1)."

I. Elijah taught, "[Freedman:] 'Rise, rise, you acacia, soar, soar, in your abundant glory, beautiful in your gold embroidery, extolled in the innermost shrine of the sanctuary, encased between the two cherubim.'"

J. Said R. Samuel bar. R. Isaac, "How much did [Moses,] son of Amram labor so as to teach the art of song to the Levites. But you beasts are able to sing such a song on your own, without instruction. All power to you!"

No. 1 reverts to the theme of indignation at Abraham's coming to an agreement with Abimelech, forcefully imposing the theme of the later history of Israel upon the story at hand. No. 2 is tacked on because of the concluding reference to No. 1. Once more we see that a composition was complete before selection for use here, and the materials in our hands indicate that the compositors were reluctant to change much that they had received. If we have to choose the single paradigmatic event in Abraham's life, it is his binding of Isaac as a sacrifice to God. This endowed his descendants with merit and gave them the example above all else:

LV:III.

1. A. Another interpretation: "The Lord tries the righteous, but the wicked and him who loves violence his soul hates" (Ps. 11:5):

B. The cited verse speaks of Abraham: "And it came to pass after these things God tested Abraham" (Gen. 22:1).

2. A. R. Abin commenced discourse by citing the following verse of Scripture: "Forasmuch as the king's word has power, and who may say to him, 'What are you doing?'" (Qoh. 8:4).

B. Said R. Abin to Rab, "The matter may be compared to the case of a master who instructs his disciple, saying to him, 'Do not lend money on interest,' while the master himself lends money on interest.

C. "So the disciple says to him, 'You tell me not to lend money on interest, but you lend money on interest.'

D. "He says to him, 'I tell you not to lend money on interest to Israelites, but it is all right to do so to the nations of the world, as it is said, 'To a foreigner you may lend on interest, but to your brother you shall not lend on interest' (Deut. 23:21). [The result of learning is an accurate knowledge of what one must and must not do.]

E. "So the Israelites said before the Holy One, blessed be he, 'Lord of the ages, "You have written in the Torah, 'You shall not take vengeance nor bear any grudge' (Lev. 19:18), but you do it yourself: 'The Lord avenges and is full of wrath, the Lord takes vengeance on his adversaries and keeps wrath for his enemies' (Nah. 1:2).'"

F. "Said the Holy One, blessed be he, to them, 'I have written in the Torah, "You shall not take vengeance nor bear any grudge" (Lev. 19:18), with reference to Israel. But as to the nations of the world: "You shall avenge the children of Israel" (Num. 31:2).'"

G. Along these same lines, it is written, "You shall not try the Lord your God" (Deut. 6:16), yet: "And it came to pass after these things God tested Abraham" (Gen. 22:1).

The message of the composite is not made explicit, because it is obvious. Israel may not test God, but God may test Israel. But that point is not the principal polemic before us. In the established context, the testing of Abraham stands for the trials of Israel, and God's testing of Abraham, hence of Israel, marks Israel in its history as special and holy, just as (we have seen at LV:I, II) Abraham was suitable for testing because he was strong and worthy of it. So through a somewhat circuitous route, asking a superficially theological question of theodicy, the compositors make a stunning point in linking Abraham's life to Israel's.

LV:VI.

1. A. "That God tested Abraham" (Gen. 22:1):

B. R. Yose the Galilean said, "He made him great, like the ensign of a ship. [The use of the word ensign derives from the shared consonants for the words "test" and "ensign."]

C. R. Aqiba said, "The word bears its literal meaning of testing, so that people should not say that he confused him or perplexed him so that he would not know what to do. [The test consisted of the three days of journeying, which gave Abraham plenty of time to think about what was going to do.]"

2. A. "And he said to him, 'Abraham!' And he said, 'Here I am'" (Gen. 22:1):

B. Said R. Joshua, "In two passages Moses compared himself to Abraham.

C. "God said to him, '"Do not glorify yourself in the presence of the king and do not stand in the place of great men"' (Prov. 25:6).

D. "Abraham said, 'Here I am.' 'Here I am, ready for the priesthood, here I am, ready for the monarchy.'

E. "He had the merit of attaining the priesthood: 'The Lord has sworn and will not repent, you are a priest for ever after the manner of Melchizedek' (Ps. 110:4).

F. "He also had the merit of attaining the monarchy: 'You are a mighty prince among us' (Gen. 23:5).

G. "Moses for his part also said, 'Here I am' (Ex. 3:4). 'Here I am, ready for the priesthood, here I am, ready for the monarchy.'

H. "But the Holy One, blessed be he, said to him, 'Do not draw nigh hither' (Ex. 3:5). 'Drawing nigh' speaks of the priesthood: 'And the common man who draws nigh shall be put to death' (Num. 1:51). 'Hither' refers to the monarchy, as it is said, 'You have brought me thus far' (2 Sam. 7:18)."

No. 1 juxtaposes two unrelated comments, Yose's interpretation of the word, "test," familiar from LV:I, and Aqiba's observation about the three days' journey. No. 2 proceeds to link Abraham to Moses, a routine and important exercise. But Abraham was greater than Moses. The upshot is to link Abraham to Moses and to show how the biography of the patriarch prefigures the life of the founder of the nation. Since Moses is usually represented as meek and mild, the comparison presents a certain irony.

LVI:VII.

1. A. "But the angel of the Lord called to him from heaven and said, 'Abraham, Abraham!' [And he said, 'Here am I']" (Gen. 22:11).

B. R. Hiyya repeated on Tannaite authority, "The repeated name represents an expression of affection and eagerness."

C. R. Eliezer said, "It means that he spoke both to him and to coming generations.

D. "You have not got a single generation in which there is no one of the standing of Abraham, and you have not got a single generation in which there is no one of the standing of Jacob, Moses, and Samuel."

2. A. "He said, 'Do not lay your hand on the lad or do anything to him, for now I know that you fear God, seeing you have not withheld your son, your only son, from me'" (Gen. 22:12):

B. Where was the knife ["Do not lay your *hand* "]?

C. Tears from the ministering angels had fallen on it and dissolved it.

D. Then he said, "So I shall strangle him."

E. He said to him, "Do not lay your hand on the lad."

F. Then he said, "Then let us at least draw a drop of blood [symbolic of the offering]."

G. He said to him, "'...or do anything to him.'"

H. "...for now I know [that you fear God]:"

I. "Now I am telling everybody that you love me: 'seeing you have not withheld your son, your only son, from me' (Gen. 22:12).

J. "And do not claim, 'Whatever sickness does not affect one's own body is no sickness,' for I credit the merit to you for this action as though I had said to you, 'Offer me yourself,' and you did not hold back."

No. 1 allows the exegete to make the important point that each generation lives out the lives of the patriarchs. No. 2 constructs a dialogue for God and Abraham. Out of the angel's statement Abraham's answers are worked out.

LVI:X.

1. A. "So Abraham called the name of that place 'The Lord will provide,' [as it is said to this day, 'On the mount of the Lord it shall be provided']" (Gen. 22:14):

B. R. Bibi the Elder in the name of R. Yohanan: "He said before him, 'Lord of all ages, from the time that you said to me, "Take your son, your only son" (Gen. 22:2), I could have replied to you, "Yesterday you said to me, 'For in Isaac shall seed be called to you' (Gen. 21:12), and now you say, 'Take your son, your only son' (Gen. 22:2)." God forbid, did I not do it? But I suppressed my love so as to carry out your will. May it always please you, Lord our God, that, when the children of Isaac will come into trouble, you remember in their behalf that act of binding and be filled with mercy for them.'"

2. A. [Jerusalem had various names.] Abraham called it "will provide." "So Abraham called the name of that place 'The Lord will provide,' [as it is said to this day, 'On the mount of the Lord it shall be provided']" (Gen. 22:14).

B. Shem called it "Salem." "And Melchizedek, king of Salem" (Gen. 14:18).

C. Said the Holy One, blessed be he, "If I call the place '...will provide,' as Abraham called it, Shem, a righteous man, will have a legitimate complaint.

D. "If I call it '...Salem,' as Shem did, then Abraham, a righteous man, will have a legitimate complaint.

E. "So therefore I will call it by the name that both of them have given it, thus: *Yire Shalem* ,' or Jerusalem ['He will see peace']."

3. A. R. Berekhiah in the name of R. Helbo: "While the place was still called Salem, the Holy One, blessed be he, made a tabernacle and prayed in it: 'In Salem also is set his tabernacle and his dwelling-place in Zion' (Ps. 76:3).

B. "And what did he say there? 'May it be pleasing for me to witness the building of the house of the sanctuary.'"

4. A. ["So Abraham called the name of that place 'The Lord will provide,' as it is said to this day, 'On the mount of the Lord it shall be provided'" (Gen. 22:14)]: This teaches that the Holy One, blessed be he, showed him the house of the sanctuary as it was built, wiped out, and built once more:

B. "So Abraham called the name of that place 'The Lord will provide'" refers to the house of the sanctuary when it was built, in line with this verse: "Three times in the year will all your males be seen...in the place where he shall choose" (Gen. 16:16).

C. "as it is said to this day, 'On the mount of the Lord'" refers to the Temple in its hour of destruction, in line with this verse: "For the mountain of Zion, which is desolate" (Lam. 5:18).'

D. "...it shall be provided" [refers to the Temple] rebuilt and restored in the coming age, in line with this verse: "When the Lord has built up Zion, when he has been seen in his glory" (Ps. 102:17).

No. 1 explains the future tense of "the Lord will provide," or "see to it," emphasizing once more the future tense of the action. No. 2 explains the name of the spot in terms of the twin etiology. No. 3 pursues the same line of thought. No. 4 reverts to the overriding theme of the correspondence of the life of the patriarch to the history of Israel, now explicitly linked. The history of the Temple is contained in Abraham's name for the place. The final judgment of Abraham finds expression in Psalm 24 and other biblical passages, read as if to speak of Abraham in particular:

LIX:V.
1. A. "You are fairer than the children of men" (Ps. 45:3):

   B. You have found praise among the beings of the upper world,

   C. as it says, "Behold, their valiant ones cry without" (Is. 33:7).

   D. You have been praised among the beings of the lower world,

   E. as it says, "You are a mighty prince among us"(Gen. 23:6).

   F. "Therefore God has blessed you forever" (Ps. 45:3).

   G. "Now Abraham was old, well advanced in years; and the Lord had blessed Abraham in all things" (Gen. 24:1).

2. A. "Who shall ascend into the mountain of the Lord, and who shall stand in his holy place? [He who has clean hands and a pure heart, who has not taken his life without cause, and who has not sworn deceitfully. He shall receive a blessing from the Lord]" (Ps. 24:3-5):

   B. "Who shall ascend into the mountain of the Lord" speaks of Abraham, as it is said, "For now I know that you fear God" (Gen. 22:12).

   C. "...and who shall stand in his holy place" speaks of Abraham, as it is said, "And Abraham got up early in the morning, to the place where he had stood before the Lord" (Gen. 19:27).

   D. "He who has clean hands," as it is said, "I will not take a thread or a shoe latchet" (Gen. 14:23).

   E. "...and a pure heart." "Far be it from you to do such a thing" (Gen. 18:25).

   F. "...who has not taken his life without cause," the life of Nimrod.

   G. "...who has not sworn deceitfully." "I have lifted up my hand to the Lord, God most high, maker of heaven and earth" (Gen. 14:22).

   H. "He shall receive a blessing from the Lord." "Now Abraham was old, well advanced in years; and the Lord had blessed Abraham in all things" (Gen. 24:1).

3. A. Abraham blessed everyone, as it is said, "And through you will all the families of the earth be blessed" (Gen. 12:3). But who blesses Abraham? The Holy One, blessed be he, blesses him, as it is said, "...and the Lord had blessed Abraham in all things" (Gen. 24:1).

   B. Moses was the ensign of Israel, as it is said, "Why strive you with me? Why do you make me the ensign before the Lord" (Ex. 17:2). But who was the ensign of Moses? It was God: "And Moses built an altar and called the name of it, 'The Lord is my ensign'" (Ex. 17:14).

   C. David was the shepherd of Israel, as it says, "'You shall shepherd my people, Israel'" (1 Chr. 11:2). But who was the shepherd of David? It was the

Holy One, blessed be he, as it is said, "The Lord is *my* shepherd, I shall not want" (Ps. 23:1).

D. Jerusalem is the light of the world, as it is said, "And nations shall walk in your light" (Is. 60:3). But who is the light of Jerusalem? It is God, as it is written, "But the Lord shall be for you an everlasting light" (Is. 60:3).

No. 1 simply interweaves a number of verses to indicate that the cited intersecting verse speaks of Abraham. No. 2 follows the same pattern. What we are given is summaries of the life and virtues of Abraham, as these illustrate passages of Psalms and are illustrated by them. No. 3 goes along its own way, making one point through three examples. It is included because it makes use of our base verse. Its basic point is that the lives of the patriarchs prefigure the entire history of Israel. In Part Four we shall see how this theme comes to full expression.

Chapter Nine

Isaac

Isaac serves as a name on which to hang various lessons. The picture of Genesis left slight alternative, since he scarcely plays so active a role in the narrative as either Abraham or Jacob. The sages before us found few lessons particular to the person of Isaac, but compensated by translating his situation -- in particular, his dealings with the kings of the land -- into theirs. So their fundamental method of interpretation, which led them to find in the biblical statement a lesson for themselves, left them well-equipped to deal in terms relevant to their own circumstance even with a somewhat shadowy personality such as Isaac. The single dominant theme, the way in which the patriarch's deed prefigured the future life of Israel, emerges in the following:

LXIV:VIII.

1. A. "And Isaac dug again the wells of water [which had been dug in the days of Abraham his father; for the Philistines had stopped them after the death of Abraham; and he gave them the names which his father had given them. But when Isaac's servants dug in the valley and found there a well of springing water, the herdsmen of Gerar quarreled with Isaac's herdsmen, saying, 'The water is ours.' So he called the name of the well Esek, because they contended with him. Then they dug another well, and they quarreled over that also, so he called its name Sitnah. And he moved from there and dug another well and over that they did not quarrel, so he called its name Rehoboth, saying 'For now the Lord has made room for us, and we shall be fruitful in the land'" (Gen. 26:18-22). "That same day Isaac's servants came and told him about the well which they had dug and said to him, 'We have found water.' He called it Shibah, therefore the name of the city is Beer Sheba to this day" (Gen. 26:32-33)]:

   B. How many wells did our father Isaac dig in Beer Sheba?

   C. R. Judah bar Simon said, "Four, corresponding to the four standards in the wilderness that marked off his descendants."

   D. And rabbis said, "Five, corresponding to the five scrolls of the Torah."

   E. "'So he called the name of the well Esek, because they contended with him:' this one corresponds to the scroll of Genesis, in which the Holy One, blessed be he, is contending in the creation of his world.

   F. "'Then they dug another well, and they quarreled over that also, so he called its name Sitnah:' this one corresponds to the scroll of Exodus, on the count that they embittered their lives with harsh labor.

G. "'But when Isaac's servants dug in the valley and found there a well of springing water:' this corresponds to the book of Leviticus, which is full of many laws.

H. "'He called it Shibah:' this one corresponds to the book of Numbers, which completes the number of the seven scrolls of the Torah."

I. But are they not only five, not seven?!

J. [No, indeed there were seven, as will now be explained:] Bar Qappara treated the portion of the book of Numbers that begins, "And it came to pass, when the ark set forward" (Num. 10:35) as one book, "And it came to pass, when the ark set forward" and the next verse as a separate book, and from the end of that section until the end of ,the book of Numbers he treated as another book.

2. A. "And he moved from there and dug another well and over that they did not quarrel, so he called its name 'Room' [Rehoboth],"

B. on account of the following explanation: "saying 'For now the Lord has made room for us, and we shall be fruitful in the land'" (Gen. 26:18-22). 2-33).

No. 1 works out a detailed reading of the verse. But the introduction of the points of correspondence between the deeds of the patriarchs and the history of Israel moves the interpretation away from a simple work of glossing. No. 2 explains the obvious. Isaac dealt with the gentile kings, and he taught his descendants whatever lessons there were to be learned.

LXIV:X.

1. A. "They said, 'We see plainly that the Lord is with you; [so we say, 'Let there be be an oath between you and us, and let us make a covenant with you, that you will do us no harm, just as we have not touched you and have done to you nothing but good and have sent you away in peace. You are now the blessed of the Lord']" (Gen. 26:29):

B. ["We have seen plainly that the Lord is with you] on the basis of the fact that we have seen your deeds and the deeds of your fathers.

C. "...'so we say, 'Let there be be an oath between you and us, and let us make a covenant with you.'"

2. A. "[...so we say,'Let there be be an oath between you and us, and let us make a covenant with you,] that you will do us no harm, just as we have not touched you and have done to you nothing but good:'"

B. [As to the meaning of the words, "nothing but good,"] the word for "nothing but" constitutes an exclusionary usage, bearing the meaning that in point of fact, they did not do them a complete favor.

3. A. In the time of R. Joshua b. Hananiah the government decreed that the house of the sanctuary should be rebuilt. Pappus and Lulianus set up money changing tables from Acco to Antioch to provide what was needed for those who came up from the Exile in Babylonia.

B. The Samaritans went and reported to him, "Let it be known to the king that if this rebellious city is rebuilt and the walls are finished, they will not pay tribute (mindah), impost (belo) or toll (halak)" (Ezra 4:13).

C. The words mindah, belo, and halak, respectively, mean land tax, poll tax, and a tax on crops [Freedman, p. 580, n. 2].

D. He said to them, "What shall we do? For the decree has already been issued [for the rebuilding to go forward]."

E. They said to him, "Send orders to them either to change its location or to add five cubits to it or to cut it down by five cubits, and they will give up the project on their own."

F. The community was assembled on the plain of Beth Rimmon, when the royal orders arrived they began to weep. They had the mind to rebel against the government.

G. They said, "Let one wise man go and calm the community down." They said, "Let R. Joshua b. Hananiah do it, because he is a scholast [Hebrew: askolostiqah] of the Torah."

H. He went up and expounded as follows: "A wild lion killed a beast and got a bone stuck in his throat. The lion said, 'To whoever will come and remove it I shall give a reward.' An Egyptian heron with a long beak came and removed the bone, then asked for his fee. The lion answered, 'Go. Now you can boast that you stuck your head into the lion's mouth whole and pulled it out whole.'

I. "So it is enough for us that we entered into dealings with this nation whole and have come forth whole." [Likewise it was enough for Isaac to have gotten out as well as he did.]

4. A. "That same day Isaac's servants came and told him about the well which they had dug and said to him , 'We have found water.' [He called it Shibah, therefore the name of the city is Beer Sheba to this day]" (Gen. 26:32-33):

B. On the basis of this statement, ["to him," which may be spelled to mean, "to him," or to mean "not,"]" we do not know whether or not they found anything.

C. On the analogy to the verse, "...and found there a well of living water" (Gen. 26:19), we know that they found water.

No. 1 contributes a minor gloss, explaining the conversation. No. 2 is inserted as a bridge to No. 3, underlining that the dealings with Abimelech in no way were so harmonious as the narrative suggests on the surface. This yields, at No. 3, the story, quite a propos, that Israel should be glad to emerge from such dealings whole and unscathed, and should expect nothing more. No. 4 clarifies the ambiguous matter of the word at hand, which, spelled one way, means "to him," and the other, "not," hence, in the latter, "we have not found...." The diverse composition yields the simple point that what is at the surface of the story cannot dictate the real meaning. There is no good to be derived from dealings with the gentiles. Isaac formed a link in the generations, from Abraham to Jacob. Of central interest is his message to Jacob, prototype of Israel:

XVI:IV.

1. A. "Let peoples serve you" (Gen. 27:29): this refers to the seventy nations.

B. "and nations bow down to you:" these are the children of Ishmael and the children of Keturah: "And the sons of Dedan were Asshurim and Letushim and Lerummim" (Gen. 25:3).

C. "Be lord over your brothers:"speaks of Esau and his chiefs.

2. A. "and may your mother's sons bow down to you:"

B. Here you say "and may your mother 's sons bow down to you," and elsewhere: "Your father' s sons will down down before you" (Gen. 49:8).

C. Since Jacob took four wives, Leah and Rachel, Zilpah and Bilah, it says, "Your father's sons," but since Isaac was married only to Rebecca, it is, "and may your mother's sons bow down to you."

3. A. "Cursed be everyone who curses you, and blessed be every one who blesses you" (Gen. 27:29):

B. By contrast: "Blessed be everyone who blesses you and cursed be everyone who curses you" (Num. 24:9). [Why the difference in the precedence of blessing and curse in the two formulations?]

C. Since Balaam hated Israel, he begins with a reference to a blessing and ends with a reference to a curse, but since Isaac loves Israel, he begins with a reference to a curse so as to conclude with a reference to a blessing.

D. Said R. Isaac bar Hiyya, "Since the wicked begin in prosperity and end in suffering, they begin with a blessing and conclude with a curse, but since the righteous begin with suffering and end with prosperity, they begin with a curse and end with a blessing."

What we may find interesting in the treatment of Isaac is the method of sages. They find a way of saying a single and constant truth, wherever they turn to discover proof and warrant for the convictions of their system and its way of life.

Chapter Ten

Jacob

Jacob stood for Israel, the Jewish people, and does today. All biblical references to "Israel" or to "Jacob" identify the man with the nation, and the nation with the man. For sages, moreover, Esau represented Rome, which, in their own time, had gone from pagan to Christian, and from the benign or neutral ruler of submissive and loyal Israel to an active enemy. Not only so, but Rome now claimed to descend from the same holy ancestor from whom Israel had come forth. So Rome not only ruled but claimed the patrimony of Israel -- an ominous turn of events. The issues at stake in the reading of the stories of Jacob and Esau and in the interpretation of Jacob's life as a set of lessons for his children proved considerable.

Sages' first task in explaining how Jacob set an example for his descendants found definition in the tale of Jacob and Esau. That is the point at which Jacob, in the biblical narrative, presented the face of a schemer and deceiver. But for sages, that mask covered a face of innocence and purity. Jacob had only the highest motives, and Isaac understood and accepted them. We begin with a passage that is already familiar, namely, how Jacob explained what was at issue, the future history of the service of sacrifice to God.

LXIII:XIII.

1. A. "Jacob said, 'First sell me your birthright.' Esau said, 'I am about to die, of what use is a birthright to me?'"

   B. He said to him, "Sell me one day that is yours."

   C. Said R. Aha, "Whoever knows how to reckon [the exile] will discover that for only one did day Jacob lived under the shadow of Esau." [Freedman, p. 568, n. 4: The verse is translated as symbolically alluding to Israel in the diaspora, with Jacob demanding, "Sell me...yours," "leave me in peace if only for a short while," and R. Aha observes that that indeed has been the case.]

2. A. "Esau said, 'I am about to die, of what use is a birthright to me?'"

   B. R. Simeon b. Laqish said, "He began to revile and blaspheme. What do I need it for: '...of what use is a birthright to me?'"

3. A. Another explanation: "I am about to die:"

   B. For Nimrod was looking for him to kill him on account of the garment that had belonged to the first man, for at the moment that Esau put it on and went out to the field, all of the wild beasts and fowl in the world came and gathered around him [and that is why he was such a good hunter].

4. A. "Jacob said, 'Swear to me first.' So he swore to him and sold his birthright to Jacob" (Gen. 25:33):

B. Why did Jacob risk his life for the right of the firstborn?

C. **For we have learned in the Mishnah: Before the tabernacle was set up, the high places were permitted, and the rite of offering was carried out by the first born. Once the tabernacle was set up, the high places were forbidden, and the rite of offering was carried out by the priests[M. Zebahim 14:4].**

D. He said, "Should that wicked man stand and make offerings?" Therefore Jacob risked his life for the right of the firstborn.

5. A. That is in line with the following verse: "I will prepare you for blood, and blood shall pursue you, surely you have hated blood, therefore shall blood pursue you" (Ez. 35:6).

B. But did Esau hate blood?

C. R. Levi in the name of R. Hama bar Hanina: "This is the blood of circumcision [which Esau did hate]."

D. R. Levi in the name of R. Samuel b. Nahman,"This refers to the blood of the offerings by the firstborn."

E. Rabbis say, "You have hated the blood of man when it is in his body, in line with this verse: 'Yes, he loved cursing and it came to him and he did not delight in blessing' (Ps. 109:17)."

F. R. Levi in the name of R. Hama bar Hanina, "He did not take pleasure in the birthright."

G. R. Huna said, "This refers to the blood of the offerings, which are called a blessing, in line with this verse: 'An altar of earth you shall make for me...I will come to you and bless you' (Ex. 20:21)."

No. 1 makes explicit what is at stake in the sale, namely, Israel's life under Esau's rule. Nos. 2, 3 revert to the body of the story and gloss details. No. 4 shows that what was at stake was a considerable issue. No. 5 takes up the cited intersecting verse, continuing the foregoing, the matter of the offerings. Esau had no right to make offerings, he had no respect for the Temple and its cult. A reading of Church fathers' treatment of the "bloody rite" of the Jerusalem Temple will justify sages' emphasis on this point.

LXV:XVIII.

1. A. "So he went in to his father and said, 'My father,' and he said, 'Here I am. Who are you, my son?' And Jacob said to his father, 'I am Esau your first born. [I have done as you told me;' now sit up and eat of my game, that you may bless me']" (Gen. 27:18-19):

B. Said R. Levi, "'I' am the one who will receive the Ten Commandments, but Esau is indeed your first born.'"

2. A. "... now sit up:"

B. Said R. Yohanan, "Said the Holy One, blessed be he, to Jacob, "You have said, "...now sit up." By your life with that same language I shall pay you your just reward: "Rise up, O Lord, and let your enemies be scattered"' (Num. 10:35)."

3. "But there is he who is swept away by want of righteousness" (Prov. 13:23) refers to Esau. Said the Holy One, blessed be he, to Esau, "You have said, 'Let my father arise' (Gen. 27:31). By the fortune of my idol I adjure you to arise.' By your life I shall pay you I shall pay you back with that very same language: 'Rise up, O Lord, and let your enemies be scattered' (Num. 10:35)."

Nos. 1, 2 amplify the discourse, redirecting the statements of Jacob to the history of Israel in the future. Each statement then bears a deeper meaning, drawn from that history. No. 3 builds on the point of No. 2, using the same verse to Esau's disadvantage that has served as praise for Jacob. The simplest statements of Scripture, bearing unambiguous meaning, turn out to say the opposite of what they seem to suggest:

LXV:XX.

1. A. "And Jacob went near to Isaac his father, who felt him and said, 'The voice is Jacob's voice, but the hands are the hands of Esau'" (Gen. 27:22):

B. "It is the sound of the voice of a wise man, but the hands are those of one who strips corpses."

2. A. "The voice is Jacob's voice:"

B. Jacob rules only by his voice [through reasoned argument].

C. "...but the hands are the hands of Esau:"

D. and Esau rules only by the power of his hands [by force].

3. A. "The voice is Jacob's voice:"

B. Said R. Phineas, "When the voice of Jacob is drawn mute, then: 'the hands are the hands of Esau.' He is called and comes."

4. A. "The voice is Jacob's voice, but the hands are the hands of Esau:"

B. Said R. Berekhiah, "When Jacob uses his voice to express anger [against God], then the hands of Esau take control, but when his voice speaks clearly, then the hands of Esau do not take control."

5. A. Said R. Abba bar Kahana, "No philosophers in the world ever arose of the quality of Balaam ben Beor and Abnomos of Gadara. All of the nations of the world came to Abnomos of Gadara. They said to him, 'Do you maintain that we can make war against this nation?'

B. "He said to them, 'Go and make the rounds of their synagogues and the study houses. If you find there children chirping out loud in their voices [and studying the Torah], then you cannot overcome them. If not, then you can conquer them, for so did their father promise them: "The voice is Jacob's voice," meaning that when Jacob's voice sounds forth in synagogues, Esau has no power.'"

Nos. 1-5 present a series of interpretations of Isaac's statement which yield a single notion. Jacob rules through measured, calm, and reasoned discourse. Jacob rules through study of the Torah. The nations of the world have no power over Jacob when Jacob studies Torah. The voice of Jacob prevails but when

Jacob does not speak up, then Esau prevails. This single message comes in a number of forms and versions. What exactly is at issue in Isaac's blessing of Jacob? It is, not surprisingly, the entire future of Israel as against the history of Rome.

LXXV:VIII.

1. A. "And Jacob sent:" (Gen. 32:3):

B. This is what Solomon said through the Holy Spirit: "Blessings are upon the head of the righteous but the mouth of the wicked conceals violence" (Prov. 10:6).

C. This verse is stated only with regard to Jacob and Esau.

D. "Blessings are upon the head of the righteous" refers to Jacob.

E. "...but the mouth of the wicked conceals violence" speaks of Esau, the wicked man.

F. Fortunate are the righteous, who are blessed both on earth and in heaven. That is the way things are: "So that he who is blessed in earth shall be blessed by the God of truth" (Is. 65:16).

G. This tells you that in response to all of the blessings which Isaac bestowed upon Jacob, the Holy One, blessed be he, responded and bestowed a blessing above.

H. Isaac blessed him as follows: "So God give you of the dew of heaven" (Gen. 27:28).

I. Correspondingly, the Holy One, blessed be he, blessed him with dew and said, "And the remnant of Jacob shall be in the midst of many peoples as dew" (Mic. 5:6).

J. Isaac blessed him as follows:"And of the fatness of the earth" (Gen. 27:28).

K. Correspondingly, the Holy One, blessed be he, blessed him with grain and said, "And he will give the rain for your seed, wherewith you sow the ground, and the bread of the increase of the ground, and it shall be fat and plentiful" (Is. 30:23).

L. Isaac blessed him as follows: "And plenty of grain and wine" (Gen. 27:28).

M. Correspondingly, the Holy One, blessed be he said, "And the Lord answered and said to his people,'Behold, I will send you grain and wine and oil'" (Joel 2;19).

N. Isaac blessed him as follows: "Let peoples serve you" (Gen. 27:29).

O. Correspondingly,the Holy One, blessed be he said, "And kings as shall be your foster-fathers" (Is. 49:23).

P. Isaac blessed him as follows: "Be lord over your brethren" (Gen. 27:29).

Q. Correspondingly, the Holy One, blessed be he said, to him through Moses, our master, "And to make you high above all the nations" (Deut. 26:19).

R. This tells you that in response to all of the blessings which Isaac bestowed upon Jacob, the Holy One, blessed be he, responded and bestowed a blessing above.

S. Rebecca, his mother, blessed him in the same way, "O you who dwell in the shadow of the most high" (Ps. 91:1). "For he will give his angels charge over you to keep you in all your ways"(Ps. 91:11).

T. The Holy Spirit answered her: "He will call upon me and I will answer him" (Ps. 91:15).

U. Now if the Holy One, blessed be he, bestowed blessings on him, why did his father and mother have to go and bless him also, as it is said, "And Isaac called Jacob and blessed him" (Gen. 28:1)?

U. It is because Isaac foresaw through the Holy Spirit that his children were destined to go into exile. He said to him, "Come and I shall give you a blessing for the Exile, that the Holy One, blessed be he, will bring you back from the exile."

V. And what was that blessing that he gave him? "He will deliver you in six troubles" (Job 5:19).

W. Therefore it is said, "Blessings are upon the head of the righteous [but the mouth of the wicked conceals violence]" (Prov. 10:6).

F-Q are tacked on because they illustrate F: the blessings that are bestowed on the righteous both in heaven and on earth. But of course they form a distinct composition.   The importance of the whole is once more to link Jacob's biography to Israel's history. None of this has any bearing on our base verse, and there is no pretense that it does. It is simply a thematic exercise, built on the pretext of comparing Jacob and Esau, but moving entirely along its own lines. Jacob further presented the model of the direct encounter with God, as point made repeatedly in the portrait of Genesis. If people wished to know God and enter into relationship with God, they had best learn the lessons Jacob taught them. The encounter found full and rich amplification:

LXVIII:X.

1. A. "And he lighted upon a certain place and stayed there that night" (Gen. 28:11):

B. [Since the word "lighted upon" bears the meaning of "encounter' we interpret as follows:] He wanted to go on but the world became a wall before him [so he bumped into the place and had to stay].

2. A. Rabbis say, "'...because the sun had set' (Gen. 28:11) teaches that the Holy One, blessed be he, made the sun set out of season, so as to talk in private with our father, Jacob.

B. "The matter may be compared to the case of the king's ally, who would come to him from time to time. The king said, 'Put out the lamps, since I want to talk with my ally in private.' So the Holy One, blessed be he, made the sun set out of season, so as to talk in private with our father, Jacob."

3. A. R. Phineas in the name of R. Hanan: "He heard the voice of the ministering angels saying, 'The sun has come! The sun has come!'

B. "So too when Joseph said, 'Lo, the sun and the moon...bowed down to me' (Gen. 37:9), Jacob said, 'Now who told him that my name is 'Sun'?"

4. A. As to those two hours early that the Holy One, blessed be he, made the sun set when Jacob went forth from his father's house, when did he restore them to him?

B. When he came back to his father's house: "And the sun rose for him" (Gen. 32:32).

C. Said the Holy One, blessed be he, to him, "You are an omen for your children. Just as, when you went forth, on your account I brought the orb of the sun down, and when you came back, I restored the orb of the sun on your account, so when your children went forth: 'She who has borne seven languishes, her spirit droops, her sun has gone down while it was yet day' (Jer. 15:(9), but when they come back: 'But to you who fear my name shall the sun of righteousness arise with healing in its wings' (Mal. 3:20)."

After the detail contributed at No. 1, we move on to three interpretations of the statement that the sun had set. In the first, No. 2, the sunset serves God's purpose in talking with Jacob. In the second, No. 3, Jacob himself is called the sun, and that ties up to No. 2. But No. 4 draws the whole together, picking up the themes of Jacob compared to the sun, on the one side, and the hours lost on the present occasion, on the other, that is, the themes of Nos. 3 and 2, respectively. Then the whole is woven into the salvific history of Israel, with exile and redemption in turn. This is explicitly linked to the exile through the motif of Jacob's leaving the land. Then, just as, when Jacob, who stands for Israel, left the land, the sun set prematurely, so when Israel returns to the Land, the sun will rise for them. It would be difficult to find a better example of a deft and subtle weaving of distinct and autonomous materials into a single fabric with a picture and a point of its own.

LXVIII:XI.

1. A. "Taking one of the stones of the place, [he put it under his head and lay down in that place to sleep]" (Gen. 28:11):

B. R. Judah said, "He took twelve stones. He said, 'So did the Holy One, blessed be he, decree that twelve tribes would come forth. Now Abraham did not produce them, and Isaac did not produce them. As for me, if these stones will stick together, I shall know that I am going to produce twelve tribes.'

C. "When he saw that the stones stuck together, he knew that he would set up the twelve tribes."

D. R. Nehemiah said, "He took three stones. He said, 'As to Abraham, the Holy One, blessed be he, joined his name to him, as to Isaac, the Holy One, blessed be he, joined his name to him, so, as for me, if these three stones will stick together, I shall know that the name of the Holy One, blessed be he, will be joined to mine.'

E. "When he saw that the stones stuck together, he understood that the name of the Holy One, blessed be he, would be joined to his."

F. Rabbis say, "Since the word 'stones" refers to the smallest plural, it must mean that he took two stones. He said, 'As to Abraham, from him came forth Ishmael and the sons of Keturah. As from Isaac, from him came forth Esau. And as to me, if these three stones will stick together, I shall know that no refuse will come forth from me.'"

2. A. R. Levi and R. Eleazar in the name of R. Yose b. Zimra: "He arranged them like a roof-gutter [Freedman] and put only one of them under his head, since he was afraid of wild beasts.' [Freedman, p. 623, n. 5: This is a reconciliation of the statement that he took stones and the one that he took *one* stone, Gen. 28:18.]"

3. A. R. Berekhiah, R. Levi in the name of R. Hama bar Haninah: "It is written, 'For lo, the Lord comes forth out of his place...and the mountains shall be molten under him" (Mic. 1:3-4).

B. "And as to him upon whom the Holy One, blessed be he, was revealed, how much the more so [will the rocks melt and fuse]!" [Freedman, p. 624, n. 1: The stones would certainly melt and fuse into one. He defends the miraculous explanation.]

4. A. R. Berekhiah in the name of R. Levi, "Those rocks that our father, Jacob, put under his head turned under him into a bed and a pillow.

B. "What was the cover that he placed over himself? 'The beams of our houses are cedars' (Song 1:17), that is, the righteous men and the righteous women, the prophets and the prophetesses."

5. A. "...he lay down in that place to sleep" (Gen. 28:11):

B. R. Judah said, "Here he slept, while during all those fourteen years that he was secluded in the land and serving as disciple for Eber, he did not sleep."

C. R. Nehemiah said, "Here he slept, while during all those twenty years that he was in the house of Laban, he never slept."

D. What did he say [while staying awake and tending the sheep]?

E. R. Joshua b. Levi said, "It was the fifteen Songs of Ascents that are in the Book of Psalms.

F. "What verse shows it? 'A song of ascents of David. If it had not been the Lord who was for us, let Israel now say' (Ps. 124:1). The 'Israel' here is our father."

G. R. Samuel bar Nahman said, "He recited the entire book of Psalms.

H. "What verse shows it? Yet you are holy, O you who are enthroned upon the praises of Israel' (Ps. 22:4), and the 'Israel' here is our father."

No. 1 lays out the several meanings to be imputed to the stones that Jacob took. No. 2 deals with the contradiction of details. No. 3 stands by itself (*pace* Freedman) and makes its own point. No. 4 proceeds to link Jacob's situation to the house of Israel, covered and protected by its righteous and prophetic men and women. No. 5 makes a point relevant to Jacob's life and drawn out of the verse at hand. Since the verse makes it explicit that here he slept, it must follow that elsewhere he did not sleep. And the further discussion flows in the wake of that observation. Obviously, the secondary expansion of Nehemiah's position can have stood entirely on its own. But including the materials underlines the view that, wherever we speak of "Israel," we can mean Jacob in his own lifetime. So we see a movement not only from the biography of the patriarch to the history of Israel but also from the history of Israel to the biography of the patriarch.

LXIX:V.

1. A. "...and your descendants shall be like the dust of the earth, and you shall spread abroad to the west and to the east and to the north, and to the south; and by you and your descendants shall all the families of the earth bless themselves'" (Gen. 28:13-14):

B. [Lacking here: Just as the dust of the earth is from one end of the world to the other, so your children will be from one end of the world to the other.]

C. Just as the dust of the earth is blessed only with water, so your children will be blessed only through the merit attained by study of the Torah, which is compared to water [hence: through water].

D. Just as the dust of the earth wears out metal utensils and yet endures forever, so Israel endures while the nations of the world come to an end.

E. Just as the dust of the world is treated as something on which to trample, so your children are treated as something to be trampled upon by the government.

F. That is in line with this verse: "And I will put it into the hand of them that afflict you" (Is. 51:23), that is to say, those who make your wounds flow [Freedman].

G. Nonetheless, it is for your good that they do so, for they cleanse you of guilt, in line with this verse: "You make her soft with showers" (Ps. 65:11). [Freedman, p. 339, n. 33: "Words of the same root are used for 'make soft' and 'who afflict you.' The passage understands the former in the sense of making the rain flow and hence the latter too -- to make the wounds flow."]

H. "That have said to your soul, Bow down, that we may go over" (Is. 51:23):

I. What did they do to them? They made them lie down in the streets and drew ploughs over them."

J. R. Azariah in the name of R. Aha: "That is a good sign. Just as the street wears out those who pass over it and endures forever, so your children will wear out all the nations of the world and will live forever."

2. A. "... and you shall spread abroad to the west and to the east and to the north, and to the south; and by you and your descendants shall all the families of the earth bless themselves" (Gen. 28:13-14):

B. Said R. Abba bar Kahana, "'You are the one who will split the sea,' in line with this verse: 'The breaker has gone up before them' (Mic. 2:13)." [The word for "the west" is "the sea," and "you shall spread" is read as "you shall break, hence the statement at hand (Freedman, p. 633, n. 1).]

3. A. R. Yose bar Haninah said, "He also showed him the divisions of the land that Ezekiel would make [at Ez. 48]."

B. But Ezekiel divided the land only from east to west?

C. Isaiah came along and spelled out matters: "For you shall spread abroad on the right hand and on the left" (Is. 54:3).

No. 1 makes its own point, pertinent in no particular way either to the present context or to the exegesis of the verse at hand. Nos. 2, 3 amplify the meaning of the verse. The former presents a play on words, thus linking the statement to Jacob to the dividing of the Red Sea. Sages did not restrict their reading of a story to a single line of thought. When we impute to them the power to preserve a multiple vision of a single incident, we find ample exemplification in the following. Jacob's dealing with Laban yields several distinct lessons. It is as if we had a drama, on which a stage is divided into a number of cubicles, so that we see the same thing happening against quite different sets and played out by distinctive groups of actors, each with its own voice, each working out its own plot.

LXXIV:III.

1. A. "He said to them, 'I see that your father does not regard me with favor as he did before. But the God of my father has been with me'" (Gen. 31:4-5):

    B. "He has been my pillar, my support" [a play on the word for "with me"].

2. A. "You know that I have served your father with all my strength; yet your father has cheated me and changed my wages ten times, but God did not permit him to harm me" (Gen. 31:6-7):

    B. Said R. Hiyya the Elder, "On every stipulation that Laban made with Jacob he reneged ten times, as it says, 'Yes, no.'" [Freedman, p. 673, n. 2: Reading "not" for "good," while "*hen*" in Aramaic is "yes," he renders: "And Laban said, 'Yes and no.'"]

    C. Rabbis say, "It was a hundred times: 'And your father has mocked me and changed my wages ten times' (Gen. 31:7), [and the word means ten times ten], for the word for 'ten times' here corresponds to the word for quorum, which is at least ten.'"

3. A. "'If he said, "The spotted shall be your wages," [then all the flock bore spotted, and if he said, "The striped shall be your wages," then all the flock bore striped. Thus God has taken away the cattle of your father and given them to me. In the mating season of the flock I lifted up my eyes and saw in a dream that the he-goats which leaped upon the flock were striped, spotted, and mottled']" (Gen. 31:8ff.):

    B. R. Berekhiah and R. Levi in the name of R. Hama b. R. Haninah: "The Holy One, blessed be he, foresaw what Laban was going to do with Jacob, and he made things come out in the end exactly in that manner. What is said is not, 'If he said,' but, 'If he will say.' [The use of the future indicates that (Freedman, p. 678, n. 1:) God anticipated and forestalled these changes of agreement.]"

    C. R. Yudan and R. Aibu in the name of R. Yohanan: "What is written is not, 'For I have seen all that Laban *has done* to you,' but '...is doing to you.'"

4. A. "'Then the angel of the God said to me in the dream, "Jacob," [and I said, "Here I am." And he said, "Lift up your eyes and see, all the goats that leap upon the flock are striped, spotted, and mottled, for I have seen all that Laban is doing to you. I am the God of Bethel, where you anointed a pillar and made a vow to me']" (Gen. 31:11-13):

    B. R. Eliezer says, "He spoke both to him and to coming generations. There is no generation in which there is none of the standing of Abraham, Jacob, Moses, and Samuel."

5. A. "'And he said, "Lift up your eyes and see, all the goats that leap upon the flock are striped, spotted, and mottled, for I have seen all that Laban is doing to you. I am the God of Bethel, where you anointed a pillar and made a vow to me'" (Gen. 31:11-13):

    B. Said R. Hunia, "What is written is not, '...going up upon the flock...,' but rather, 'those that are going up,' meaning that they would mount on their own."

    C. R. Tanhuma said, "They were carried in a rain shower."

    D. Rabbis say, "They were carried in clouds of glory."

6. A. "Thus God has taken away the cattle of your father and given them to me" (Gen. 31:9):

    B. "It is like one who saves something out of the garbage."

The glosses, item by item, emphasize three themes, first, God's help to Jacob, second, Laban's deceit, third, the stake that Israel in its history has in the lives of the patriarchs and matriarchs. If the message were restated in contemporary terms, it would be that while the Labans of the world deceive the Israelites of the world, God knows what is going on, and Israel does not lack its Jacobs to save the people. These seem to me recurrent motifs. Jacob stands for Israel in yet another way. He presents the most human and mortal face of the patriarchs, detailed, unlike Isaac, flawed and frail, unlike the mighty Abraham. So when the Scripture says thast Jacob feared, Jacob's heirs can identify with him. But then they have to learn the lesson of the situation of Israel, which is that they have every reason to hope, and none at all to fear.

LXXVI:I.

1. A. "Then Jacob was greatly afraid and distressed" (Gen. 32:7):

    B. R. Phineas in the name of R. Reuben opened by citing this verse: "Trust in the Lord with all your heart' (Prov. 3:5).

    C. "To two men did the Holy One, blessed be he, give assurances, and both of them nonetheless were afraid, the select among the patriarchs and the select among the prophets.

    D. "The select among the patriarchs was Jacob: 'For the Lord has chosen Jacob for himself' (Ps. 135:4).

    E. "The Holy One, blessed be he, had said to him, 'Lo, I shall be with you' (Gen. 28:15), yet: 'Then Jacob was greatly afraid and distressed.'

    F. "...and the select among the prophets: this was Moses, our master: 'Had not Moses, his chosen...' (Ps. 106:23).

    G. "The Holy One, blessed be he, had said to him, 'Certainly I will be with you' (Ex. 3:12).

    H. "But he was afraid: 'And the Lord said to Moses, "Do not fear him, for I have delivered him into your hand"' (Num. 21:34). Since he had to say, 'Do not fear him,' it is certain that he did fear him, for otherwise there was no need to make that statement."

2. A. R. Berekhiah and R. Helbo in the name of R. Samuel bar Nahman, "The Israelites were deserving of complete destruction in the time of Haman [for they lost hope], except that they took the position that had been taken by the elder, saying, 'If our father, Jacob, to whom the Holy One, blessed be he, gave assurances, was afraid, as to us, how much the more so!'"

    B. "Then Jacob was greatly afraid" (Gen. 32:7).

No. 1 makes the obvious point that, after the promises God had made to Jacob, he should not have been afraid. This is then drawn into line with Moses' fear and shown to be perfectly natural. No. 2 makes essentially the same point, again linking Israel's history to Jacob's biography. The next compositions go over the same ground. The message to contemporary Israel is to have faith.

LXXVII:

1. A. "And Jacob was left alone" (Gen. 32:24):

    B. "There is none like unto God, O Jeshurun" (Deut. 33:26):

    C. R. Berekhiah in the name of R. Judah bar Simon, "The sense of the verse is this: 'There is none like God. But who is like God? It is Jeshurun, specifically, the proudest and the noblest among you. [Freedman, p. 710, n. 2: Jeshurun is derived from the word for upright or noble.]'

    C. "You find that everything that the Holy One, blessed be he, is destined to do in the age to come he has already gone ahead and done through the righteous in this world.

    D. "The Holy One, blessed be he, will raise the dead, and Elijah raised the dead.

    E. "The Holy One, blessed be he, will hold back rain, and Elijah held back rain.

    F. "The Holy One, blessed be he, made what was little into a blessing [and so increased it in volume], and Elijah made what was little into a blessing.

    G. "The Holy One, blessed be he, visits barren women [and makes them fruitful], and Elisha visits barren women [and makes them fruitful].

    H. "The Holy One, blessed be he, made what was little into a blessing [and so increased it in volume], and Elisha made what was little into a blessing.

    I. "The Holy One, blessed be he, made the bitter sweet, and Elisha made the bitter sweet.

    J. "The Holy One blessed be he made the bitter sweet through something that was bitter, and Elisha made the bitter sweet through something that was bitter."

2. A. R. Berekhiah in the name of R. Simon: "There is none like unto God, O Jeshurun:'

    B. "The sense of the verse is this: 'There is none like God. But who is like God? It is the elder, Israel.

    C. "What is written concerning the Holy One, blessed be he? 'And the Lord alone shall be exalted' (Is. 2:11).

    D. "So too of Jacob: 'And Jacob was left alone.'"

The point of the choice of the intersecting verse emerges at No. 2, which is surely part of the unitary composition begun at No. 1. That is, we have two views of who is like God, one identifying the righteous in general, the other Jacob in particular. The point in common in No. 2 then draws us back to the word-choice in the present verse, referring to Jacob as "alone," in the same sense as Is. 2:11 speaks of God alone Freedman understands this to mean that Jacob was unique in virtue. The task of hopeful Israel? It is to reach out to the gentiles to bring them under the wings of God's presence. This is what Abraham had done, and this remained the task of Israel.

LXXXIV:IV.

1. A. "Jacob dwelt in the land of his father's sojournings, in the land of Canaan:"

B. [Since the word "sojournings" contains the consonants for the word for "proselyte," it is as if we read, "in the land in which his ancestors had made proselytes, and so we note:] Abraham made proselytes, for its is written, "And Abraham took Sarai his wife...and the souls that they had made in Haran" (Gen. 12:5).

C. R. Eleazar in the name of R. Yose b. Zimra: "If all of the nations of the world should come together to try to create a single misquito, they could not put a soul into it, and yet you say, 'And the soul that they had made'? But this refers to the proselytes."

D. Then why should not the text say, "The proselytes whom they had converted." Why stress, "whom they had made"?

E. This serves to teach you that whoever brings a gentile close [to the worship of the true God] is as if he had created him anew.

F. And why not say, "That he had made"? Why, "That they had made"?

G. Said R. Huniah, "Abraham converted the men and Sarah the women."

H. Jacob likewise made converts: "Then Jacob said to his household and to all that were with him, 'Put away the strange gods that are among you'...And they gave to Jacob all the foreign gods" (Gen. 35:2ff.).

I. In regard to Isaac we have no explicit statement of the same matter. Yet where do we find that Isaac did so?

J. It has been taught by R. Hoshaia in the name of R. Judah bar Simon, "Here it is said, 'Jacob dwelt in the land of his father's sojournings, in the land of Canaan.' [Since the word "sojournings" contains the consonants for the word for "proselyte," it is as if we read, "in the land in which his ancestors had made proselytes:] 'among the proselytes of his father.'"

The point is fully exposed in the play on the word "sojourning." At issue then is the interpretation of the base verse. All three of the patriarchs engaged in winning proselytes to God's worship. The stress on that fact suggests the issue proved lively in the time of the exegete-compositors.

Chapter Eleven

The Matriarchs

While with Isaac, sages had to impart detail and dimension to a small and shadowy figure, in the case of the matriarchs they took as their task the opposite exercise. The matriarchs, particularly Sarah, Rebecca, and Rachel, play substantial roles in the narrative. Their place in the life of their families and their influence over the future history of Israel surely find ample demonstration in particular in the persons of Sarah at the beginning and Rebecca, Jacob's mother. Indeed, if we had to point to a single truly effective personality in the book of Genesis, apart from God, we should have to point to Rebecca. But in the hands of the sages whose comments are assembled in Genesis Rabbah, none of the matriarchs finds a role commensurate to her stature in the biblical record. That is not to suggest sages do not recognize the matriarchs' special role. On the contrary, they see them as critical to the unfolding of Israel's history in Genesis.Rachel and Rebecca, in particular, exercise prophetic gifts.

LXXII:VI.

1. A. "[And Leah conceived again and she bore Jacob a sixth son.] Then Leah said, 'God has endowed me with a good dowry; now my husband will honor me, [because I have borne him six sons,' so she called his name Zebulun]" (Gen 30:20):

   B. As to a field, so long as you manure it and hoe it, it produces fruit. [The name of Zebulun and of the verb, "endowed with a good dowry" are connected to the word for "manure," which shares the same consonants. Hence (Freedman, p. 666, n.1:) "The more children I bear the more he will love me."]

2. A. "Afterwards she bore him a daughter and called her name Dinah" (Gen. 30:21):

   B. If a man's wife was pregnant and he said, "May it please God that my wife give birth to a male child," lo, this is a vain prayer {m. Ber. 9:3].

   C. A member of the house of R. Yannai said, "The cited paragraph of the Mishnah treats a case in which the wife is already sitting on the labor stool [by which point the matter is decided, one way or the other, anyhow]."

   D. Said R. Judah bar Pazzi, "Even if the the wife is already sitting on the labor stool, the sex of the child can change, in line with this verse: 'O house of Israel, cannot I do with you as this potter? says the Lord. Behold, as the clay in the potter's hand, so are you in my hand, O House of Israel' (Jer. 18:6)."

E. An objection was raised from the following verse: "Afterwards she bore him a daughter and called her name Dinah." [There was no issue of changing the birth of that child at the last minute.]

F. He said to them, "In point of fact, while Dinah was taking shape, in the main she was to be male, but on account of the prayer of Rachel, who had said, 'May the Lord add to me another son!' (Gen. 30:24), she was turned into a girl-child.. [Freedman, p. 666, n. 7: Since Jacob was only destined to beget twelve sons, this one had to be a daughter.]"

3. A. Said R. Haninah b. Pazzi, "The matriarchs were prophetesses, and Rachel was one of them. 'May the Lord add to me more sons' is not what she said, rather, '...another son.'

B. "She said, 'Jacob is going to produce yet one more son, and would that it come forth from me.'

C. Said R. Haninah, "The matriarchs got together and said, 'We have enough males, let this one be remembered with a male child.'"

No. 1 explains the name of Zebulun. No. 2 makes use of the base verse as part of the repertoire of proofs for the cited proposition. The point is that God can change the sex of a child even at the last minute, for the reasons given. Then No. 3, which does belong, exploits what No. 2 has introduced. So Nos. 2-3 appear to have come together before the entire set found its place here.

LXVII:IX.

1. A. "But the words of Esau her older son were told to Rebecca, [so she sent and called Jacob her younger son and said to him, 'Behold your brother Esau comforts himself by planning to kill you. Now therefore my son, obey my voice; arise, flee to Laban my brother in Haran, and stay with him a while, until your brother's fury turns away; until your brother's anger turns away, and he forgets what you have done to him; then I will send and fetch you from there. Why should I be bereft of you both in one day?]" (Gen. 27:42-45):

B. R. Haggai in the name of R. Isaac, "The matriarchs were prophets, and Rebecca was one of the matriarchs [and that is how she knew what Esau was thinking of doing]."

C. R. Berekhiah in the name of R. Isaac: "Even a common person will not plough one furrow within another. Will the prophets do so? And yet you find: 'Do not touch my anointed ones and do no harm to my prophets' (Ps. 105:15)."

No. 1 answers the question of who told Rebecca what she knew. She is represented as a prophet. But when it comes to heroic women, Ruth, the ancestress of the Messiah, finds a place in the conventional repertoire leading to the Messiah but none of the matriarchs figure in that same standard list.

LXVIII:VI.

1. A. "Now Jacob left Beer-sheba" (Gen. 28:10):

B. Was he the only one who went [that the statement is made concerning Jacob alone]?

C. Did not any number of ass-drivers and camel-drivers go forth with him?

D. R. Azariah in the name of R. Judah bar Simon, R. Hanan in the name of R. Samuel bar R. Isaac: "When a righteous man is in a town, he is its glory, he is its praise, he is its honor. When he leaves there, its glory leaves there, its praise leaves there, its honor leaves there."

E. Along these same lines: "And she went forth out of the place where she was" (Ruth 1:7).

F. Was she the only one who went [that the statement is made concerning Ruth alone]?

G. Did not any number of ass-drivers and camel-drivers go forth with her?

H. R. Azariah in the name of R. Judah bar Simon, R. Hanan in the name of R. Samuel bar R. Isaac: "When a righteous man is in a town, he is its glory, he is its praise, he is its honor. When he leaves there, its glory leaves there, its praise leaves there, its honor leaves there."

I. That reply serves well in the case of Ruth, for she was alone, that righteous woman, as the ornament of the place. But here was not Isaac there too?

J. R. Azariah in the name of R. Yudan b. R. Simon, "The merit attained by an individual righteous person cannot compare to that attained by two [so that even when one remains, the departure of the other is still noticeable (Freedman, p. 619, n. 4)]."

The composition is worked out on its own terms, not for the purpose of a verse-by-verse exegesis of Genesis but to make a syllogistic point about the importance of a righteous person to the place in which that person is located. The comparison of the statements concerning Jacob and Ruth then contributes to the larger argument. But from our perspective drawing a parallel between Jacob and Ruth admits to the circle of the heroic figures not only the Messiah but the mother of the Messiah. Not only do the matriarchs play their role, they also provide a source of merit for future Israel, no less than the merit of the patriarchs. That is the important point, for the sages at hand, to be found in Genesis. Women as much as men participate in the supernatural transaction of merit.

LXXIII:I.

1. A. "Then God remembered Rachel, and God hearkened to her and opened her womb. She conceived and bore a son and said, 'God has taken away my reproach,' and she called his name Joseph, saying, 'May the Lord add to me another son!'" (Gen. 30:22-24):

B. "Remember me, O Lord, when you favor your people, O think of me at your salvation" (Ps. 106:4):

C. Said R. Eleazar, "On the New Year were Sarah, Rachel, and Hannah remembered: 'Then God remembered Rachel.'"

The use of "remembered" applies in all three instances, and the present one accounts for the inclusion of the entire syllogism here.

LXXIII:II.

1. **A.** "He has remembered his mercy and his faithfulness to the house of Israel; all the ends of the earth have seen the salvation of our God" (Ps. 98:3):

B. "He has remembered his mercy" refers to Abraham: "Mercy to Abraham" Mic. 7:20).

C. "... and his faithfulness" refers to Jacob: "You will show faithfulness to Jacob" (Mic. 7:20).

D. "...to the house of Israel" the elder.

E. Who was the house of our father, Abraham? Was it not Rachel?

F. In regard to all of the others it is written, "And the children of Leah, the first born of Jacob was Reuben...and the children of Zilpah, Leah's maid, were Gad and Asher...and the children of Bilhah, Rachel's maid, were Dan and Naphtali" (Gen. 35:23-26).

G. But in connection with the children of Rachel it is written, "The sons of Rachel, Jacob's wife: Joseph and Benjamin" (Gen. 46:19). [Only Rachel is designated as Jacob's wife.]

2. **A.** Another matter: "He has remembered his mercy and his faithfulness to the house of Israel."

B. "Then God remembered Rachel, [and God hearkened to her and opened her womb. She conceived and bore a son and said, 'God has taken away my reproach,' and she called his name Joseph, saying, 'May the Lord add to me another son!']" (Gen. 30:22-24).

Both exercises work out the theme of God's remembering Rachel. The important contribution of No. 1 comes at 1.E., in which Rachel in particular is made subject to divine remembrance. No. 2 looks to be an abbreviated statement of what is fully exposed at No. 1.

LXXIII:VI.

1. **A.** "[Then God remembered Rachel, and God hearkened to her and opened her womb. She conceived and bore a son and said, 'God has taken away my reproach,'] and she called his name Joseph, saying, 'May the Lord add to me another son!'" (Gen. 30:22-24):

B. "Another" means "different," in respect to the exile. [This is now explained.]

C. Said R. Judah bar Simon, "It was not to the place to which the ten tribes were sent into exile that the tribes of Judah and Benjamin were sent into exile.

D. "The ten tribes were sent into exile on the other side of the Sambatyon river, while the tribes of Judah and Benjamin have been scattered among all lands."

2. **A.** "Another son:"

B. This is in respect to dissension.

C. For R. Phineas in the name of R. Simon said, "On account of the prayer of Rachel, the tribes of Judah and Benjamin did not take part with the ten tribes [in the revolt against the Davidic dynasty (following Freedman)]."

D. "'Another' means, the conduct of others."

Nos. 1, 2 link Rachel's prayer to the later history of Israel, once more finding in the lives of the matriarchs and patriarchs a foretaste of Israel's fate. The major proposition sages found in Genesis maintained that Israel's blessing derived from its particular, corporeal descent from Abraham, Isaac, and Jacob. That meant, also, the matriarchs played the principal part in the transmission of the blessing of Israel. So the following spells out the place of the matriarchs in the future history of Israel, and we see clearly that the matriarchs, in this most important aspect of the sacred history of Israel, enjoyed full parity with the patriarchs (in what is, admittedly, a patriarchal document).

LX:XIII.

1. A. "And the sent away Rebecca, their sister, and her nurse, and Abraham's servant and his men. And they blessed Rebecca and said to her, ['Our sister, be the mother of thousands of ten thousands, and may your descendants possess the gate of those who hate them']" (Gen. 24:60):

B. Said R. Aibu, "They were impoverished and poor, and had nothing to give her as a dowry but words."

2. A. "...'Our sister, be the mother of thousands of ten thousands, and may your descendants possess the gate of those who hate them'" (Gen. 24:60):

B. R. Berekhiah and R. Levi in the name of R. Hama bar Hanina: "On what account was Rebecca not visited [with children] until Isaac prayed for her? It was so that the nations of the world should not say, 'It was our prayer [through her brother] that was fruitful. Rather: 'And Isaac prayed to the Lord for his wife' (Gen. 25:21)."

3. A. R. Berekhiah in the name of R. Levi: "It is written, 'The blessing of the destroyer came upon me' (Job 29:13).

B. "'The blessing of the destroyer' refers to Laban the Syrian: 'An Aramean tried to destroy my father' (Deut. 26:5).

C. "'...The blessing of the destroyer came upon me' refers to Rebecca. This is the blessing: 'Our sister, be the mother of thousands of ten thousands, and may your descendants possess the gate of those who hate them.'"

4. A. "Our sister, be the mother of thousands of ten thousands, and may your descendants possess the gate of those who hate them:"

B. From her came forth thousands from Esau and tens of thousands from Jacob.

C. "Thousands from Esau:" "The thousands of Teman, the thousands of Omar" (Gen. 36:15).

D. "...and tens of thousands from Jacob:" "I made you into ten thousands, even as the growth of the field" (Ez. 16:7).

E. Some say, "Both derived from Israel: 'And when it rested, he said, "Return O Lord unto the ten thousands of the thousands of Israel'" (Num. 10:36)."

After a minor gloss, the principal problem of the cited verse moves to the fore. It is the fact that the gentiles blessed their sister, with the question of whether they had the power of giving such a blessing. So the first point is that when Rebecca was blessed with children, it was on account of Isaac, not the blessing of her brother and mother. Further, the blessing was unbalanced, so Esau was less than Jacob.

Part Four

LIVES OF THE FOUNDERS,
HISTORY FOR THE CHILDREN

Chapter Twelve

Abraham and Israel's History

Sages read Genesis as the history of the world with emphasis on Israel. So the lives portrayed, the domestic quarrels and petty conflicts with the neighbors, all serve to yield insight into what was to be. While many times up to this point we have come across that simple truth, we now turn to a detailed examination of how sages spelled out the historical law at hand. For, as we have seen, just as the deeds of the patriarchs taught lessons on how the children were to act, so the lives of the patriarchs signaled the history of Israel. These propositions really laid down the same judgment, one for the individual and the family, the other for the community and the nation. Every detail of the narrative therefore served to prefigure what was to be, and Israel found itself, time and again, in the revealed facts of the history of the creation of the world, the decline of humanity down to the time of Noah, and, finally, its ascent to Abraham, Isaac, and Israel.

Sages read Genesis as history. What in fact does that mean? It was literally and in every detail a book of facts. Genesis constituted an accurate and complete testimony to things that really happened just as the story is narrated. While, therefore, sages found in Genesis deeper levels of meaning, uncovering the figurative sense underlying a literal statement, they always recognized the literal facticity of the statements of the document. The following picture of the way in which facts of Scripture settled claims of living enemies makes the matter clear. To sages Genesis reported what really happened. But, as we see throughout, Genesis also spelled out the meanings and truth of what happened.

LXI:VII.

1. A. "But to the sons of his concubines, Abraham gave gifts, and while he was still living, he sent them away from his son Isaac, eastward to the east country" (Gen. 25:6):

   B. In the time of Alexander of Macedonia the sons of Ishmael came to dispute with Israel about the birthright, and with them came two wicked families, the Canaanites and the Egyptians.

   C. They said, "Who will go and engage in a disputation with them."

   D. Gebiah b. Qosem [the enchanter] said, "I shall go and engage in a disputation with them."

   E. They said to him, "Be careful not to let the Land of Israel fall into their possession."

F. He said to them, "I shall go and engage in a disputation with them. If I win over them, well and good. And if not, you may say, 'Who is this hunchback to represent us?'"

G. He went and engaged in a disputation with them. Said to them Alexander of Macedonia, "Who lays claim against whom?"

H. The Ishmaelites said, "We lay claim, and we bring our evidence from their own Torah: 'But he shall acknowledge the firstborn, the son of the hated' (Deut. 21;17). Now Ishmael was the firstborn. [We therefore claim the land as heirs of the first-born of Abraham.]"

I. Said to him Gebiah b. Qosem, "My royal lord, does a man not do whatever he likes with his sons?"

J. He said to him, "Indeed so."

K. "And lo, it is written, 'Abraham gave all that he had to Isaac' (Gen. 25:2)."

L. [Alexander asked,] "Then where is the deed of gift to the other sons?"

M. He said to him, "'But to the sons of his concubines, Abraham gave gifts, [and while he was still living, he sent them away from his son Isaac, eastward to the east country]' (Gen. 25:6)."

N. [The Ishmaelites had no claim on the land.] They abandoned the field in shame.

O. The Canaanites said, "We lay claim, and we bring our evidence from their own Torah. Throughout their Torah it is written, 'the land of Canaan.' So let them give us back our land."

P. Said to him Gebiah b. Qosem, "My royal lord, does a man not do whatever he likes with his slave?"

Q. He said to him, "Indeed so."

R. He said to him, "And lo, it is written, 'A slave of slaves shall Canaan be to his brothers' (Gen. 9:25). So they are really our slaves."

S. [The Cannanites had no claim to the land and in fact should be serving Israel.] They abandoned the field in shame.

T. The Egyptians said, "We lay claim, and we bring our evidence from their own Torah. Six hundred thousand of them left us, taking away our silver and gold utensils: 'They despoiled the Egyptians' (Ex. 12:36). Let them give them back to us."

U. Gebiah b. Qosem said, "My royal lord, six hundred thousand men worked for them for two hundred and ten years, some as silversmiths and some as goldsmiths. Let them pay us our salary at the rate of a *denar* a day."

V. The mathematicians went and added up what was owing, and they had not reached the sum covering a century before the Egyptians had to forfeit what they had claimed. They abandoned the field in shame.

V. [Alexander] wanted to go up to Jerusalem. The Samaritans said to him, "Be careful. They will not permit you to enter their most holy sanctuary."

W. When Gebiah b. Qosem found out about this, he went and made for himself two felt shoes, with two precious stones worth twenty-thousand pieces of silver set in them. When he got to the mountain of the house [of the Temple], he said to him, "My royal lord, take off your shoes and put on these two felt slippers, for the floor is slippery, and you should not slip and fall."

X. When they came to the most holy sanctuary, he said to him, "Up to this point, we have the right to enter. From this point onward, we do not have the right to enter."

Y. He said to him, "When we get out of here, I'm going to even out your hump."

Z. He said to him, "You will be called a great surgeon and get a big fee."

2. A. "[But to the sons of his concubines, Abraham gave gifts, and while he was still living,] he sent them away from his son Isaac, eastward to the east country]' (Gen. 25:6):

B. He said to them, "Go as far to the east as you can, so as not to be burned by the flaming coal of Isaac."

C. But because Esau came to make war with Jacob, he took his appropriate share on his account: "Is this your joyous city, whose feet in antiquity, in ancient days, carried her afar off to sojourn? Who has devised this against Tyre, the crowning city" (Is. 23:7).

D. Said R. Eleazar, "Whenever the name of Tyre is written in Scripture, if it is written out [with all of the letters], then it refers to the province of Tyre. Where it is written without all of its letters [and so appears identical to the word for enemy], the reference of Scripture is to Rome. [So the sense of the verse is that Rome will receive its appropriate reward.]"

E. [As to the sense of the word for] "the crowning city,"

F. R. Abba bar Kahana said, "It means that they surrounded the city like a crown."

G. R. Yannai, son of R. Simeon b. R. Yannai, said, "They surrounded it with a fence of thorns."

No. 1 is deposited here because of the case of the Ishmaelites, Abraham's children, deprived as they were of their inheritance. That issue pressed on the consciousness of the exegete-compositors. No. 2 carries forward the eschatological reading of the incident. Israel's later history is prefigured in the gift to Isaac and the rejection of the other sons. The self-evidence that Esau's reward will be recompense for his evil indicates that the passage draws upon sarcasm to make its point. Sages essentially looked in the facts of history for the laws of history. We may compare them to social scientists or social philosophers, trying to turn anecdotes into insight and to demonstration how we may know the difference between impressions and truths. Genesis provided facts. Careful sifting of those facts will yield the laws that dictated why things happened one way, rather than some other. The language, as much as the substance., of the narrative provided facts demanding careful study. We understand why sages thought so if we call to mind their basic understanding of the Torah. To them (as to many today, myself included) the Torah came from God and in every detail contained revelation of God's truth. Accordingly, just as we study nature and derive facts demanding explanation and yielding law, so we study Scripture and find facts susceptible of explanation and yielding truth.

Let us begin with an exemplary case of how sages discovered social laws of history in the facts of Scripture. What Abraham did corresponds to what Balaam did, and the same law of social history derives proof from each of the two contrasting figures.

LV:VIII.

1. A. "And Abraham rose early in the morning, [saddled his ass, and took two of his young men with him, and his son Isaac, and he cut the wood for the burnt offering and arose and went to the place which God had told him]" (Gen. 22:3):

B. Said R. Simeon b. Yohai, "Love disrupts the natural order of things, and hatred disrupts the natural order of things.

C. "Love disrupts the natural order of things we learn from the case of Abraham: '...he saddled his ass.' But did he not have any number of servants? But that proves love disrupts the natural order of things.

D. "Hatred disrupts the natural order of things we learn from the case of Balaam: 'And Balaam rose up early in the morning and saddled his ass' (Num. 22:21). But did he not have any number of servants? But that proves hatred disrupts the natural order of things.

E. "Love disrupts the natural order of things we learn from the case of Joseph: 'And Joseph made his chariot ready' (Gen. 46:29). But did he not have any number of servants? But that proves love disrupts the natural order of things.

F. "Hatred disrupts the natural order of things we learn from the case of Pharoah: 'And he made his chariot ready' (Ex. 14:6). But did he not have any number of servants? But that proves hatred disrupts the natural order of things."

2. A. Said R. Simeon b. Yohai, "Let one act of saddling an ass come and counteract another act of saddling the ass. May the act of saddling the ass done by our father Abraham, so as to go and carry out the will of him who speak and brought the world into being counteract the act of saddling that was carried out by Balaam when he went to curse Israel.

B. "Let one act of preparing counteract another act of preparing. Let Joseph's act of preparing his chariot so as to meet his father serve to counteract Pharaoh's act of preparing to go and pursue Israel."

C. R. Ishmael taught on Tannaite authority, "Let the sword held in the hand serve to counteract the sword held in the hand.

D. "Let the sword held in the hand of Abraham, as it is said, 'Then Abraham put forth his hand and took the knife to slay his son' (Gen. 22:10) serve to counteract the sword taken by Pharoah in hand: 'I will draw my sword, my hand shall destroy them' (Ex. 15:9)."

We see that the narrative is carefully culled for probative facts, yielding laws. One fact is that there are laws of history. The other is that laws may be set aside, by either love or hatred. Yet another law of history applies in particular to Israel, as distinct from the foregoing, deriving from the life of both Israel and the nations, Abraham and Balaam. What follows presents the law that Israel never is orphaned of holy and heroic leaders.

LVIII:II.

1. A. "The sun rises and the sun goes down" (Qoh. 1:5):

B. Said R. Abba, "Now do we not know that the sun rises and the sun sets? But the sense is this: before the Holy One, blessed be he, makes the sun of one righteous man set, he brings up into the sky the sun of another righteous man.

C. "On the day that R. Aqiba died, Our Rabbi [Judah the Patriarch] was born. In his regard, they recited the following verse: 'The sun rises and the sun goes down' (Qoh. 1:5).

D. "On the day on which Our Rabbi died, R. Adda bar Ahbah was born. In his regard, they recited the following verse: 'The sun rises and the sun goes down' (Qoh. 1:5).

E. "On the day on which R. Ada died, R. Abin was born. In his regard, they recited the following verse: 'The sun rises and the sun goes down' (Qoh. 1:5).

F. "On the day on which R. Abin died, R. Abin his son was born. In his regard, they recited the following verse: 'The sun rises and the sun goes down' (Qoh. 1:5).

G. "On the day on which R. Abin died, Abba Hoshaiah of Taraya was born. In his regard, they recited the following verse: 'The sun rises and the sun goes down' (Qoh. 1:5).

H. "On the day on which Abba Hoshaiah of Taraya died, R. Hoshaiah was born. In his regard, they recited the following verse: 'The sun rises and the sun goes down' (Qoh. 1:5).

I. "Before the Holy One, blessed be he, made the sun of Moses set, he brought up into the sky the sun of Joshua: 'And the Lord said to Moses, Take you Joshua, the son of Nun' (Num. 27:18).

J. "Before the Holy One, blessed be he, made the sun of Joshua set, he brought up into the sky the sun of Othniel, son of Kenaz: 'And Othniel the son of Kenaz took it' (Joshua 15:17).

K. "Before the Holy One, blessed be he, made the sun of Eli set, he brought up into the sky the sun of Samuel: 'And the lamp of God was not yet gone out, and Samuel was laid down to sleep in the Temple of the Lord' (1 Sam. 3:3)."

L. Said R. Yohanan, "He was like an unblemished calf."

M. [Reverting to K:] "Before the Holy One, blessed be he, made the sun of Sarah set, he brought up into the sky the sun of Rebecca: 'Behold Milcah also has borne children' (Gen. 22:20). 'Sarah lived a hundred and twenty-seven years. These were the years of the life of Sarah' (Gen. 23:1)."

One rule of Israel's history is yielded by the facts at hand. Israel is never left without an appropriate hero or heroine. The relevance the long discourse becomes clear at the end. Here is an example of how the language of Scripture yields laws of history.

XLII:III.

1. A. R. Tanhuma and R. Hiyya the Elder state the following matter, as does R. Berekhiah in the name of R. Eleazar [the Modite], "The following exegetical principle came up in our possession from the exile.

B. "Any passage in which the words, 'And it came to pass' appear is a passage that relates misfortune."

C. Said R. Samuel bar Nahman, "There are five such passages marked by the words, 'and it came to pass,' that bear the present meaning.

D.   "'And it came to pass in the days of Amraphel, king of Shinar...these kings made war with Bera, king of Sodom' (Gen. 14:1).

E.   "The matter [of Abram's defending the local rulers] may be compared to the ally of a king who came to live in a province. On his account the king felt obligated to protect that entire province. Barbarians came and attacked him. Now when the barbarians came and attacked him, the people said, 'Woe, the king is not going to want to protect the province the way he used to [since it has caused him trouble]. That is in line with the following verse of Scripture, 'And they turned back and came to En Mishpat [source of justice], that is Kadesh [holy] [and subdued all the country of the Amalekites]' (Gen. 14:7)." [This concludes the first of the five illustrations.] [Lev. R. XI:VII.2.E adds: So too, Abraham was the ally of the King, the Holy One, blessed be he, and in his regard it is written, 'And in you shall all the families of the earth be blessed' (Gen. 12:4). So it was on his account that the Holy One, blessed be he, felt obligated to protect the entire world.]

F.   Said R. Aha, "They sought only to attack the orb of the Eye of the world. The eye that had sought to exercise the attribute of justice in the world did they seek to blind: 'That is Kadesh' (Gen. 14:7)."

G.   Said R. Aha, "It is written, 'that is...,' meaning, that is the particular one who has sanctified the name of the Holy One, blessed be he, by going down into the fiery furnace."

H.   [Reverting to the discourse suspended at the end of E:] When the barbarians came and attacked, they began to cry, "Woe, woe!"

I.   "And it came to pass in the days of Amraphel" (Gen. 14:1).

2. A.   "And it came to pass in the days of Ahaz" (Is. 7:1):

B.   "The Aramaeans on the east and the Philistines on the west devour Israel with open mouth" (Is. 9:12):

C.   The matter [of Israel's position] may be compared to the case of a king who handed over his son to a tutor, who hated the son. The tutor thought, "If I kill him now, I shall turn out to be liable to the death penalty before the king. So what I'll do is take away his wet-nurse, and he will die on his own."

D.   So thought Ahaz, "If there are no kids, there will be no he-goats. If there are no he-goats, there will be no flock. If there is no flock, there will be no Shepherd, if there is no Shepherd, there will be no world."

E.   So did Ahaz plan, "If there are no children, there will be no adults. If there are no adults, there will be no disciples. If there are no disciples, there will be no sages. If there are no sages, there will be no prophets. If there are no prophets, the Holy One, blessed be he, will not allow his presence to come to rest in the world." [Lev. R.: ...Torah. If there is no Torah, there will be no synagogues and schools. If there are no synagogues and schools, then the Holy One, blessed be he, will not allow his presence to come to rest in the world.]

F.   That is in line with the following verse of Scripture: "Bind up the testimony, seal the Torah among my disciples" (Is. 8:16).

G.   R. Huna in the name of R. Eleazar: "Why was he called Ahaz? Because he seized (ahaz) synagogues and schools."

H.   R. Jacob in the name of R. Aha: "Isaiah said, 'I will wait for the Lord, who is hiding his face from the house of Jacob, and I will hope in him' (Is. 8:17). You have no more trying hour than that moment concerning which it is written, 'And I shall surely hide my face on that day' (Deut. 31:18).

I. "From that hour: 'I will hope in him' (Is. 8:17). For he has said, 'For it will not be forgotten from the mouth of his seed' (Deut. 31:21).

J. "What good did hoping do for Isaiah?

K. "'Behold I and the children whom the Lord has given me are signs and portents in Israel from the Lord of hosts who dwells on Mount Zion' (Is. 8:18). Now were they his children? Were they not his disciples? But this teaches that they were precious to him so that he regarded them as his children."

L. [Reverting to G:] Now since everyone saw that Ahaz had seized the synagogues and schools, they began to cry out, "Woe, woe!' Thus: "And it came to pass [marking the woe] in the days of Ahaz" (Is. 7:1).

3. A. "And it came to pass in the days of Jehoiakim, son of Josiah" (Jer. 1:3).

B. "I look on the earth and lo, it was waste and void" (Jer. 4:23).

C. The matter may be compared to the case of royal edicts which came into a province. What did the people do? They took the document, tore it up and burned the bits in fire. That is in line with the following verse of Scripture: "And it came to pass, as Jehudi read three or four columns, that is, three or four verses, the king would cut them off with a penknife and throw them into the fire in the brazier until the entire scroll was consumed in the fire that was in the brazier" (Jer. 36:23).

D. When the people saw all this, they began to cry out, "Woe, woe."

E. "And it came to pass in the days of Jehoiakim" (Jer. 1:3).

4. A. "And it came to pass in the days in which the judges ruled" (Ruth 1:1). "There was a famine in the land" (Ruth 1:1).

B. The matter may be compared to a province which owed taxes in arrears to the king, so the king sent a revenuer to collect. What did the inhabitants of the province do? They went and hung him, hit him, and robbed him. They said, "Woe is us, when the king gets word of these thing. What the king's representative wanted to do to us, we have done to him."

C. So too, woe to the generation that has judged its judges.

D. "And it came to pass in the days in which the judges themselves were judged" (Ruth 1:1).

5. A. "And it came to pass in the days of Ahasuerus" (Est. 1:1). "Haman undertook to destroy, to slay, and to annihilate all the Jews, young and old, women and children, in one day" (Est. 3:13).

B. The matter may be compared to the case of a king who had a vineyard, and three of his enemies attacked it. One of them began to clip off the small branches, the next began to take the pendants off the grapeclusters, and the last of them began to uproot the vines altogether.

C. Pharaoh [began by clipping off the small branches]: "Every son that is born will you throw into the river" (Ex. 1:22).

D. Nebuchadnezzar [began to clip off the pendants of the grapeclusters,] deporting the people: "And he carried away captive the craftsmen and smiths, a thousand" (2 Kgs. 24:16).

E. R. Berekhiah in the name of R. Judah and rabbis:

F. R. Berekhiah in the name of R. Judah: "There were a thousand craftsmen and a thousand smiths."

G. Rabbis say, "This group and that group all together added up to a thousand."

H. The wicked Haman began to uproot the vines altogether. He uprooted Israel from its roots: "To destroy, to slay, and to annihilate all the Jews" (Est. 3:13).

I. When everybody saw that [Ahasuerus had sold and Haman had bought the Jews], they began to cry, "Woe, woe."

J. "And it came to pass in the days of Ahasuerus" (Est. 1:1).

6. A. R. Simeon b. Abba in the name of R. Yohanan: "Any context in which the words, 'And it came to pass...,' appear serves to signify either misfortune or good fortune. If it is a case of misfortune, it is misfortune without parallel. If it is a case of good fortune, it is good fortune without parallel."

B. R. Samuel b. Nahman came and introduced this distinction: "Any context in which the words, 'And it came to pass...' occur signifies misfortune, and any context in which the words, 'And it shall come to pass...' are used signifies good fortune."

C. They objected [to this claim], "And God said, 'Let there be light,' and it came to pass that there was light" (Gen. 1:3).

D. He said to them, "This too does not represent good fortune, for in the end the world did not enjoy the merit of actually making use of that light."

E. R. Judah [b. R. Simeon] said, "With the light that the Holy One, blessed be he, created on the first day of creation, a person could look and see from one side of the world to the other. When the Holy One, blessed be he, foresaw that there would be wicked people, he hid it away for the [exclusive use of the] righteous. 'But the path of the righteous is as the light of the dawn that shines more and more to the perfect day' (Prov. 4:18)."

F. They further objected, "And it came to pass that there was evening and morning, one day" (Gen. 1:5).

G. He said to them, "This too does not signify good fortune. For whatever God created on the first day of creation is destined to be wiped out. That is in line with the following verse of Scripture: 'For the heaven shall vanish away like smoke, and the earth shall wax old like a garment' (Is. 51:6)."

H. They further objected, "And it came to pass that there was evening and it came to pass that there was morning, a second day..., a third day..., a fourth day..., a fifth day..., a sixth day..." (Gen. 1:8, 13, 19, 23, 31).

I. He said to them, "This too does not signify good fortune. For everything which God created on the six days of creation was incomplete and would require further processing. Wheat has to be milled, mustard to be sweetened, [lupine to impart sweetness]."

J. They further objected, "And it came to pass that the Lord was with Joseph, and Joseph was a prosperous man" (Gen. 39:2).

K. He said to them, "This too does not signify good fortune, for on this account that she-bear [Potiphar's wife] came his way."

L. They further objected, "And it came to pass on the eighth day that Moses called Aaron and his sons for consecration in the priesthood" (Lev. 9:1).

M. He said to them, "This too does not signify good fortune, for on that same day Nadab and Abihu died."

N. They further objected, "And it came to pass on the day on which Moses made an end of setting up the tabernacle" (Num. 7:1).

O. He said to them, "This too does not signify good fortune. For on the day on which the Temple was built, the tabernacle was hidden away."

P. They further objected, "And it came to pass that the Lord was with Joshua and his fame was in all the land" (Joshua 6:27).

Q. He said to them, "This too does not signify good fortune, for he still had to tear his garments [on account of the defeat at Ai, Joshua 7:6]."

R. They further objected, "And it came to pass that the king dwelt in his palace, and the Lord gave him rest round about" (2 Sam. 7:1).

S. He said to them, "This too does not signify good fortune. On that very day Nathan the prophet came to him and said, 'You will not build the house' (1 Kgs. 8:19)."

T. They said to him, "We have given our objections, now you give your proofs about good fortune."

U. He said to them, "'And it shall come to pass in that day that living waters shall go out of Jerusalem' (Zech. 14:8). 'And it shall come to pass in that day that a great horn shall be blown' (Is. 27:13). 'And it shall come to pass in that day that a man shall rear a youngling' (Is. 7:21). 'And it shall come to pass in that day that the Lord will set his hand again a second time to recover the remnant of his people' (Is. 11:11). 'And it shall come to pass in that day that the mountains shall drop down sweet wine' (Joel 4:18). [All of these represent good fortune without parallel.]"

V. They said to him, "'And it shall come to pass on the day on which Jerusalem is taken...' (Jer. 38:28)."

W. He said to them, "This too does not signify misfortune but good fortune [without parallel], for on that day the Israelites received a full pardon for all their sins.

X. "That is in line with what R. Samuel b. Nahman said, 'The Israelites received a full pardon for all their sins on the day on which the Temple was destroyed. That is in line with the following verse of Scripture, "The punishment of your iniquity is completed, daughter of Zion, and he will no more take you away into exile" (Lam. 4:22).'"

The fundamental syllogism, not stated at all, is that Israel's history follows rules that can be learned in Scripture. Nothing is random, all thing connected, and fundamental laws of history dictate the sense and meaning of what happens. These laws are stated in the very language of Scripture. The long discussion obviously is constructed independent of any of the verses used as proof-texts. It serves equally well in any number of contexts, not only here but also at Lev. R. XI:VII, as indicated. The differences in the versions of Gen. R. and Lev. R. are minor and signify nothing of consequence. The sole point of intersection is at No. 1. When we turn to the biography of Abraham, we expect to find the history of Israel, detail by detail, and so we do.

XLII:IV.

1. A. "And it came to pass in the days of Amraphael" (Gen. 14:1):

B. He had three names, Kush, Nimrod, and Amraphael.

C. Kush, because he was in fact a Kushite.

D. Nimrod, because he made the world rebel (MRD).

E.   Amraphael, for he [Freedman:] made a declaration (*amar imrah*) , "I will cast down."

F.   [Freedman translates the words that follow in this way:]   [Another interpretation is] that he made sport of the world, also that he made sport of Abraham, again, that he ordered Abraham to be thrown into the furnace. [Freedman, p. 346, n. 3: "The translation is conjectural. Neither the text nor its meaning is certain."]

2.   A.   "Arioch, king of Ellasar" (Gen. 14:1):

B.   Said R. Yose of Milhayya, "How come hazel nuts are called *elsarin* ? Because they come from Ellasar."

3.   A.   "Chedorlaomer king of Elam and Tidal king of Goiim" (Gen. 14:1):

B.   Said R. Levi, "There is a place there which in Latin bears that name. The people took a man and made him king over them."

C.   Said R. Yohanan, "'Tidal' was his name."

4.   A.   Another matter: "And it came to pass in the days of Amraphael, king of Shinar" (Gen. 14:1) refers to Babylonia.

B.   "Arioch, king of Ellasar" (Gen. 14:1) refers to Greece.

C.   "Chedorlaomer, king of Elam" (Gen. 14:1) refers to Media.

D.   "And Tidal, king of Goiim [nations]" (Gen. 14:1) refers to the wicked government [Rome], which conscripts troops from all the nations of the world.

E.   Said R. Eleazar bar Abina, "If you see that the nations contend with one another, look for the footsteps of the king-messiah. You may know that that is the case, for lo, in the time of Abraham, because the kings struggled with one another, a position of greatness came to Abraham."

Obviously, No. 4 presents the most important reading of Gen. 14:1, since it links the events of the life of Abraham to the history of Israel and even ties the whole to the messianic expectation. I suppose that any list of four kings will provoke inquiry into the relationship of the entries of that list to the four kingdoms among which history, in Israel's experience, is divided. The process of history flows in both directions. Just as what Abraham did prefigured the future history of Israel, so what the Israelites later on were to do imposed limitations on Abraham.

XLIII:II.

1.   A.   "And he went in pursuit as far as Dan" (Gen. 14:14):

B.   Idolatry hits both beforehand and afterward.

C.   Before hand: "He went in pursuit as far as Dan [but could not go further than that]" (Gen. 14:14).

D.   Afterward: "The snorting of his horses is heard from Dan" (Jer. 8:15). [Freedman, p. 353, n. 4: The meaning is that the evil effects of idolatry are felt both before and after it is actually practiced. Because Jeroboam was destined to set up a golden calf at Dan (1 Kgs. 12:19), Abraham was weakened now when he came to that place and so could pursue them no further. Similarly, even after it was destroyed, Jeremiah speaks of terror raging in Dan.]

No. 5 draws a more general conclusion from the fact that Abram got as far as Dan but went no further. Jerusalem will constantly figure in the story of Abraham. The future service of sacrifice to God was prefigured in the transaction with Melchizedek.

XLIII:VI.

6. A. "And Melchizedek, king of Salem, brought out bread and wine; he was priest of God Most High" (Gen. 14:18):

B. "And, O daughter of Sor, the richest of the people shall entreat your favor with a gift" (Ps. 45:13).

C. "Daughter of Sor" speaks of Abraham, who vexed kings and was vexed by kings. [This is a play on the letters in the word *Sor*, treating them as not the name of a place but as the root for the word to vex or distress (Freedman).]

D. "They shall entreat your favor with a gift" (Ps. 45:13).

E. "And Melchizedek, king of Salem, brought out bread and wine" (Gen. 14:18).

2. A. "*Melchi* [king] *Zedek* [righteous]": This place [namely, Jerusalem, that is, the Salem of which Gen. 14:18 speaks] justifies the people who live there [hence, he was king over righteous people].

3. A. "And the king of *Zedek*" (Gen. 14:18):

B. "The Lord of *Zedek*" (Joshua 10:7).

C. Jerusalem is called "righteousness" [*Zedek*]: "Righteousness lodged in her" (Is. 1:21).

4. A. "King of Salem" (Gen. 14:18):

B. [Reading the word for Salem as *shalom* , meaning whole, we interpret in the following way:] R. Isaac the Babylonian said, "It is because he was born circumcized."

5. A. "Brought out bread and wine" (Gen. 14:18):

B. R. Samuel bar Nahman: "He handed over to him the laws governing the priesthood.

C. "The bread stands for the show-bread, and the wine stands for the drink-offerings."

D. Rabbis say, "He revealed the Torah to him: 'Come, eat of my bread and drink of the wine which I have mingled' (Prov. 9:5)."

6. A. "He was priest of God Most High" (Gen. 14:18):

B. R. Abba bar Kahana: "Every reference to wine that is mentioned in the Torah makes its mark except for the present reference. [That is, wine always causes trouble, but for the present case.]"

C. Said R. Levi, "Even this one is no exception. For on this basis it was revealed to him, 'And they shall serve them and they shall afflict them' (Gen. 15:13)." [Freedman, p. 356, n. 12: "This was Abraham's punishment for complying with the request of the king of Sodom, 'Give me the persons,' Gen. 14:21, instead of converting them to the true faith. Levi perhaps holds that this complaisance was due to the convivial and friendly mood induced by the drinking of wine."]

No. 1 begins discourse with the introduction of an intersecting verse, read in line with the base-verse. Nos. 2, 3, and 4 go over the name of the king. No. 5 then links the present passage to the later history of Israel, for it is taken for granted that "Salem" and Jerusalem are one and the same place. So Melchizedek was the priest of Jerusalem even before the Temple was built. Once more the history of Israel is joined to the life of Abraham. One recalls that in the fourth century numerous places in the Holy Land found association, if only after the fact, with the life and deeds of Jesus. But we need not suppose the view of Salem and Jerusalem began only in the time of the composition of our document. No. 6 makes its own point, independent of the cited verse.

XLIII:VIII.

1. A. "And blessed be God Most High, who has delivered your enemies into your hand" (Gen. 14:20):

B. [Since the word for "deliver" yields the letters that serve for the word for plans or schemes,] R. Huna said, "It is that he turned your plans against your enemies."

C. R. Yudan said, "How many schemes did I work out to place them under your hand. They were friendly with one another, sending one another dry dates and other gifts. But I made them rebel against one another so that they would fall into your hand."

2. A. "And Abram gave him a tenth of everything" (Gen. 14:20):

B. R. Judah in the name of R. Nehorai: "On the strength of that blessing the three great pegs on which the world depends, Abraham, Isaac, and Jacob, derived sustenance.

C. "Abraham: 'And the Lord blessed Abraham in *all* things' (Gen. 24:1) on account of the merit that 'he gave him a tenth of *all* things' (Gen. 14:20).

D. "Isaac: 'And I have eaten of *all*' (Gen. 27:33), on account of the merit that 'he gave him a tenth of *all* things' (Gen. 14:20).

E. "Jacob: 'Because God has dealt graciously with me and because I have all' (Gen. 33:11) on account of the merit that 'he gave him a tenth of *all* things' (Gen. 14:20).

3. A. Whence did Israel gain the merit of receiving the blessing of the priests?

B. R. Judah said, "It was from Abraham: '*So* shall your seed be' (Gen. 15:5), while it is written in connection with the priestly blessing: '*So* shall you bless the children of Israel' (Num. 6:23)."

C. R. Nehemiah said, "It was from Isaac: 'And I and the lad will go *so* far' (Gen. 22:5), therefore said the Holy One, blessed be he, '*So* shall you bless the children of Israel' (Num. 6:23)."

D. And rabbis say, "It was from Jacob: 'So shall you say to the house of Jacob' (Ex. 19:3) (in line with the statement, '*So* shall you bless the children of Israel' (Num. 6:23)."

4. A. When shall "I magnify your children like the stars"?

B. R. Eleazar and R. Yose bar Hanina:

C. One of them said, "When I shall be revealed to them with the word '*so* :' 'So shall you say to the house of Jacob' (Ex., 19:3).

D. The other said, "When I shall be revealed to them through their leaders and give a message invoking the word '*so* :' 'So says the Lord, Israel is my son, my firstborn' (Ex. 4:22)."

No. 1 works out a play on the root for "deliver," thereby explaining exactly what God contributed to the salvation of Abram. No. 2 once more links the blessing at hand with the history of Israel. Now the reference is to the word "all," which joins the tithe of Abram to the blessing of his descendants. Since the blessing of the priest is at hand, No. 3 treats the origins of the blessing., But I see no clear point of intersection with the verse at hand. No. 4 is attached because of its discussion of Ex. 19:3, and not because of its relevance to the matter at hand. Therefore Nos. 3 and 4 were joined before the whole was inserted here. Time and again events in the lives of the patriarchs prefigure the four monarchies, among which, of course, the fourth, last, and most intolerable was Rome. Here is another such exercise in the recurrent proof of a single proposition.

XLIV:XVII.

4. A. "[And it came to pass, as the sun was going down,] lo, a deep sleep fell on Abram, and lo, a dread and great darkness fell upon him" (Gen. 15:12):

B. "...lo, a dread" refers to Babylonia, as it is written, "Then was Nebuchadnezzar filled with fury" (Gen. 3:19).

C. " and darkness" refers to Media, which darkened the eyes of Israel by making it necessary for the Israelites to fast and conduct public mourning.

D. "...great..." refers to Greece.

E. R. Simon said, "The kingdom of Greece set up one hundred and twenty commanders, one hundred and twenty hyparchs, and one hundred and twenty generals."

F. Rabbis said, "It was sixty of each, as it is written, 'Serpents, fiery serpents, and scropions' (Gen. 8:15). Just as the scorpion produces sixty eggs at a time, so the kingdom of Greece set up sixty at a time."

G. "...fell upon him" refers to Edom, as it is written, "The earth quakes at the noise of their fall" (Jer. 49:21).

H. Some reverse matters:

I. "...fell upon him" refers to Babylonia, since it is written, "Fallen, fallen is Babylonia" (Is. 21:9).

J. "...great..." refers to Media, in line with this verse: "King Ahasuerus did make great" (Est. 3:1).

K. " and darkness" refers to Greece, which darkened the eyes of Israel by its harsh decrees.

L. "...lo, a dread" refers to Edom, as it is written, "After this I saw...,a fourth beast, dreadful and terrible" (Dan. 7:7).

No. 4 successfully links the cited passage once more to the history of Israel. Israel's history falls under God's dominion. Whatever will happen carries out

God's plan. The fourth kingdom is part of that plan, which we can discover by carefully studying Abraham's life and God's word to him.

XLIV:XVIII.

1. A. "Then the Lord said to Abram, 'Know of a surety [that your descendants will be sojourners in a land that is not theirs, and they will be slaves there, and they will be oppressed for four hundred years; but I will bring judgment on the nation which they serve, and afterward they shall come out with great possessions']" (Gen. 15:13-14):

B. "Know" that I shall scatter them.

C. "Of a certainty" that I shall bring them back together again.

D. "Know" that I shall put them out as a pledge [in expiation of their sins].

E. "Of a certainty" that I shall redeem them.

F. "Know" that I shall make them slaves.

G. "Of a certainty" that I shall free them.

2. A. "...that your descendants will be sojourners in a land that is not theirs and they will be slaves there, and they will be oppressed for four hundred years:"

B. It is four hundred years from the point at which you will produce a descendant. [The Israelites will not serve as slaves for four hundred years, but that figure refers to the passage of time from Isaac's birth.]

C. Said R. Yudan, "The condition of being outsiders, the servitude, the oppression in a land that was not theirs all together would last for four hundred years, that was the requisite term."

No. 1 parses the cited verse and joins within its simple formula the entire history of Israel, punishment and forgiveness alike. No. 2 parses the verse to follow, trying to bring it into line with the chronology of Israel's later history.

XLIV:XIX.

1. A. "But I will also bring judgment on the nation which they serve" (Gen. 15:14):

B. Said R. Helbo, "Rather than, 'and that nation,' the passage states, 'But I will *also* bring judgment on the nation which they serve' (Gen. 15:14). Also they, also Egypt and the four kingdoms who will enslave you [will God judge]."

2. A. "I will bring judgment" (Gen. 15:14):

B. R. Eleazar in the name of R. Yose: "With these two letters, namely, the letters that form the word for 'judge,' the Holy One, blessed be he, promised our ancestor that he would redeem his children. But should they carry out an act of repentence, he will redeem them with seventy-two letters [and not only with two]."

C. Said R. Yudan, "The verse that follows presents seventy-two letters [in illustration of the foregoing statement]: 'Or has God tried to go and take him a nation from the midst of another nation, by trials, by signs, and by wonders, and by war, and by a mighty hand, and by an outstretched arm, and by great terrors' (Deut. 4:34). Here there are seventy-two letters. But if you propose that there are seventy five, not seventy-two, take off the three letters that make up the second reference to the word 'nation,' which do not count."

D. R. Abin said, "It is by his name that he will redeem them, and the name of the Holy One, blessed be he, contains seventy-two letters."

No. 1 deals with the object of the verb "judge," and No. 2 presents its own proposition on the character of ultimate redemption. The issue here is not particular to the verse at hand. The proposition is that God has unconditionally promised to redeem Israel, but if Israel repents, then the redemption will come with greater glory. If Abraham, Isaac, and Jacob stand for Israel later on, then Ishmael, Edom, and Esau represent Rome. Hence whatever sages find out about those figures tells them something about Rome and its character, history, and destiny. Here is Ishmael's lesson:

XLV:IX.
1. A. "He shall be a wild ass of a man, [his hand against every man and every man's hand against him, and he shall dwell over against all his kinsmen]" (Gen. 16:12):

B. R. Yohanan and R. Simeon b. Laqish:

C. R. Yohanan said, "[The term is used figuratively.] For most people grow up in a settled community, while he grew up in the wilderness."

D. R. Simeon b. Laqish said, "'A wild ass of a man' is meant literally, for most people plunder property, but he plundered lives."

2. A. "...his hand against every man and every man's hand against him" (Gen. 16:12):

B. [Reading the consonants for "every...against him" with different vowels, we produce the meaning:] His hand and the hand of his dog were alike. Just as his dog ate carrion, so he ate carrion.

3. A Said R. Eleazar, "When is it the case that 'his hand is against every man and every man's hand against him'?

B. "When he comes concerning whom it is written: 'And wheresoever the children of men, the beasts of the field and the fowl of the heaven dwell, has he given them into your hand' (Dan. 2:38). [Freedman, p. 386, n. 2: In the days of Nebuchadnezzar, whose ruthless policy of conquest aroused the whole world against him.]

C. "That is in line with the following verse of Scripture: 'Of Kedar and of the kingdoms of Hazor, which Nebuchadrezzar smote' (Jer. 49:28). His name is spelled, 'Nebuchadrezzar' because he shut them up in the wilderness and killed them. [Freedman, p. 386, n. 4: A play on the name, which, with the present spelling, ends in *asar*, spelled with an *alef*, as though it were *asar*, spelled with an *ayin* and yielding the meaning, shut up.]"

4. A. ["...and he shall dwell over against all his kinsmen]" (Gen. 16:12):

B. Here the word-choice is "dwell" while later on it is "he fell" (Gen. 25:18).

C. So long as Abraham was alive, "he [Ishmael] shall dwell." Once he died, "he fell." [His father's merit no longer protected him.]

D. Before he laid hands on the Temple, "he shall dwell." After he laid hands on the Temple, "he fell."

E. In this world "he shall dwell." In the world to come, "he fell."

No. 1 takes up the interpretation of the metaphor used for Ishmael. No. 2 carries forward the same theme, interpreting the passage in a literal way. Nos. 3-4 move from the figure of Ishmael to those like him, Nebuchadnezzar, then Rome. The Temple was destroyed by each of these persons, in the tradition of Ishmael. The conclusion then provides the hope to Israel that the enemy will perish, at least in the world to come. So the passage is read as both a literal statement and also as an effort to prefigure the history of Israel's suffering and redemption. Ishmael, standing now for Christian Rome, claims God's blessing, but Isaac gets it, as Jacob will take it from Esau.

XLVII:V.

1. A. "God said, 'No, but Sarah your wife [shall bear you a son, and you shall call his name Isaac. I will establish my covenant with him as an everlasting covenant for his descendants after him.] As for Ishmael, I have heard you. Behold, I will bless him and make him fruitful and multiply him exceedingly. He shall be the father of twelve princes, and I will make him a great nation]'" (Gen. 17:19-20).

B. R. Yohanan in the name of R. Joshua b. Hananiah, "In this case the son of the servant-woman might learn from what was said concerning the son of the mistress of the household:

C. "'Behold, I will bless him' refers to Isaac.

D. "'...and make him fruitful' refers to Isaac.

E. "'...and multiply him exceedingly' refers to Isaac.

F. "'...As for Ishmael, I have informed you' through the angel. [The point is, Freedman, p. 401, n. 4, explains, Ishmael could be sure that his blessing too would be fulfilled.]"

G. R. Abba bar Kahana in the name of R. Birai: "Here the son of the mistress of the household might learn from the son of the handmaiden:

H. "'Behold, I will bless him' refers to Ishmael.

I. "'...and make him fruitful' refers to Ishmael.

J. "'...and multiply him exceedingly' refers to Ishmael.

K. "And by an argument *a fortiori* : 'But I will establish my covenant with Isaac' (Gen. 17:21)."

2. A. Said R. Isaac, "It is written, 'All these are the twelve tribes of Israel' (Gen. 49:28). These were the descendants of the mistress [Sarah].

B. "But did Ishmael not establish twelve?

C. "The reference to those twelve is to princes, in line with the following verse: 'As princes and wind' (Prov. 25:14). [But the word for *prince* also stands for the word *vapor* , and hence the glory of the sons of Ishmael would be transient (Freedman, p. 402, n. 2).]

D. "But as to these tribes [descended from Isaac], they are in line with this verse: 'Sworn are the tribes of the word, selah' (Hab. 3:9). [Freedman, p. 402, n. 3: The word for *tribe* and for *staff* or *rod*, in the cited verse, are synonyms, both meaning tribes, both meaning rods, and so these tribes would endure like rods that are planted.]"

Nos. 1 and 2 take up the problem of the rather fulsome blessing assigned to Ishmael. One authority reads the blessing to refer to Isaac, the other maintains that the blessing refers indeed to Ishmael, and Isaac will gain that much more. No. 2 goes over the same issue, now with the insistence that the glory of Ishmael will pass like vapor, while the tribes of Isaac will endure as well planted rods. The polemic against Edom/Rome, with its transient glory, is familiar. We should not limit saves' powers of interpretation to the exposition of lines of structure of whole stories. Details, as much as the main point, yielded laws of history. Here is how sages take up the detail of Rebecca's provision of a bit of water, showing what that act had to do with the history of Israel later on.

XLVIII:X.

2. A. "Let a little water be brought" (Gen. 18:4):

B. Said to him the Holy One, blessed be he, "You have said, 'Let a little water be brought' (Gen. 18:4). By your life, I shall pay your descendants back for this: 'Then sang Israel this song," spring up O well, sing you to it'" (Num. 21:7)."

C. That recompense took place in the wilderness. Where do we find that it took place in the Land of Israel as well?

D. "A land of brooks of water" (Deut. 8:7).

E. And where do we find that it will take place in the age to come?

F. ""And it shall come to pass in that day that living waters shall go out of Jerusalem" (Zech. 14:8).

G. ["And wash your feet" (Gen. 18:4)]: [Said to him the Holy One, blessed be he,] "You have said , 'And wash your feet.' By your life, I shall pay your descendants back for this: 'Then I washed you in water' (Ez. 16:9)."

H. That recompense took place in the wilderness. Where do we find that it took place in the Land of Israel as well?

I. "Wash you, make you clean" (Is. 1:16).

J. And where do we find that it will take place in the age to come?

K. "When the Lord will have washed away the filth of the daughters of Zion" (Is. 4:4).

L. [Said to him the Holy One, blessed be he,] "You have said, 'And rest yourselves under the tree' (Gen. 18:4). By your life, I shall pay your descendants back for this: 'He spread a cloud for a screen' (Ps. 105:39)."

M. That recompense took place in the wilderness. Where do we find that it took place in the Land of Israel as well?

N. "You shall dwell in booths for seven days" (Lev. 23:42).

O. And where do we find that it will take place in the age to come?

P. "And there shall be a pavilion for a shadow in the day-time from the heat" (Is. 4:6).

Q. [Said to him the Holy One, blessed be he,] "You have said, 'While I fetch a morsel of bread that you may refresh yourself' (Gen. 18:5). By your life, I shall pay your descendants back for this: 'Behold I will cause to rain bread from heaven for you' (Ex. 16:45)"

R. That recompense took place in the wilderness. Where do we find that it took place in the Land of Israel as well?

S. "A land of wheat and barley" (Deut. 8:8).

T. And where do we find that it will take place in the age to come?

U. "He will be as a rich cornfield in the land" (Ps. 82:16).

V. [Said to him the Holy One, blessed be he,] "You ran after the herd ['And Abraham ran to the herd' (Gen. 18:7)]. By your life, I shall pay your descendants back for this: 'And there went forth a wind from the Lord and brought across quails from the sea' (Num. 11:27)."

W. That recompense took place in the wilderness. Where do we find that it took place in the Land of Israel as well?

X. "Now the children of Reuben and the children of Gad had a very great multitude of cattle" (Num. 32:1).

Y. And where do we find that it will take place in the age to come?

Z. ""And it will come to pass in that day that a man shall rear a young cow and two sheep" (Is. 7:21).

AA. [Said to him the Holy One, blessed be he,] "You stood by them: 'And he stood by them under the tree while they ate' (Gen. 18:8). By your life, I shall pay your descendants back for this: 'And the Lord went before them' (Ex. 13:21)."

BB. That recompense took place in the wilderness. Where do we find that it took place in the Land of Israel as well?

CC. "God stands in the congregation of God" (Ps. 82:1).

DD. And where do we find that it will take place in the age to come?

EE. "The breaker is gone up before them...and the Lord at the head of them" (Mic. 2:13).

No. 2 presents a sizable and beautifully disciplined construction, making one point again and again. Everything that Abraham did brought a reward to his descendants. The enormous emphasis on the way in which Abraham's deeds prefigured the history of Israel, both in the wilderness, and in the Land, and, finally, in the age to come, provokes us to wonder who held that there were children of Abraham beside Israel. The answer then is clear. We note that there are five statements of the same proposition, each drawing upon a clause in the base verse. The extended statement moreover serves as a sustained introduction to the treatment of the individual clauses that now follow, item by item. Obviously, it is the merit of the ancestors that connects the living Israel to the lives of the patriarchs and matriarchs of old.

XLVIII:XII.

3. A. R. Jonah and R. Levi in the name of R. Hama b. R. Hanina: "The wilderness of Sin [Ex. 16:1ff.] and the wilderness of Alush [Num. 33:13] are the same place.

B. "On account of what merit did the Israelites merit having mana given to them? It was because of the statement, 'knead it and make cakes.' [The word for knead is *lushi*, hence because of the kneading of the dough by Sarah, the later Israelites had the merit of receiving mana in the wilderness of Alush which is the same as the wilderness of Sin, where, in the biblical account, the mana came down, so Ex. 16:1ff.]"

The important contribution is at No. 3, at which the merit of Sarah's action stands for the later Israelites. The point-for-point emphasis on that theme presents no surprises. The reciprocity of the process of interpreting Israel's history in light of the founders' lives and the founders lives through the later history of Israel infuses the explanation of the debate over Sodom. Never far from sages' minds is the entire sweep and scope of Israel's long history. Never distant from the lips of the patriarchs and matriarchs is the message of Israel's destiny.

XLIX:X.

1. A. ""And the Lord said, 'If I find at Sodom [fifty righteous in the city, I will spare the whole place for their sake]'" (Gen. 18:26):

B. R. Judah bar Simon in the name of R. Joshua b. Levi: "'For it is for God to have said, "I have forgiven"' (Job 34:31).

C. "So: 'I will spare the whole place for their sake' (Gen. 18:26)."

D. "I shall not take a pledge" (Job 34:31) means, "I shall not exact a surety," in line with the use of the same root in this verse: "If you take your neighbor's garment as a pledge" (Ex. 22:25).

E. [Speaking in the name of God:] "Yet people complain [using the consonants for the word for exact a surety] against me, claiming that I do not judge rightly."

F. "Apart from me, I will see" (Job 34:32): [God speaks:] "Even without me, you go and examine my judgment. If I have made a mistake, 'You teach me' (Job 34:32), and 'if I have committed an injustice' to the earlier generation, 'I will not do it again' to the later generations."

2. A. "To him will I keep silence, and to his branches" (Job 41:4): [God further speaks to Abraham:] "For you I shall keep silent, and for the branches that come forth from you."

B. This is addressed to Abraham, who said, "Far be it from you to do such a thing" (Gen. 18:25).

C. It is further addressed to Moses, who said, "Lord, why are you angry against your people" (Ex. 32:11).

D. ...to Joshua, who said, "Why have you brought this people over the Jordan" (Joshua 7:7).

E. ...to David, who said, "Why do you stand afar off, O Lord" (Ps. 10:1).

3. A. "Or his proud talk, or his fair array of words" (Job 41:4):

B. Grace infused [Abraham's] extended speech when he sought mercy for the Sodomites.

The two intersecting verses drawn from Job, Job 34:31 and 41:4, cast fresh light on Abraham's statement at hand. No. 1 assigns a long response to God, in which he accepts Abraham's plea. No. 2 assembles a range of examples of Abraham's descendants' following his example, and No. 3 reverts to the case at hand. This is a striking and successful amplification of a base verse and its case through the invoking intersecting verses. The upshot is to introduce into Abraham's discourse the entire history of Israel.

LIII:IV.

1. A. "For ever, O Lord, your word stands fast in heaven" (Ps. 119:89):

   B. But does God's word not stand fast on earth?

   C. But what you said to Abraham in heaven, "At this season I shall return to you" (Gen. 18:14) [was carried out:]

   D. "The Lord remembered Sarah as he had said and the Lord did to Sarah as he had promised" (Gen. 21:1).

2. A. R. Menahamah and R. Nahman of Jaffa in the name of R. Jacob of Caesarea opened discourse by citing the following verse: "'O God of hosts, return, we beseech you' (Ps. 80:15).

   B. "'Return and carry out what you promised to Abraham: "Look from heaven and behold" (Ps. 80:15). "Look now toward heaven and count the stars"' (Gen. 15:5).

   C. "'And be mindful of this vine' (Ps. 80:15). 'The Lord remembered Sarah as he had said and the Lord did to Sarah as he had promised' (Gen. 21:1)."

3. A. R. Samuel bar Nahman opened discourse with this verse: "God is not a man, that he should lie" (Num. 23:19).

   B. Said R. Samuel bar Nahman, "The beginning of this verse does not correspond to its end, and the end does not correspond to its beginning.

   C. "'God is not a man that he should lie' (Num. 23:18), but the verse ends, 'When he has said, he will not do it, and when he has spoken, he will not make it good' (Num. 23:18).

   D. "[That obviously is impossible. Hence:] When the Holy One, blessed be he, makes a decree to bring good to the world: 'God is not a man that he should lie' (Num. 23:18).

   E. "But when he makes a decree to bring evil on the world: 'When he has said, he [nonetheless] will not do it, and when he has spoken, he will not make it good' (Num. 23:18).

   F. "When he said to Abraham, 'For through Isaac shall your descendants be named,' 'God is not a man that he should lie' (Num. 23:18).

   G. "When he said to him, 'Take your son, your only son' (Gen. 22:2), 'When he has said, he will not do it, and when he has spoken, he will not make it good' (Num. 23:18).

   H. "When the Holy One, blessed be he, said to Moses, 'I have surely remembered you' (Ex. 3:16), 'God is not a man that he should lie' (Num. 23:18).

   I. "When he said to him, 'Let me alone, that I may destroy them' (Deut. 9:14), 'When he has said, he will not do it, and when he has spoken, he will not make it good' (Num. 23:18).

   J. "When he said to Abraham, 'And also that nation whom they shall serve will I judge' (Gen. 15:14), 'God is not a man that he should lie' (Num. 23:18).

   K. "When he said to him, 'And they shall serve them and they shall afflict them for four hundred years' (Gen. 15:13), 'When he has said, he will not do it, and when he has spoken, he will not make it good' (Num. 23:18).

   L. "When God said to him, 'I will certainly return to you' (Gen. 18:10, 'God is not a man that he should lie' (Num. 23:18).

   M. "'The Lord remembered Sarah as he had said and the Lord did to Sarah as he had promised' (Gen. 21:1)."

The point of No. 1 is now familiar. No. 2 makes the same statement, now in a somewhat more complex composition. No. 3 presents a magnificent exposition of its simple syllogism, the relevance of which is self-evident. The main point is that God will always carry out his word when it has to do with a blessing, but God may well go back on his word when it has to do with punishment. The later events in the history of Israel are drawn together to make this important point. The same powerful principle that Israel's history takes place in eternity, so considerations of what comes first and what happens later -- that is, priority and order -- do not apply, -- opens many passages to deep and nuanced interpretation, as in what follows.

LIII:V.
1. A. "Who has kept with your servant, David my father" (1 Kgs. 8:24):
   B. This refers to Abraham [even though it speaks of David].
   C. "That which you did promise him" (1 Kgs. 8:24) "At the set time I will return to you" (Gen. 18:14).
   D. "Yes, you spoke with your mouth and have fulfilled it with your hand as it is this day" (1 Kgs. 8:24).
   E. "And the Lord remembered Sarah" (Gen. 21:1).
2. A. "Who makes the barren woman dwell in her house" (Ps. 113:9):
   B. That verse refers to Sarah: "And Sarai was barren" (Gen. 11:30).
   C. "As a joyful mother of children" (Ps. 113:9).
   D. "Sarah has given children suck" (Gen. 21:7).
3. A. "And the Lord remembered Sarah as he had said" (Gen. 21:1):
   B. R. Judah said, "'And the Lord remembered Sarah as he had said' (Gen. 21:1). refers to what he had stated to her by an act of saying, while 'And he did to Sarah as he had spoken' (Gen. 21:1) alludes to statements that he made to her with an act of speaking."
   C. R. Nehemiah said, "'And the Lord remembered Sarah as he had said' (Gen. 21:1). refers to what he had stated to her through an angel, while 'And he did to Sarah as he had spoken' (Gen. 21:1) alludes to statements that he made to her himself."
4. A. R. Judah says, "'And the Lord remembered Sarah' (Gen. 21:1) by giving her a son, 'and the Lord did to Sarah as he had promised' (Gen. 21:1) by giving her the blessing of milk."
   B. Said to him R. Nehemiah, "And had she already been informed about the matter of milk? But this teaches that the Holy One, blessed be he, restored her youth to her."
5. A. R. Abbahu [in the name of R. Yose b. R. Hanina]: "'I shall place fear of her over all the nations of the world, so that they will not abuse her by calling her barren.'"
   B. R. Yudan [in the name of R. Simeon b. Laqish]: "She had no ovary, so the Holy One, blessed be he, formed an ovary for her."
6. A. "The Lord remembered Sarah" (Gen. 21:1):
   B. Said R. Aha, "The Holy One, blessed be he, takes care of [and remembers] bailments. Amalek entrusted to the Holy One bundles of thorns, so he returned him bundles of thorns: 'I remember what Amalek did to Israel' (1 Sam. 15:2).

C. "Sarah entrusted to the Holy One, blessed be he, the religious duties and good deeds that she had performed, and he returned to her the reward of doing religious duties and good deeds: 'The Lord remembered Sarah' (Gen. 21:1)."

Nos. 1 and 2 present interweavings of verses, making points in an elegant way. No. 3 then reads the base verse in terms of its broader meaning. Judah wants to distinguish things God has said from those that he has spoken, and Nehemiah finds his own distinction for the same terms. What follows, however, has no place here. It has been revised from its original appearance, XLVII:II, at which point it made sense. No. 5 makes that certain, since it is completely irrelevant to the present context. We therefore see what the framers were willing to do to revise what they had received -- and what they were not willing to do. Overall they simply inserted whole compositions, even though only small parts of those compositions had a place. But where they did make changes, as here, we can readily discern what was original and what has emerged as the revised version. No. 6 draws its own contrast, resting on the usages of the word "remember" of Amalek and Sarah. It produces the effect of linking the life of Sarah to the history of Israel. The lives of the patriarchs and matriarchs therefore prefigure the life of israel, as we have seen throughout.

LIII.X.

1. A. "And the child grew and was weaned, [and Abraham made a great feast on the day that Isaac was weaned]" (Gen. 21:8):

   B. R. Hoshaia the Elder said, "He was weaned from the evil impulse."

   B. Rabbis say, "He was weaned from relying upon milk."

2. A. "...and Abraham made a *great* feast on the day that Isaac was weaned" (Gen. 21:8):

   B. R. Judah said, "The *Great* One of the ages was there."

   C. R. Yudan in the name of R. Yose bar Haninah: "'The king made a great feast' (Est. 2:18). The *Great* One of the ages was there. That is in line with this verse: 'For the Lord will again rejoice over you for good' (Deut. 30:9), in the days of Mordecai and Esther, 'As he rejoiced over your fathers' (Deut. 30:9), in the days of Abraham, Isaac, and Jacob."

3. A. Said R. Judah, "'A great feast' refers to a feast for the great ones of the age. Og and all the great ones were there. They said to Og, 'Did you not say that Abraham was a barren mule, who cannot produce a child?'

   B. "He said to them, 'Now what is this gift of his? Is he not puny? If I put my finger out on him, I can crush him.'

   C. "Said to him the Holy One, blessed be he, 'Now are you treating my gift with contempt? By your life, you will see a thousand myriads of his children, and you will fall in the end to his children.'

   D. "So it is said: 'And the Lord said to Moses, "Fear him not, for I have delivered him into your hand"' (Num. 21:34)."

   E. [Freedman:] (R. Levi said, "The cradle was rocked for the first time in the house of our father Abraham.")

F. [Continuing A-D,] for R. Joshua bar Nehemiah said, "Those thirty-one kings whom Joshua killed were all present at the feast made by Abraham."

G. But there were not thirty-one. The matter accords with what R. Berekhiah and R. Helbo, R. Parnakh in the name of R. Yohanan [said], "'The king of Jericho, one' (Joshua 12:9). Scripture states, 'One,' meaning, 'he and his regent.'"

No. 1 contrasts figurative and literal interpretations of the verse. No. 2 explicitly links Isaac's feast with the miracle in the time of Esther, and, should we miss the point, further links the two matters explicitly. The recurrent appeal to the events of the Book of Esther should not be missed. No. 3 succeeds still more effectively in introducing the theme of Israel's history. So the feast for Isaac prefigures the redemption of Israel. The reciprocal flow of merit found its counterpart in the two-way exchange of penalty as well. When Abraham erred, his descendants would pay the price.

LIV:IV.

1. A. "Abraham set seven ewe lambs of the flock apart" (Gen. 21:28):

    B. Said the Holy One, blessed be he, to him, "You have given him seven ewe lambs. By your life I shall postpone the joy of your descendants for seven generations.

    C. "You have given him seven ewe lambs. By your life matching them his descendants [the Philistines] will kill seven righteous men among your descendants, and these are they: Hofni, Phineas, Samson, Saul and his three sons.

    D. "You have given him seven ewe lambs. By your life, matching them the seven sanctuaries of your descendants will be destroyed, namely, the tent of meeting, the altars at Gilgal, Nob, Gibeon, Shiloh, and the two eternal houses of the sanctuary.

    E. "You have given him seven ewe lambs. [By your life, matching them] my ark will spend seven months in the fields of the Philistines."

2. A. R. Jeremiah in the name of R. Samuel bar R. Isaac: "If the mere chicken of one of them had been lost, would he not have gone looking for it by knocking on doors, so as to get it back, but my ark spent seven months in the field and you pay not mind to it. I on my own will take care of it: 'His right hand and his holy arm have wrought salvation for him' (Ps. 98:1).

    B. "That is in line with this verse: 'And the kine took the straight way' (1 Sam. 6:12). They went straight forward, turning their faces to the ark and [since the word for 'straight forward' contains the consonants for the word for 'song'] singing."

    C. And what song did they sing?

    D. R. Meir said, " 'The song of the sea. Here it is said, 'They went along...lowing as they went' (1 Sam. 6:12), and in that connection: 'For he is highly exalted' (Ex. 15:1). [The word for lowing' and the word for 'exalted' share the same consonants.]"

    E. R. Yohanan said, "'O sing to the Lord a new song' (Ps. 98:1)."

    F. R. Eleazar said, "'O Give thanks to the Lord, call upon his name' (Ps. 105:1)."

G. Rabbis said, "'The Lord reigns, let the earth rejoice' (Ps. 97:1)."

H. R. Jeremiah said, "The three: 'O sing to the Lord a new song, sing to the Lord, all the earth' (Ps. 96:1). 'The Lord reigns, let the peoples tremble' (Ps. 99:1)."

I. Elijah taught, "[Freedman:] 'Rise, rise, you acacia, soar, soar, in your abundant glory, beautiful in your gold embroidery, extolled in the innermost shrine of the sanctuary, encased between the two cherubim.'"

J. Said R. Samuel bar. R. Isaac, "How much did [Moses,] son of Amram labor so as to teach the art of song to the Levites. But you beasts are able to sing such a song on your own, without instruction. All power to you!"

No. 1 reverts to the theme of indignation at Abraham's coming to an agreement with Abimelech, forcefully imposing the theme of the later history of Israel upon the story at hand. No. 2 is tacked on because of the concluding reference to No. 1. The binding of Isaac, critical in sages' reading of lessons taught by Abraham's deeds for the direction of their descendants, formed the centerpiece of their quest for the laws of history as well. At each point, in each detail, they discovered not only what we going to happen but also why. The single most important paradigm for history therefore emerged from the deed at Moriah.

LVI:I.

1. A. "On the third day Abraham lifted up his eyes and saw the place afar off" (Gen. 22:4):

B. "After two days he will revive us, on the third day he will raise us up, that we may live in his presence" (Hos.16:2).

C. On the third day of the tribes: "And Joseph said to them on the third day, 'This do and live'" (Gen. 42:18).

D. On the third day of the giving of the Torah: "And it came to pass on the third day when it was morning" (Ex. 19:16).

E. On the third day of the spies: "And hide yourselves there for three days" (Josh 2:16).

F. On the third day of Jonah: "And Jonah was in the belly of the fish three days and three nights" (Jonah 2:1).

G. On the third day of the return from the Exile: "And we abode there three days" (Ezra 8:32).

H. On the third day of the resurrection of the dead: "After two days he will revive us, on the third day he will raise us up, that we may live in his presence" (Hos. 16:2).

I. On the third day of Esther: "Now it came to pass on the third day that Esther put on her royal apparel" (Est. 5:1).

J. She put on the monarchy of the house of her fathers.

K. On account of what sort of merit?

L. Rabbis say, "On account of the third day of the giving of the Torah."

M. R. Levi said, "It is on account of the merit of the third day of Abraham: 'On the third day Abraham lifted up his eyes and saw the place afar off' (Gen. 22:4)."

2. A. "...lifted up his eyes and saw the place afar off" (Gen. 22:4):

B. What did he see? He saw a cloud attached to the mountain. He said, "It would appear that that is the place concerning which the Holy One, blessed be he, told me to offer up my son."

The third day marks the fulfillment of the promise, at the end of time of the resurrection of the dead, and, at appropriate moments, of Israel's redemption. The reference to the third day at Gen. 22:2 then invokes the entire panoply of Israel's history. The relevance of the composition emerges at the end. Prior to the concluding segment, the passage forms a kind of litany and falls into the category of a liturgy. Still, the recurrent hermeneutic which teaches that the stories of the patriarchs prefigure the history of Israel certainly makes its appearance.

LVI:II.

1. A. He said, "Isaac, my son, do you see what I see?"

B. He said to him, "Yes."

C. Her said to the two lads, "Do you see what I see?"

D. They said to him, "No."

E. He said, "Since you do not see, 'Stay here with the ass' (Gen. 22:5), for you are like an ass."

F. On the basis of this passage we learn that slaves are in the category of asses.

G. Rabbis derive proof from the matter of the giving of the Torah: "Six days you shall labor and do all your work, you...your daughter, your man-servant, your maid-servant, your cattle" (Ex. 20:10).

2. A. Said R. Isaac, "Will this place [the Temple mount] ever be distant from its owner [God]? Never, for Scripture says, 'This is my resting place for ever; here I will dwell, for I have desired it' (Ps. 132:14).

B. "It will be when the one comes concerning whom it is written, 'Lowly and riding upon an ass' (Zech. 1:9)."

3. A. "I and the lad will go thus far [and worship and come again to you]" (Gen. 22:5):

B. Said R. Joshua b. Levi, "[He said,] 'We shall go and see what will be the end of "thus."'" [Freedman, p. 492, n. 5: God had said, "Thus shall your seed be" (Gen. 15:5). So the sense is, "We will see how that can be fulfilled, now that I am to lose my son."]

4. A. "...and we will worship [through an act of prostration] and come again to you" (Gen. 22:5):

B. He thereby told him that he would come back from Mount Moriah whole and in peace [for he said that *we* shall come back].

5. A. Said R. Isaac, "And all was on account of the merit attained by the act of prostration.

B. "Abraham returned in peace from Mount Moriah only on account of the merit owing to the act of prostration: '...and we will worship [through an act of prostration] and come [then, on that account] again to you' (Gen. 22:5).

C. "The Israelites were redeemed only on account of the merit owing to the act of prostration: And the people believed...then they bowed their heads and prostrated themselves' (Ex. 4:31).

D. "The Torah was given only on account of the merit owing to the act of prostration: 'And worship [prostrate themselves] you afar off' (Ex. 24:1).

E. "Hannah was remembered only on account of the merit owing to the act of prostration: 'And they worshipped before the Lord' (1 Sam. 1:19).

F. "The exiles will be brought back only on account of the merit owing to the act of prostration: 'And it shall come to pass in that day that a great horn shall be blown and they shall come that were lost...and that were dispersed...and they shall worship the Lord in the holy mountain at Jerusalem' (Is. 27:13).

G. "The Temple was built only on account of the merit owing to the act of prostration: 'Exalt you the Lord our God and worship at his holy hill' (Ps. 99:9).

H. "The dead will live only on account of the merit owing to the act of prostration: 'Come let us worship and bend the knee, let us kneel before the Lord our maker' (Ps. 95:6)."

No. 1 explains both how Abraham knew it was the place and also why he left the lads behind. No. 2 then takes up the language of "seeing the place from afar," and by a play on the words, asks whether this place will ever be made far from its owner, that is, God. The answer is that it will not. No. 3 draws a lesson from the use of "thus" in the cited verses. The sizable construction at No. 4 makes a simple point, to which our base verse provides its modest contribution. But its polemic is hardly simple. The entire history of Israel flows from its acts of worship ("prostration") and is unified by a single law. Every sort of advantage Israel has ever gained came about through worship. Hence what is besought, in the elegant survey, is the law of history. The Scripture then supplies those facts from which the governing law is derived.

LVI:IX.

1. A. "And Abraham lifted up his eyes and looked, and behold, behind him was a ram, [caught in a thicket by his horns. And Abraham went and took the ram and offered it up as a burnt offering instead of his son]" (Gen. 22:13):

    B. What is the meaning of the word for "behind"?

    C. Said R. Yudan, "'Behind' in the sense of 'after,' that is, after all that happens, Israel nonetheless will be embroiled in transgressions and perplexed by sorrows. But in the end, they will be redeemed by the horns of a ram: 'And the Lord will blow the horn' (Zech. 9:14)."

    C. Said R. Judah bar Simon, "'After' all generations Israel nonetheless will be embroiled in transgressions and perplexed by sorrows. But in the end, they will be redeemed by the horns of a ram: 'And the Lord God will blow the horn' (Zech. 9:14)."

    D. Said R. Hinena bar Isaac, "All through the days of the year Israelites are embroiled in transgressions and perplexed by sorrows. But on the New Year they take the ram's horn and sound it, so in the end, they will be redeemed by the horns of a ram: 'And the Lord God will blow the horn' (Zech. 9:14)."

E. R. Abba bar R. Pappi, R. Joshua of Siknin in the name of R. Levi: "Since
our father, Abraham, saw the ram get himself out of one thicket only to be
trapped in another, the Holy One, blessed be he, said to him, 'So your
descendants will entangled in one kingdom after another, struggling from
Babylonia to Media, from Media to Greece, from Greece to Edom. But in the
end, they will be redeemed by the horns of a ram: 'And the Lord God will blow
the horn...the Lord of Hosts will defend them' (Zech. 9:14-5).

2. A. "... And Abraham went and took the ram and offered it up as a burnt
offering instead of his son]" (Gen. 22:13):

B. R. Yudan in the name of R. Benaiah: "He said before him, 'Lord of all
ages, regard the blood of this ram as though it were the blood of Isaac, my son,
its innards as though they were the innards of Isaac my son.'"

C. That [explanation of the word "instead"] accords with what we have
learned in the Mishnah: "Lo, this is instead of that, this is in
exchange for that, this is in place of that" -- lo, such is an act
of exchanging [one beast for another in the sacrificial rite, and
both beasts then are held to be sanctified] [M. Tem. 5:5].

D. R. Phineas in the name of R. Benaiah: "He said before him, 'Lord of all
ages, regard it as though I had offered up my son, Isaac, first, and afterward had
offered up the ram in his place.'"

E. That [sense of the word "instead"] is in line with this verse: "And Jothan
his son reigned in his stead" 2 Kgs. 15:7).

F. That accords with what we have learned in the Mishnah: [If one says,
"I vow a sacrifice] like the lamb," or "like the animals of the
Temple stalls" [it is a valid vow] [M. Ned. 1:3].

G. R. Yohanan said, "That is in the sense of 'like the lamb of the daily
whole offering.'" [One who made such a statement has vowed to bring a lamb.]

H. R. Simeon b. Laqish said, "...'like the ram of Abraham, our father.'" [One
who has made such a statement has vowed to bring a ram.]

I. There they say, "...'like the offspring of a sin-offering.'"

J. Bar Qappra taught on Tannaite authority, "...'like a lamb which has never
given suck [thus, a ram]."

The power of No. 1 is to link the life of the private person, affected by
transgression, and the history of the nation, troubled by its wandering among the
kingdoms. From the perspective of the Land of Israel, the issue is not Exile but
the rule of foreigners. In both cases the power of the ram's horn to redeem the
individual and the nation finds its origin in the Binding of Isaac. The exegetical
thrust, linking the lives of the patriarchs to the life of the nation, thus brings the
narrative back to the paradigm of individual being, so from patriarch to nation to
person. The path leads in both directions, of course, in a fluid movement of
meaning. No. 2 works on the language of "instead," a technical term in the cult,
and so links the Binding of Isaac to the Temple cult.

LVI:XI.

1. A. "And the angel of the Lord called to Abraham a second time from heaven
and said, 'By myself I have sworn, [says the Lord, because you have done this
thing, and have not withheld your son, your only son, I will indeed bless you

and I will multiply your descendants as the stars of heaven and as the sand which is on the seashore. And your descendants shall possess the gate of their enemies, and by your descendants shall all the nations of the earth bless themselves, because you have obeyed my voice']" (Gen. 22:15-17):

B. What need was there for taking such an oath?

C. He said to him, "Take an oath to me that you will never again test me or Isaac my son."

2. A. What need was there for taking such an oath?

B. R. Levi in the name of R. Hama bar Hanina, "He said to him, 'Take an oath to me that you will never again test me.'

C. "The matter may be compared to the case of a king who was married to a noble lady. She produced a first son from him, and then he divorced her, [remarried her, so she produced] a second son, and he divorced her again, a third son, and he divorced her again. When she had produced a tenth son, all of them got together and said to him, 'Take an oath to us that you will never again divorce our mother.'

D. "So when Abraham had been tested for the tenth time, he said to him, 'Take an oath to me that you will never again test me.'"

3. A. Said R. Hanan, "'...because you have done this thing...'! It was the tenth trial and he refers to it as '...this [one] thing...'? But this also is the last, since it outweighs all the rest.

B. "For if he had not accepted this last trial, he would have lost the merit of all that he had already done."

3. A. "...I will indeed bless you [and I will multiply your descendants as the stars of heaven and as the sand which is on the seashore. And your descendants shall possess the gate of their enemies, and by your descendants shall all the nations of the earth bless themselves, because you have obeyed my voice]" (Gen. 22:17):

B. [Since the Hebrew makes use of the verb, "bless," two times, translated "indeed bless," we explain the duplicated verb to mean] a blessing for the father, a blessing for the son.

C. [Similarly, the duplicated verb for "multiply" means] myriads for the father and myriads for the son.

4. A. "...And your descendants shall possess the gate of their enemies...:"

B. Rabbi said, "This refers to Palmyra. Happy is he who will witness the fall of Palmyra, since it participated in both destructions of the Temple."

C. R. Yudan and R. Hanina:

D. One of them said, "At the destruction of the first Temple it provided eighty thousand archers."

E. The other said, "At the destruction of the Temple it supplied eight thousand archers."

5. A. "So Abraham returned to his young men[and they arose and went together to Beersheba and Abraham dwelt at Beersheba]" (Gen. 22:19):

B. And where was Isaac?

C. R. Berekhiah in the name of Rabbis over there [in Babylonia]: "He had sent him to Shem to study Torah with him. [Why the emphasis on Torah-study?]

D. "The matter may be compared to the case of a woman who got rich from her spinning. She said, 'Since it is from this spindle that I got rich, it will never leave my hand.'"

E. R. Yose bar Haninah said, "He sent him away by night, on account of the evil eye."

F. For from the moment that Hananiah, Mishael, and Azariah came up out of the fiery furnace, their names are not mentioned again in the narrative. So where had they gone?

G. R. Eleazar said, "They died in spit."

H. R. Yose bar Haninah said, "They died on account of the evil eye."

I. R. Joshua b. Levi said, "They changed their residence and went to Joshua b. Yehosedeq to study Torah, in line with this verse: 'Hear now, O Joshua the high priest, you and your fellows that sit before you, for they are men that are a sign' (Zech. 3:8)."

J. R. Tanhum bar Abina in the name of R. Hinena: "It was on that stipulation that Hananiah, Mishael, and Azariah descended to the fiery furnace,

No. 1 spells out the matter of the oath, which is an unusual and weighty procedure. No. 2 then carries forward a statement made in No. 1, though it has no bearing upon the larger issue. No. 3 and No. 4 gloss the base verse. No. 5 answers a basic question left open by the narrative. F-J were included in the composition before the whole was inserted here, and hence the syllogism preceded the exegesis.

Chapter Thirteen

Isaac and Jacob and Israel's History

While Abraham founded Israel, Isaac and Jacob carried forth the birthright and the blessing. This they did through the process of selection, ending in the assignment of the birthright to Jacob alone. The lives of all three patriarchs flowed together, each being identified with the other as a single long life. This immediately produces the proposition that the historical life of Israel, the nation, continued the individual lives of the patriarchs. The theory of who is Israel, therefore, rested on genealogy: Israel is one extended family, all being children of the same fathers and mothers, the patriarchs and matriarchs of Genesis. This theory of Israelite society, and of the Jewish people in the time of the sages of Genesis Rabbah, made of the people a family, and of genealogy, a kind of ecclesiology. The importance of that proposition in countering the Christian claim to be a new Israel cannot escape notice. Israel, sages maintained, is Israel after the flesh, and that in a most literal sense. But the basic claim, for its part, depended upon the facts of Scripture, not upon the logical requirements of theological dispute. Here is how those facts emerged in the case of Isaac.

LXIII:III.

1. A. "These are the descendants of Isaac, Abraham's son: Abraham was the father of Isaac" (Gen. 25:19):

B. Abram was called Abraham: "Abram, the same is Abraham" (1 Chr. 1:27).

C. Isaac was called Abraham: ""These are the descendants of Isaac, Abraham's son, Abraham."

D. Jacob was called Israel, as it is written, "Your name shall be called more Jacob but Israel" (Gen. 32:29).

E. Isaac also was called Israel: "And these are the names of the children of Israel, who came into Egypt, Jacob and his" (Gen. 46:8).

F. Abraham was called Israel as well.

G. R. Nathan said, "This matter is deep: 'Now the time that the children of Israel dwelt in Egypt' (Ex. 12:40), and in the land of Canaan and in the land of Goshen 'was four hundred and thirty years' (Ex. 12:40)." [Freedman, p. 557, n. 6: They were in Egypt for only 210 years. Hence their sojourn in Canaan and Goshen must be added, which means, from the birth of Isaac, Hence the children of Israel commence with Isaac. And since he was Abraham's son, it follows that Abraham was called Israel.]

The polemic at hand, linking the patriarchs to the history of Israel, claiming that all of the patriarchs bear the same names, derives proof, in part, from the base verse. But the composition in no way rests upon the exegesis of the base verse. Its syllogism transcends the case at hand. The importance of Isaac in particular derived from his relationship to the two nations that would engage in struggle, Jacob, who was and is Israel, and Esau, who stood for Rome. By himself, as a symbol for Israel's history Isaac remained that same shadowy figure whom we encountered earlier. Still, Isaac plays his role in setting forth the laws of Israel's history .

LXV:XIII.

1. A. "[He said, 'Behold I am old; I do not know the day of my death.] Now then take your weapons, [your quiver and your bow, and go out to the field and hunt game for me, and prepare for me savory food, such as I love, and bring it to me that I may eat; that I may bless you before I die']" (Gen. 27:2-4):

B. "Sharpen your hunting gear, so that you will not feed me carrion or an animal that was improperly slaughtered.

C. "Take your *own* hunting gear, so that you will not feed me meat that has been stolen or grabbed."

2. A. "Your quiver:"

B. [Since the word for "quiver" and the word for "held in suspense" share the same consonants, we interpret the statement as follows:] he said to him, "Lo, the blessings [that I am about to give] are held in suspense. For the one who is worthy of a blessing, there will be a blessing."

3. A. Another matter: "Now then take your weapons, your quiver and your bow and go out to the field:"

B. "Weapons" refers to Babylonia, as it is said, "And the weapons he brought to the treasure house of his god" (Gen. 2:2).

C. "Your quiver" speaks of Media, as it says, "So they suspended Haman on the gallows" (Est. 7:10). [The play on the words is the same as at No. 2.]

D. "And your bow" addresses Greece: "For I bend Judah for me, I fill the bow with Ephraim and I will story up your sons, O Zion, against your sons, O Javan [Greece]" (Zech. (9:13).

E. "and go out to the field" means Edom: "Unto the land of Seir, the field of Edom" (Gen. 32:4).

4. A. "And prepare for me savory food:"

B. R. Eleazar in the name of R. Yose b. Zimra: "Three statements were made concerning the tree, that it was good to eat, a delight to the eyes, and that it added wisdom,

C. "and all of them were stated in a single verse:

D. "'So when the woman saw that the tree was good for food,' on which basis we know that it was good to eat;

E. "'and that it was a delight to the eyes', on which basis we know that it was a delight for the eyes,

F. "'and that the tree was to be desired to make one wise,' on which basis we know that it added to one's wisdom.

G. "That is in line with the following verse of Scripture: 'A song of wisdom of Ethan the Ezrahite' (Ps. 89:1)" [and the root for "song of wisdom" and that for "to make one wise" are the same].

H. "So did Isaac say, '"And prepare for me savory food." I used to enjoy the appearance [of food], but now I get pleasure only from the taste.'

I. "And so did Solomon say, 'When goods increase, those who eat them are increased, and what advantage is there to the owner thereof, saving the beholding of them with his eyes' (Qoh. 5:10).

J. "The one who sees an empty basket of bread and is hungry is not equivalent to the one who sees a full basket of bread and is satisfied."

5. A. "And Rebecca was listening when Isaac spoke to his son Esau. So when Esau went to the field to hunt for game and bring it..." (Gen. 27:5):

B. If he found it, well and good.

C. And if not, "...to bring it" even by theft or violence.

No. 1 begins with the imputation of some deeper meanings fo Isaac's statement, showing him to be more perspicacious than the narrative before us. No. 2 broadens the range of meaning, making the matter of the blessing more conditional than the narrative suggests. Isaac now is not sure who will get the blessing; his sense is that it will go to whoever deserves it. No. 3 then moves from the moral to the national, making the statement a clear reference to the history of Israel (as though, by this point, it were not obvious). What the author of the item at hand contributes, then, is the specific details. What the compositor does is move the reader's mind from the philological to the moral to the national dimension of exegesis of the statements at hand. No. 4 works out the meaning of the request for tasty food; the main point is that Isaac wants highly spiced food, since he cannot see what he is eating. If one knows he has something to eat, that often satisfies; not seeing is not knowing. No. 5 contributes a familiar motif. Esau steals, but Jacob takes only what is lawful. Isaac foresaw the entire history of Israel.

LXV:XXIII.

1. A. ["See the smell of my son is as the smell of a field which the Lord has blessed" (Gen. 27:27):] Another matter: this teaches that the Holy One, blessed be he, showed him the house of the sanctuary as it was built, wiped out, and built once more.

B. "See the smell of my. son:" This refers to the Temple in all its beauty, in line with this verse: "A sweet smell to me shall you observe" (Num. 28:2).

C. "...is as the smell of a field:" This refers to the Temple as it was wiped out, thus: "Zion shall be ploughed as a field" (Mic. 3:12).

D. "...which the Lord has blessed:" This speaks of the Temple as it was restored once more in the age to come, as it is said, "For there the Lord commanded the blessing, even life for ever" (Ps. 133:3).

The conclusion explicitly links the blessing of Jacob to the Temple throughout its history. The concluding proof-text presumably justifies the entire identification of the blessing at hand with what was to come.

LXVI:II.

1. A. R. Berekhiah opened [discourse by citing the following verse:] "'Return, return, O Shulamite, return, return that we may look upon you' (Song 7:1):

B. "The verse at hand refers to 'return' four times, corresponding to the four kingdoms in which Israel enters in peace and from which Israel comes forth in peace.

C. "'O Shulamite:' the word refers to the nation who every day is blessed with a blessing ending with peace [which shares the consonants of the word at hand], as it is said, 'And may he give you peace' (Num. 7:26).

D. "It is the nation in the midst of which dwells the Peace of the ages, as it is said, 'And let them make me a sanctuary that I may dwell among them' (Ex. 25:8).

E. "It is the nation to which I am destined to give peace: 'And I will give peace in the land' (Lev. 26:6).

F. "It is the nation over which I am destined to spread peace: 'Behold, I will extend peace to her like a river' (Is. 66:12)."

G. R. Samuel bar Tanhum, R. Hanan bar Berekiah in the name of R. Idi: "It is the nation that makes peace between me and my world. For if it were not for that nation, I would destroy my world."

H. R. Hana in the name of R. Aha: "'When the earth and all the inhabitants thereof are dissolved' (Ps. 75:4), as in the statement, 'All the inhabitants of Canaan are melted away' (Ex. 15:15).

I. "'I' (Ps. 75:4), that is, when they accepted upon themselves [the Ten Commandments, beginning,] 'I am the Lord your God' (Ex. 20:2), I established the pillars of it' (Ps. 75:4), and the world was set on a solid foundation."

J. Said R. Eleazar bar Merom, "This nation preserves [makes whole] the stability of the world, both in this age and in the age to come."

K. R. Joshua of Sikhnin in the name of R. Levi: "This is the nation on account of the merit of which whatever good that comes into the world is bestowed. Rain comes down only for their sake, that is, 'to you' [as in the base verse], and the dew comes down only 'to you.'

L. "May God give you of the dew of heaven."

The point of this rather sizable composition comes at the end, but the intersecting verse is worked out in its own terms. We have a philosophy of Israel among the nations, stating in one place every component. We begin with a reference to the four kingdoms, but then we move out of that item to the name of the Shulamite, and, third, we proceed to work on the theme of Israel as the nation of peace. Once the praise of Israel forms the focus, we leave behind the issue of peace and deal with the blessings that come to the world on Israel's account. Only at that point does the base verse prove relevant. I could not begin to speculate on the origins of this complex composition -- unitary or incremental. What is important to us is the reason for its selection and inclusion on the part of those responsible for the document before us, and their interest is self-evident. But whether they took existing materials and tacked on their point, or whether the composition existed in this form prior to its selection and inclusion, we cannot now know. Whatever future history finds adumbration in the life of Jacob derives from the struggle with Esau. Israel and Rome -- these two contend for the world. Still, Isaac plays his part in the matter. Rome does have a legitimate claim, and that claim demands recognition -- an amazing, if grudging concession on the part of sages that Christian Rome at least is Esau.

LXVII:IV.

1. A   "When Esau heard the words of his father, he cried out with an exceedingly great and bitter cry [and said to his father, 'Bless me, even me also, O my father!']" (Gen. 27:34):

   B.   Said R. Hanina, "Whoever says that the Holy One, blessed be he, is lax, may his intestines become lax.   While he is patient, he does collect what is coming to you.

   C.   "Jacob made Esau cry out one cry, and where was he penalized?   It was in the castle of Shushan: 'And he cried with a loud and bitter cry' (Est. 4:1)."

2. A.   "But he said, 'Your brother came with guile and he has taken away your blessing'" (Gen. 33:35):

   B.   R. Yohanan said, "[He came] with the wisdom of his knowledge of the Torah."

3. A.   "Esau said, 'Is he not rightly named Jacob? [For he has supplanted me these two times.   He took away my birthright and behold, now he has taken away my blessing.'   Then he said, 'Have you not reserved a blessing for me?']" (Gen. 27:36):

   B.   "'He took away my birthright, and I kept silence, and now he has taken away my blessing.'"

4. A.   "Then he said, 'Have you not reserved a blessing for me?'" (Gen. 27:36):

   B.   --even an inferior one?

The stunning concession for Christianity should not be missed.   Rome really is Israel's brother.   The history of the two brothers forms a set of counterpoints, the rise of one standing for the decline of the other.   The ultimate end, Israel's final glory, will permanently mark the subjugation of Esau.   The point of No. 1 is to link the present passage to the history of Israel's redemption later on.   In this case, however, the matter concerns Israel's paying recompense for causing anguish to Esau.   No. 2 introduces Jacob's knowledge of Torah in place of Esau's view of Jacob as full of guile.   The remainder of the entries provides minor glosses.

LXVII:V.

1. A. "Isaac answered Esau,['Behold I have made him your lord and all his brothers I have given to him for servants, and with grain and wine I have sustained him. What then can I do for you, my son?']" (Gen. 27:37):"

B. Said R. Berekhiah, "'Behold I have made him your lord and all his brothers I have given to him for servants' is the seventh of the blessings Isaac passed out [to Jacob].

C. "Why then does he mention it first?

D. "The sense is this: 'I made him king over you, and your blessings belong to him.'"

E. "A slave and everything he owns belongs to his master: all his brothers I have given to him for servants, and with grain and wine I have sustained him.'"

2. A. "... What then can I do for you, my son?'" (Gen. 27:37): [Since the word for "now" uses the consonants of the word for "bread," we interpret:] "Indeed for you the bread is baked [in that you will have prosperity also]."

C. R. Yohanan said, "Leave him alone, for his bread is baked for him everywhere."

D. R. Simeon b. Laqish said, "Leave him alone, for anger [which shares the consonants used for the word "now"] and wrath are handed over to him."

3. A. R. Simlai, and some say it in the name of R. Abbahu, "Said the Holy One, blessed be he, 'You have said, "What then can I do for you, my son?"

B. "[Isaac replied, "'Yet let favor be shown to him" (Is. 26:10).'

C. "[God said,] "'He is wicked" (Is. 26:10).'

D. "''Has he not learned righteousness?'"

E. "'Did he not honor his parents?'

F. "''In the land of uprightness will he deal wrongfully.'"

G. "He said to him, 'He is destined to lay his hands on the sanctuary.'

H. "He said to him, 'If so, give him prosperity in this world: "and let him not behold the majesty of the Lord" in the world to come.'"

No. 1 amplifies the discourse between Isaac and Esau. No. 2 works on the word "now," which yields consonants bearing diverse meanings. The passage falls into the category of philological exegesis. Employing the cited verse of Isaiah, No. 3 then constructs a colloquy between Isaac and God. Apart from the struggle with Esau, Jacob still serves as a model and paradigm of Israel's history. For example, his dream of the ladder to heaven encompassed all of Israel's history,. with stress not on Esau but on Sinai.

LXVIII:XII.

3. A. Bar Qappara taught on Tannaite authority, "There is no dream without a proper interpretation.

B. "'That there was a ladder:'refers to the ramp to the altar.

C. "'...set up on the earth:' that is the altar, 'An altar of dirt you will make for me' (Ex. 20:24).

D. "'...and the top of it reached to heaven:' these are the offerings, for their fragrance goes up to heaven.

E. "'...and behold, the angels of God:' these are the high priests.

F. "'...were ascending and descending on it:' for they go up and go down on the ramp.

G. "'And behold, the Lord stood above it:' 'I saw the Lord standing by the altar' (Amos 9:1)."

4. A. Rabbis interpreted the matter to prefigure Sinai: "'And he dreamed:

B. "'...that there was a ladder:' this refers to Sinai.

C. "'...set up on the earth:' 'And they stood at the lower part of the mountain' (Ex. 19:17).

D. "'...and the top of it reached to heaven:' 'And the mountain burned with fire into the heart of heaven' (Deut. 4:11).

E. "'...and behold, the angels of God:' these are Moses and Aaron.

F. "'...were ascending:' 'And Moses went up to God' (Ex. 19:3).

G. "'...and descending on it:' "And Moses went down from the mount' (Ex. 19:14).

F. "'...And behold, the Lord stood above it:' 'And the Lord came down upon Mount Sinai' (Ex. 19:20)."

5. A. Salomaini in the name of R. Simeon b. Laqish: "He showed him a throne with three legs."

B. R. Joshua of Sikhnin in the name of R. Levi: "'And you are the third of the three legs.'"

C. That accords with the view of R. Joshua in the name of R. Levi: "'For the portion of the Lord is his people, Jacob the cord of his inheritance' (Deut. 32:9): as a cord cannot be made of less than three strands [so there were three patriarchs, and hence he told Jacob that he would be the third of the three]."

D. R. Berekhiah said, "He showed him a world and a third of the world.

E. "'Ascending' [in the plural] speaks of at least two angels, and 'descending' speaks of two, and each angel in size is a third of the world [thus a world and a third].

F. "And how do we know that an angel is the size of a third of the world? 'His body also was like the beryl and his face as the appearance of lightning' (Dan. 10:6)."

6. A. R. Hiyya the Elder and R. Yannai:

B. One of them said, "'They were going up and coming down' on the ladder."

C. The other said, "'They were going up and coming down' on Jacob."

D. The one who says, "'They were going up and coming down' on the ladder," has no problems.

E. As to the one who says, "'They were going up and coming down' on Jacob," the meaning is that they were raising him up and dragging him down, dancing on him, leaping on him, abusing him.

F. For it is said, "Israel, in whom I will be glorified" (Is. 49:3).

G. [So said the angels,] "Are you the one whose visage is incised above?" They would then go up and look at his features and go down and examine him sleeping.

H. The matter may be compared to the case of a king who was in session and judging cases in a judgment chamber. So people go up to the basilica and find him asleep. They go down to the judgment chamber and find him judging cases.

I. Above whoever speaks in favor of Israel rises up, and whoever condemns Israel goes down. Below, whoever speaks in his favor goes down, and whoever condemns him goes up.

7. A. The angels who accompany a person in the Land do not accompany him outside of the Land.

B. "Ascending" are the ones who accompanied him in the land, and "descending" are the ones who will accompany him outside of the land.

8. A. R. Levi in the name of R. Samuel: "Because the ministering angels revealed the mystery of the Holy One, blessed be he, [telling Lot what he was about to do], they were sent into exile from their appropriate dwelling for a hundred and thirty eight years."

B. R. Tanhuma stated it in the word for "stalk," which contains the letters of a numerical value adding up to 138.

C Said R. Hama bar Hanina, "It was because they puffed themselves up, saying, 'for *we* are about to destroy this place' (Gen. 19:13)."

D. When did they return? Here: "ascending" and only then "descending." [Freedman, p. 627, n. 3: The banished angels were now permitted to reascend to heaven and then bidden to descend to accompany Jacob.]

No. 3 reads the dream in terms of the Temple cult, and No. 4 in terms of the revelation of the Torah at Sinai, and No. 5 has the dream refer to the patriarchs. At LXVIII:XIII we complete the repertoire of parabolic interpretations of the base verse. No. 5 bears a sizable addendum, 5.D-F. No. 6 then goes over the matter of the ascent and the descent of the angels. It presents a number of separate themes, first the notion that the angels were curious about this Jacob, so they came down to see him. The other theme is the link from Jacob to Israel's condition, with the rueful observations at 6.I to make the point. I find the composite somewhat confusing, and I may have erred in not further dividing it. No. 7 works over the same issue, namely, the identification of the angels and their purpose in going up and down the ladder. No. 8 connects these angels to the ones who brought Lot out of Sodom.

LXX:VI.

1. A. "...so that I come again to my father's house in peace, then the Lord shall be my God" (Gen. 28:20-22):

B. R. Joshua of Sikhnin in the name of R. Levi: "The Holy One, blessed be he, took the language used by the patriarchs and turned it into a key to the redemption of their descendants.

C. "Said the Holy One, blessed be he, to Jacob, 'You have said, "Then the Lord shall be my God." By your life, all of the acts of goodness, blessing, and consolation which I am going to carry out for your descendants I shall bestow only by using the same language:

D. ""Then in that day, living waters shall go out from Jerusalem" (Zech. 14:8). "Then in that day a man shall rear a young cow and two sheep" (Is. 7:21). "Then, in that day, the Lord will set his hand again the second time to recover the remnant of his people" (Is. 11:11). "Then, in that day, the mountains shall drop down sweet wine" (Joel 4:18). "Then, in that day, a great horn shall be blown and they shall come who were lost in the land of Assyria" (Is. 27:13).'"

The union of Jacob's biography and Israel's history yields the passage at hand. It is important only because it says once again what we have now heard throughout our survey of Genesis Rabbah -- but makes the statement as explicit as one can imagine.

LXX:X.

1. A. "Jacob said to them, 'My brothers, where do you come from?' They said, 'We are from Haran'" (Gen. 29:40):

B. R. Yose bar Haninah interpreted the verse at hand with reference to the Exile.

C. "'Jacob said to them, "My brothers, where do you come from"' They said, "We are from Haran:" that is, 'We are flying from the wrath of the Holy One, blessed be he.' [Here there is a play on the words for "Haran" and "wrath," which share the same consonants.]

D. "'He said to them, "Do you know Laban the son of Nahor?"' The sense is this, 'Do you know him who is destined to bleach your sins as white as snow?' [Here there is a play on the words for "Laban" and "bleach," which share the same consonants.]

E. "'They said, "We know him." He said to them, "Is it well with him?" They said, "It is well."' On account of what sort of merit?

F. [Yose continues his interpretation:] "'[The brothers go on,] "...and see, Rachel his daughter is coming with the sheep'" (Gen. 29:6-7).

G. "That is in line with this verse: 'Thus says the Lord, "A voice is heard in Ramah, lamentation and bitter weeping, Rachel weeping for her children. She refuses to be comforted." Thus says the Lord, "Refrain your voice from weeping...and there is hope for your future," says the Lord, and your children shall return to their own border'" (Jer. 31:15-16)."

Now the history of the redemption of Israel is located in the colloquy between Jacob and Laban's sons.

LXX:XV.

1. A. "Now Laban had two daughters, the name of the older was Leah, and the name of the younger was Rachel" (Gen. 29:16):

B. They were like two beams running from one end of the world to the other.

C. This one produced captains and that one produced captains, this one produced kings and that one produced kings, this one produced liontamers and that one produced liontamers, this one produced conquerers of nations and that one produced conquerers of nations, this one produced those who divided countries and that one produced dividers of countries.

D. The offering brought by the son of this one overrode the prohibitions of the Sabbath, and the offering brought by the son of that one overrode the prohibitions of the Sabbath.

E. The war fought by this one overrode the prohibitions of the Sabbath, and the war fought by this one overrode the prohibitions of the Sabbath.

F. To this one were given two nights, and to that one were given two nights.

G. The night of Pharaoh and the night of Sennacherib were for Leah, and the night of Gideon for for Rachel, and the night of Mordecai was for Rachel, as it is said, "On that night the king could not sleep" (Est 6:1).

2 . A. "The name of the older [greater] was Leah...:"

B. She was greater in the gifts that came to her, receiving the priesthood forever and the throne forever.

C. "...and the name of the younger [lesser] was Rachel" (Gen. 29:16):

D. She was lesser in the gifts she received, Joseph for a while, Saul. for a while.

No. 1 links the whole history of Israel to the two daughters of Laban and their offspring. No. 2 effects the same exercise.

LXX:XX.

1 . A. "[So Jacob did so and completed her work; then Laban gave him his daughter Rachel to wife]...So Jacob went in to Rachel also, and he loved Rachel more than Leah, and served Laban for another seven years" (Gen. 29:28-30):

B. Said R. Judah bar Simon, "Under ordinary circumstances a worker works with a householder assiduously for two or three hours, but then he gets lazy at his work. But here just as the labor committed for the first years was complete, so the labor given in the latter seven years was hard and complete.

C. "Just as the first years were worked out in good faith, so the last years were worked out in good faith."

2 . A. Said R. Yohanan, "It is written, 'And Jacob fled into the field of Aram, and Israel served for wife, and for a wife he kept sheep' (Hos. 12:13).

B. "He said to them, 'Your example is like Jacob. Just as Jacob was subjugated before he had married a wife and was also subjugated after he had married a wife, so you, before your redeemer was born, have been subjugated, and after your redeemer has been born you are still subjugated."

No. 1 makes a minor observation. No. 2 then joins the present story to the history of Israel. The subjugation after the birth of the redeemer is supposed to refer to the fact that the redeemer was born on the day the Temple was destroyed [Freedman, p. 651, n.1]. Once more, Israel's disaster is Rome's triumph -- but the opposite also will be the case.

LXXIII:VII.

1 . A. "When Rachel had borne Joseph, [Jacob said to Laban, 'Send me away, that I may go to my own home and country. Give me my wives and my children for whom I have served you and let me go; for you know the service which I have given you']" (Gen. 30:25):

B. Once the "satan" of Esau was born [namely, Joseph], then: "Jacob said to Laban, 'Send me away, that I may go to my own home and country.'"

C. For R. Phineas in the name of R. Samuel bar Nahman: "It is a tradition that Esau will fall only by the hand of the descendants of the children of Rachel: 'Surely the youngest of the flock shall drag them away' (Jer. 49:20).

D. "And why does Scripture call them 'the youngest of the flock'? Because they are the youngest of the tribes."

The tendency to link the present tale to the history of Israel finds another statement here. The fact of C-D is taken for granted at B.

LXXV:VI.

1. A. "And I have an ox, an ass [flocks, manservants and maidservants" (Gen. 32:5):

B. R. Judah said, "From a single ox, many oxen came forth, and from a single ass, many asses came forth."

C. [As to the use of the singular] R. Nehemiah said, "It is the way people say it: 'an ass, a camel' [meaning a collective noun]."

D. Rabbis said, "'An ox' refers to the priest who was anointed for war: 'His firstling bullock, majesty is his name' (Deut. 33:17).

E. "'An ass' refers to the anointed king-messiah: 'Lowly, and riding upon an ass' (Zech. 9:9).

F. "Flocks" speaks of Israel: 'And you are my sheep, the sheep of my pasture' (Ez. 34:31).

G. "'And manservants and maidservants' refers to Israel: "Behold as the eyes of the servants unto the hand of their master' (Ps. 123:2)."

The messianic theme finds a place in the tale at hand.

LXXV:XIII.

1. A. At that moment Jacob stood up in prayer before the Holy One, blessed be he. He said before him, "Lord of all ages, You have written in your Torah, 'And whether it be cow or ewe, you shall not kill it and its young both in one day' (Lev. 22:28).

B. "If this wicked man comes and destroys all of them at once, what will come of the Torah?

C. "By your leave, 'Save me, I pray you' (Gen. 32:12)."

D. What did he do? He sent him a present, so as to blind him, as it is said, "For a gift blinds the eyes of the wise" (Deut. 16:19).

E. And the word "wise" refers only to the Edomites, as in the following verse: "I will destroy the wise men out of Edom" (Ob. 1:8).

2. A. "These he delivered into the hand of his servants, every drove by itself, [and said to his servants, 'Pass on before me, and put a space between drove and drove']" (Gen. 32:17):

B. What is the meaning of the statement, "...and put a space"?

C. Said Jacob before the Holy One, blessed be he, "Lord of all ages, if troubles come upon my children, do not let it happen that they come in quick succession, but let them have a respite from their troubles."

D. At that moment he lifted up his eyes and saw Esau, and he raised his eyes on high and wept and sought mercy for himself before the Holy One, blessed be he.

E. God listened to his prayer and promised him that he would save them from all their troubles on account of the merit he had attained: "The Lord answer you in the day of trouble, the name of the God of Jacob set you up on high" (Ps. 20:2).

No. 1 expands on the situation of Jacob before he met Esau, now invoking for God the rule that mother and child may not be killed on one day. The sending of gifts is then explained as a shrewd, not a craven act. Israel's salvation is prefigured in Jacob's victory over the angel.

LXXVIII:V.

1. A. "The sun rose upon him as he passed Penuel, limping because of his thigh" (Gen. 32:21):

B. Said R. Berekhiah, "The sun shown only to heal him, but as for others, it was merely gave light."

C. R. Huna in the name of R. Aha: "The sun served to heal Jacob, but it burned up Esau and his commanders.

D. "Said the Holy One, blessed be he, to him, 'You are a sign for your children. Just as the sun served to heal you, but it burned up Esau and his commanders, so your children will find that the sun serves to heal them but to burn up the nations.'

E. "As to healing them: 'But for you that fear my name shall the sun of righteousness arise with healing in its wings' (Ma. 3:20).

F. "As to burning up the nations: 'For behold the day comes, it burns as a furnace' (Mal. 3:19)."

2. A. "Limping upon his thigh" (Gen. 32:31):

B. R. Joshua b. Levi went to Rome. When he got back to Acre, R. Hinena came out to receive him and found him limping on this thigh.

C. He said to him, "You are like your ancestor: 'Limping upon his thigh' (Gen. 32:31)."

Berekhiah's comment, no. 1, links Jacob's life to Israel's destiny in the future. The upshot of No. 2 is to make the same point, now in the setting of the life of a sage. Much that he said serves to illuminate Israel's future history.

LXXVIII:XIII.

1. A. "[Then Esau said, 'Let us journey on our way, and I will go before you.'] But Jacob said to him, 'My lord knows [that the children are frail, and that the flocks and herds giving suck are a care to me; and if they are overdriven for one day, all the flocks will die. Let my lord pass on before his servant, and I will lead on slowly, according to the pace of the cattle which are before me and and according to the pace of the children, until I come to my lord in Seir']" (Gen. 33:12-14):

B. Said R. Berekhiah, "'My lord knows that the children are frail' refers to Moses and Aaron.

C. "...and that the flocks and herds giving suck are a care to me' speaks of Israel: 'And you, my flock, the flock of my pasture, are men' (Ez. 34:31)."

D. R. Huna in the name of R. Aha: "If it were not for the tender mercies of the Holy One, blessed be he, ' 'and if they are overdriven for one day, all the flocks will die' in the time of Hadrian."

E. R. Berekhiah in the name of R. Levi: "'My lord knows that the children are frail' speaks of David and Solomon.

F. "'...the flocks and herds' refers to Israel: ' 'And you, my flock, the flock of my pasture, are men' (Ez. 34:31).

G. Said R. Huna in the name of R. Aha, "If it were not for the tender mercies of the Holy One, blessed be he, ' 'and if they are overdriven for one day, all the flocks will die' in the time of Haman."

The event at hand now is identified with other moments in the history of Israel.

LXXXII:X.

1. A. "So Rachel died and she was buried on the way to Ephrath, [that is, Bethlehem, and Jacob set up a pillar upon her grave; it is the pillar of Rachel's tomb, which is there to this day. Israel journeyed on and pitched his tent beyond the tower of Eder]" (Gen. 35:16-21):

B. Why did Jacob bury Rachel on the way to Ephrath?

C. Jacob foresaw that the exiles would pass by there [en route to Babylonia].

D. Therefore he buried here there, so that she should seek mercy for them: "A voice is heard in Ramah...Rachel weeping for her children...Thus says the Lord, 'Keep your voice from weeping...and there is hope for your future'" (Jer. 31:15-16).

The deeds of the patriarchs aim at the needs of Israel later on. The link between the lives of the patriarchs and the history of Israel forms a major theme in the exegetical repertoire before us.

XCVI:I.

1. A. "And Jacob lived in the land of Egypt seventeen years, so the days of Jacob, the years of his life, were a hundred and forty-seven years" (Gen. 47:28):

B. [The basis of the question to follow is explained by Freedman, p. 885, n. 1: This passage is the beginning of a new lection, which normally is separated from the previous one by the space of nine letters, while sections in the same lection are separated by not less than three letters' space. This one, however, is separated from the previous one by the space of one letter only, and is therefore called closed.] Why then is this passage, among all of the passages that are in the Torah, closed [and not open, as explained by Freedman]?

C. At the point at which our father, Jacob, died, the subjugation of Israel by Egypt began.

2. A.   Why then is this passage, among all of the passages that are in the Torah, closed?

B.   Because Jacob wanted to reveal the mysteries of the end, and they were closed off from him.

3. A.   Why then is this passage among all of the passages that are in the Torah, closed?

B.   Because from him all of the troubles of the world were closed off [since he enjoyed life in Egypt].

The question receives three answers, two of them linking Israel's history to Jacob's life.

Chapter Fourteen

Joseph, the Tribal Fathers, and Israel's History

Along with Abraham, Isaac, and Jacob, Joseph take up an important role in the revelation of Israel's history. His brothers, founders of the tribes bearing their names, obviously give their testimony too to what will happen in the time to come. Since Jacob, in Genesis 49, and Moses, in Deuteronomy 32 treat the brothers of Joseph, founders of the tribes, as precursors of what was to happen in the future history of Israel as well as at the end of days, none of these modes of reading the book of Genesis presents surprises. Since both Jacob and Moses explicitly spoke of the sons of Jacob as paradigms of history, the sages understood the text precisely as the Torah itself told them to understand it. That is, the sages simply took seriously and at face value the facts in hand, as any scientist or philosopher finds facts and reflects upon their meaning and the implications and laws deriving from them. So sages' mode of reading derived from an entirely inductive and scientific, philosohical mode of thought. The laws of history begin with the principle that the merit of the founders sustains the children to come. The model for the transaction in merit -- which underlines and explains the theory of genealogy as the foundation of Israel's social entity, -- comes to expression in the life of Joseph. Joseph both derived benefit from the merit of his ancestors and handed on merit to his descendants.

LXXXIV:V.

2. A. "These are the generations of the family of Jacob. Joseph [being seventeen years old, was shepherding the flock with his brothers]" (Gen. 37:2):

    B. These generations came along only on account of the merit of Joseph.

    C. Did Jacob go to Laban for any reason other than for Rachel?

    D. These generations thus waited until Joseph was born, in line with this verse: "And when Rachel had borne Joseph, Jacob said to Laban, 'Send me away'" (Gen. 30:215).

    E. Who brought them down to Egypt? It was Joseph.

    F. Who supported them in Egypt? It was Joseph.

    G. The sea split open only on account of the merit of Joseph: "The waters saw you, O God" (Ps. 77:17). "You have with your arm redeemed your people, the sons of Jacob and Joseph" (Ps. 77:16).

    H. R. Yudan said, "Also the Jordan was divided only on account of the merit of Joseph."

No. 2 asks why only Joseph is mentioned as the family of Jacob. The inner polemic is that the merit of Jacob and Joseph would more than suffice to overcome Esau/Rome. Joseph's life, as much as Abraham's or Jacob's, represents the history of Israel and its meaning.

LXXXVI:I.

1. A. "Now Joseph was taken down to Egypt, [and Potiphar, an officer of Pharaoh, the captain of the guard, an Egyptian, bought him from the Ishmaelites who had brought him down there] (Gen. 39:1):

B. "I drew them with cords of a man, [with bands of love. Yet I was to them as those who lift up a yoke, on account of their jaws. I reached out food to them]" (Hos. 11:4):

C. "I drew them with cords of a man:" this refers to Israel: "Draw me, we will run after you" (Song 1:4).

D. "With bands of love" (Hos. 11:4): "I have loved you, says the Lord" (Mal. 1:2).

E. "Yet I was to them as those who lift up a yoke:" "For I raised their enemies over them." Why so?

F. "On account of their jaws:" On account of something that they issued from their jaws, saying to the golden calf, "These are your Gods, Israel" (Ex. 32:8).

G. And at the end: "I reached out food to them:" [God says,] "I provided much food for them. 'May he be as a rich grain field in the land' (Ps. 72:16)."

2. A. Another interpretation: "I drew them with cords of a man:" this refers to Joseph: "And they drew and lifted up Joseph" (Gen. 37:28).

B. "...with bands of love:" "Now Israel loved Joseph" (Gen. 37:3).

C. "...Yet I was to them as those who lift up a yoke:" [God speaks,] "I raised up his enemies over him, and who is this? It is the wife of Potiphar." All this why?

D. "...on account of their jaws:" It was on account of something that they issued from their jaws, saying, "And Joseph brought an evil report of them to their father" (Gen. 37:2).

E. But in the end, "...I reached out food to them:" "I gave him much food: "And Joseph was the governor over the land" (Gen. 42:6).

No. 1 reads the base verse in line with the history of Israel, No. 2 in the terms of Joseph's biography. The former composition is noteworthy in the diversity of its exegetical reference-points, citing Malachi, Song of Songs, Exodus, and Psalms. The later, by contrast, is uniform and more successful in a disciplined reading of one thing in the light of some other. I see the former as diffuse, the latter as cogent. But there is a clear correspondence between No. 1 and No. 2, since the purpose of the exegete-compositors is to compare the history of Israel to the life of Joseph, and that comparison is successfully carried out.

LXXXVII:VI.

1. A. "And although she spoke to Joseph [day after day, he would not listen to her, to lie with her or to be with her. But one day, when he went into the house to do his work and none of the men of the house was there in the house, she caught him by his garment, saying, 'Lie with me.' But he left his garment in her hand and fled and got out of the house]" (Gen. 39:10-13):

B. R. Yudan in the name of R. Benjamin bar Levi: "As to the sons of Levi, the trials affecting them were the same, and the greatness that they achieved was the same.

C. "...the trials affecting them were the same: 'And although she spoke to Joseph [day after day.' 'Now it came to pass, when they spoke to him day by day'; (Est. 3:4). [Mordecai, descended from Benjamin, was nagged every day.] 'He would not listen to her.' 'And he did not listen to them' (Est. 3:4).

D. "...and the greatness that they achieved was the same: 'And Pharaoh took off his signet ring from his hand and put it upon Joseph's hand' (Gen. 41:42). 'And the king took off his ring, which he had taken from Haman and gave it to Mordecai' (Est. 8:2).

E. "'And arrayed him in fine linen clothing and put a gold chain about his neck' (Gen. 41:42). 'And Mordecai went forth from the presence of the king in royal apparel of blue and white, and with a great crown of gold and with a robe of fine linen and purple' (Est. 8:15)F. "'And he made Joseph ride in the second chariot which he had' (Gen. 41:43). 'And cause Mordecai to ride on horseback through the street of the city' (Est. 6:9).

G. "'And they cried before him, Abrech' (Gen. 41:43). 'And proclaimed before Mordecai, "Thus shall it be done to the man"' (Est. 6:11)."

2. A. "...he would not listen to her, to lie with her or to be with her:"

B. "...to lie with her" in this world, that he would not have children with her.

C. "...or to be with her" in the world to come.

3. A. "...he would not listen to her, to lie with her or to be with her:"

B. "...to lie with her:" even lying without sexual relations.

4. A. A noble lady as R. Yose, "Is it possible that Joseph, at the age of seventeen, in his full vigor, could have done such a thing?"

B. He produced for her a copy of the book of Genesis. He began to read the story of Reuben and Judah. He said to her, "If these, who were adults and in their father's domain, were not protected by the Scripture [but were revealed by Scripture in all their lust], Joseph, who was a minor and on his own, all the more so [would have been revealed as lustful, had he done what the lady thought he had]."

The parallel drawn between Joseph and Benjamin=Mordecai permits the exegete to draw a parallel between the life of Joseph and the history of Israel. No. 2 expands on the base verse, and No. 3 presents an argument in favor of its authenticity, at the same time linking the present story to the two that have preceded.

LXXXVIII:I.

1. A. "Some time after this, the butler of the king of Egypt and his baker offended [Hebrew: sinned against] their lord the king of Egypt" (Gen. 40:1):

B. "Deliver me from all my transgressions, make me not the reproach of the base" (Ps. 89:9):

C. R. Hama bar Haninah said, "[Because they own this world,] the nations of the world ought not to have had among them sickly or weak people. Why are there sickly and weak people among them? It is so that they should not ridicule Israel, saying to them, 'Are you not a nation of sickly and weak people?'

D. "This is on the count of the following verse: '...make me not the reproach of the base.'"

E. R. Samuel bar Nahman said, "[Because they own this world,] the nations of the world ought not to have had among them people who produce scabs. And why are there such people among them? It is so that they should not ridicule Israel, saying to them, 'Are you not a nation of lepers?'

F. ""This is on the count of the following verse: '...make me not the reproach of the base.'"

2. A. Another interpretation: "Deliver me from all my transgressions, make me not the reproach of the base" (Ps. 89:9):

B. This refers to Joseph.

C. Since it is written, "And she called the men of her house" (Gen. 39:14), meaning that she put his name into everyone's mouth, the Holy One, blessed be he, said, "It is better that they turn against one another and not against that righteous man."

D. Thus: "Some time after this, the butler of the king of Egypt and his baker offended [Hebrew: sinned against] their lord the king of Egypt" (Gen. 40:1).

The effect of the dual exegesis of the intersecting verse is to link Israel's experience to Joseph's, Nos. 1, 2 in order. The comment on the intersecting verse at No. 1 can readily stand on its own, but, joined to No. 2, illuminates the purpose of God in having Joseph thrown into prison and further comments on Israel's life among the nations. In all, this is a good example of what is achieved in the intersecting verse/base verse construction. God of course governed Joseph's destiny, detail by detail, and as this becomes clear, the Jewish reader concludes that God's providence and benevolence continues to dictate what is to happen to Israel, even though that fact does not always prove self-evident.

LXXXVIII:III.

1. A. "And Pharaoh was angry with his two officers" (Gen. 40:2):

B. R. Judah bar Simon, R. Hanan in the name of R. Yohanan: "'Come and see the works of God' (Ps. 66:5).

C. "He made servants angry with their masters so as to bestow greatness on the righteous, he made masters angry with their servants in order to bestow greatness on the righteous.

D. "Thus: 'And Pharaoh was angry with his two officers' so as to bestow greatness on Joseph.

E.   "'Bigthan and Teresh were angry' (Est. 2:21) with Ahasuerus, so that he might bestow greatness on Mordecai."

2 . A.   [(Freedman:) As to the plots of Bigthan and Teresh against Ahasuerus:] R. Yudan said, "These are the views:

B.   "Rab said, 'Short daggers did they hide in their shoes.'

C.   "R. Hanan said, 'They made an instrument with which to strangle him.'

D.   "Samuel said, 'They hid a snake in his dish.'

E.   "In respect to all these views: 'Inquisition was made of the matter and it was found to be so' (Est. 2:23)."

No. 1 once more links the story of Joseph's personal rise to greatness to Israel's national rise to greatness in the time of Mordecai. Obviously, No. 2 was attached to No. 1 before the whole complex was used here. The importance for the present purpose is obvious.

LXXXVIII:V.

1 . A.   ["So the chief butler told his dream to Joseph and said to him, 'In my dream there was a vine before me, and on the vine there were three branches; as soon as it budded, its blossoms shot forth, and the clusters ripened into grapes. Pharaoh's cup was in my hand, and I took the grapes and pressed them into Pharaoh's cup and placed the cup in Pharaoh's hand. And I took the grapes and pressed them into Pharaoh's cup and placed the cup in Pharaoh's hand'" (Gen. 49:11-13)]. "...there was a vine before me:" this refers to Israel: "You plucked up a vine out of Egypt" (Ps. 80:9).

B.   "...and on the vine there were three branches:" this refers to Moses, Aaron, and Miriam.

C.   "...as soon as it budded, its blossoms shot forth:"   specifically, the blossoming of the redemption of Israel.

D.   "...and the clusters ripened into grapes:" as soon as the vine budded, it blossomed, and as soon as the grapes blossomed, the clusters ripened.

2 . A.   "'Pharaoh's cup was in my hand, and I took the grapes and pressed them into Pharaoh's cup and placed the cup in Pharaoh's hand. And I took the grapes and pressed them into Pharaoh's cup and placed the cup in Pharaoh's hand.'...' you shall place Pharaoh's cup in his hand:'"

B.   On what basis did sages ordain that there should be four cups of wine for Passover?

C.   R. Hunah in the name of R. Benaiah: "They correspond to the four times that redemption is stated with respect to Egypt: 'I will bring you out...and I will deliver you...and I will redeem you...and I will take you' (Ex. 6:6-7)."

D.   R. Samuel b. Nahman said, "They correspond to the four times that 'cups' are mentioned here: 'Pharaoh's *cup* was in my hand, and I took the grapes and pressed them into Pharaoh's *cup* and placed the *cup* in Pharaoh's hand. And I took the grapes and pressed them into Pharaoh's *cup* .'"

E.   R. Levi said, "They correspond to the four kingdoms."

F.   R. Joshua b. Levi said, "They correspond to the four cups of fury that the Holy One, blessed be he, will give the nations of the world to drink: 'For thus says the Lord, the God of Israel, to me, "Take this cup of the wine of fury"' (Jer. 25:15). 'Babylon has been a golden cup in the Lord's hand' (Jer. 51:7). 'For in the hand of the Lord there is a cup' (Ps. 75:9). 'And burning wind shall be the portion of their cup' (Ps. 11:6).

G. "And in response to these, the Holy One, blessed be he, will give Israel four cups of salvation to drink in the age to come: 'O Lord, the portion of my inheritance and of my cup, you maintain my lot' (Ps. 16:5). 'You prepare a table before me in the presence of my enemies, you have anointed my head with oil, my cup runs over' (Ps. 23:5). 'I will lift up the cup of salvations and call upon the name of the Lord' (Ps. 116:13).

H. "What is said is not 'cup of salvation' but 'cup of salvations,' one in the days of the Messiah, the other in the time of Gog and Magog."

3. A. Joseph said to him, "[Since the dream refers to Israel's coming redemption,] you have brought me a good gospel, so I shall now give you a good gospel: 'within three days Pharaoh will lift up your head and restore you to your office.'"

4. A. "But remember me, when it is well with you, and do me the kindness, I pray you, to make mention of me to Pharaoh, and so get me out of this house. For I was indeed stolen out of the land of the Hebrews, and here also I have done nothing that they should put me into the dungeon'" (Gen. 40:14-15):

B. Said R. Aha, "On the basis of the use of the verb 'stolen' twice [in the statement, 'indeed stolen,'] we learn that he was stolen twice."

5. A. "...that they should put me into the dungeon:"

B. Said R. Abin, "The meaning is that they put [One] with me in prison. [Freedman, p. 817, n. 4: The divine Presence accompanied me.]"

No. 1 reads the vision in light of the story of Israel's redemption from Egypt. No. 2 then brings the point home, by linking Israel's redemption specifically to aspects of the language of the vision. Obviously, our base verse plays only a modest role in the grand vision of No. 2. No. 3 carries forward No. 2 and therefore cannot be understood without it. If, as it would appear, No. 2 is an independent composition, then No. 3 surely was added afterward, at the level of redactional composition, to link the whole still more tightly to our context and to exploit in the service of that context the enormous conceptions introduced in No. 2. Nos. 4, 5 provide minor glosses.

LXXXIX:I.

1. A. "At it came to pass at the end of two years, [Pharaoh dreamed that he was standing by the Nile]" (Gen. 41:1):

B. "He sets an end to darkness...the stones of thick darkness and the shadow of death" (Job. 28:3):

C. A span of time has been assigned to the world, decreeing how many years it would spend in darkness.

D. What is the scriptural evidence? "He sets an end to darkness...the stones of thick darkness and the shadow of death" (Job. 28:3).

E. For all that time that the impulse to do evil is in the world, darkness and gloom are in the world. When the impulse to do evil is uprooted from the world, darkness and deep gloom will pass from the world.

2. A. Another interpretation of the verse: "He sets an end to darkness...the stones of thick darkness and the shadow of death" (Job. 28:3):

B. A span of time was assigned to the Joseph, decreeing how many years he would spend in prison.

C. Once the end came, Pharaoh had his dream: "At it came to pass at the end of two years, [Pharaoh dreamed that he was standing by the Nile]" (Gen. 41:1).

The cited verse introduces at No. 1 the theme of the prevailing interpretation of Joseph's life, which has emphasized his power to sin and his regeneration. So the underlying point is that Joseph's impulse to do evil reached the end of its allotted span of time, at which point the end of his period of suffering also came. Since Joseph's story has repeatedly been linked to Israel's history, with strong emphasis on the links between Joseph and Mordecai, the deeper message addresses Israel's condition and links its impulse to sin with its degraded condition.

XCIII:XII.
1. A. "Then he fell upon his brother Benjamin's necks and wept, and Benjamin wept upon his necks:"

B. [The Hebrew repeatedly uses the plural for the word "neck," so we ask:] how many necks did Benjamin have?

C. Said R. Eleazar, "He foresaw through the Holy Spirit that two sanctuaries were destined to be built in the share of Benjamin and were destined to be destroyed."

D. "...and Benjamin wept upon his necks:"

E. He foresaw that the tabernacle of Shilo was destined to be built in the share of Joseph and destined to be destroyed.

2. A. "And he wept out loud" (Gen. 45:2):

B. Just as Joseph conciliated his brothers only through weeping, so the Holy One, blessed be he, will redeem Israel only through weeping.

C. So it is said, "They shall come with weeping and with supplications will I lead them, I will cause them to walk by rivers of waters" (Jer. 31:9).

No. 1 goes over familiar ground, again linking the lives of the patriarchs to the history of Israel. No. 2 makes the same point, with much greater power. The founders of the tribes, Joseph's brothers, take up the task of telling future Israel what is going to happen. Clearly sages invested a great deal of effort in sorting out precisely how the tribes in later times worked out the destinies announced in the beginning.

LXXXII:IV.
1. A. "And God said to him, 'I am God Almighty; be fruitful and multiply; [a nation and a company of nations shall come from you, and kings shall spring from you. The land which I gave to Abraham and Isaac I will give to you and I will give the land to your descendants after you]'" (Gen. 35:11-13):

B. R. Yudan in the name of R. Isaac: "I reflected on the meaning of this statement that Jacob should be fruitful, for Reuben was already born, and Simeon was already born, and Benjamin had already been conceived, though still in his mother's womb. [So what sort of future procreation was going to take place as a result of this blessing?] Then I realized that, 'nation' refers to Benjamin, and 'a company of nations' speaks of Manasseh and Ephraim."

2. A. R. Berekhiah and R. Helbo in the name of R. Samuel bar Nahman: "'...kings shall spring from you' refers to Jeroboam and Jehu [who descend from Manasseh and Ephraim, hence kings descend also from the children Jacob will have in the future (Freedman, p. 754, n. 7)]."

B. Rabbis say, "It is hardly possible that Abner, who was a righteous man, should oppose the monarchy of the house of David. [Yet Abner opposed David and favored Ishboshet, son of Saul.]

C. "But what happened is that he made an exegesis [that in fact was in error] and so favored the kingship of Ishbosheth.

D. "That is in line with this verse: '...kings shall spring from you.' That refers to Saul and Ishbosheth. [Freedman, p. 755, n. 1: He held that the reference must be actually to Jacob's unborn son, Benjamin, thus *two* kings would have to descend from Benjamin, and these would be Saul and his son, not David.]"

3. A. Why did they draw the tribe of Benjamin in and to expel them in connection with the incident of the concubine at Gieah?

B. They consulted a verse of Scripture and drew them near, and they read a verse of Scripture and sent them out.

C. They read a verse of Scripture and drew them near: "...a nation and a company of nations shall come from you, and kings shall spring from you."

D. They read a verse of Scripture and expelled them: "Ephraim and Manasseh even as Reuben and Simeon shall be mine" (Gen. 48:5).

Once we make reference, No. 1, to Benjamin and the unborn descendants of Jacob, we naturally review the later history of Benjamin and his tribe, first with reference to the monarch of Saul, then with respect to the concubine at Gibeah, Nos. 2, 3. The recurrence of Benjamin as a prototype of salvation will prove striking as our document unfolds.

LXXXII:XI.

1. A. "While Israel dwelt in that land, [Reuben went and lay with Bilhah, his father's concubine, and Israel heard of it. Now the sons of Jacob were twelve. The sons of Leah: Reuben, Jacob's first born, Simeon, Levi, Judah, Issachar, and Zebulun. The sons of Rachel: Joseph and Benjamin. The sons of Bilhah, Rachel's maid, Dan and Naphtali. The sons of Zilpah, Leah's maid, Gad and Asher. These were the sons of Jacob who were born to him in Paddan-aram]" (Gen. 35:22-26):

B. Said R. Simon, "It is difficult before the Holy One, blessed be he, to pull up a name from its proper place in the genealogical chain.

C. "'And the sons of Reuben, the first born of Israel' -- for he was the firstborn, but, since he defiled his father's bed, his birthright was given to the sons of Joseph, the son of Israel, yet not so that he was to be reckoned in the genealogy as firstborn' (1 Chr. 5:1).

D. "What this indicates is that the birthright as to property was taken away from him, but not the birthright as to genealogy. [Thus we see, 'Reuben, Jacob's first born,' and that in the very context of the matter of Bilhah.]"

E. R. Levi and R. Simon:

F. One of them said, "It is not for Reuben to be reckoned in the genealogy [as the firstborn]."

G. The other of them said, "The genealogy lists not Joseph but Reuben as firstborn."

H. R. Haggai in the name of R. Isaac: "Even in the hour of his disgrace, the genealogy involving the firstborn is assigned only to Reuben.

I. "That is in line with this verse: 'While Israel dwelt in that land, Reuben went and lay with Bilhah, his father's concubine, and Israel heard of it. Now the sons of Jacob were twelve. The sons of Leah: Reuben, Jacob's first born...'"

J. R. Yudan in the name of R. Aha: "Reuben was firstborn as to conception, firstborn as to birth, firstborn as to the right of the firstborn, firstborn as to inheritance, firstborn as to transgression, firstborn as to repentance."

K. R. Azariah said, "Also firstborn as to prophecy: 'The Lord spoke first with Hosea [descended from Reuben]' (Hos. 1:2)."

The issue is fully exposed, namely, the relationship of Reuben's action to his status as firstborn. The base verse plays its role in demonstration, J, that Reuben retained his rights, with the insertion of the fact that he repented to validate that fact. Reuben then serves as a prototype for Israel's life, with special reference to the power of repentance. The brothers teach not only theological virtues, such as repentance, but also moral ones. In the following, their very honesty in regard to what they had done proves they were not hypocrites.

LXXXIV:IX.

1. A. "But when his brothers saw that their father loved him more than all his brothers, they hated him and could not speak peaceably to him" (Gen. 37:3-4):

B. Said R. Ahva bar Zeira, "Out of the disgrace of the progenitors of the tribes you may learn their glory.

C. "Later on: 'And Absalom spoke to Amnon neither good nor bad' (2 Sam. 13:22). He kept what was in his heart to himself.

D. "But here 'But when his brothers saw that their father loved him more than all his brothers, they hated him and could not speak peaceably to him.' What was in their heart was also in their mouth. [They were not hypocrites.]"

The point is well taken, made by contrasting two verses. While the composition in no way serves as an exegesis of the verse at hand, it does make an important point, which is that people should not be hypocrites. In the future, the tribes would enjoy blessings on account of the merit of their ancestors, a familiar law of history.

LXXXIV:XV.

1. A. ["But when Reuben heard it, he delivered him out of their hands, saying, 'Let us not take his life.' And Reuben said to them, 'Shed no blood, cast him into this pit here in the wilderness but lay no hand upon him,' that he might rescue him out of their hand, to restore him to his father" (Gen. 37:21-22)]: "But when Reuben heard it:"

   B. Where had Reuben been?

   C. R. Judah said, "Each one of the brothers had been serving his father for one day, and that day was the day assigned to Reuben."

   D. R. Nehemiah said, "[He said,] 'I am the firstborn, and this rotten deed will be assigned only to me.'"

   E. Rabbis said, "'He regards me as his brother, and shall I not save him? I had supposed that I was rejected on account of that foul deed that I did, but he counts me with my brothers: "and behold, the sun, the moon, and eleven stars were bowing down to me." Should I not save him?'

   F. "The Holy One, blessed be he, said to him, 'You were the first to undertake to save a life. By your life, when the cities of refuge are set aside first, they will fall only within your boundaries. That is in line with this verse: "Bezer in the wilderness, in the table-land, for the Reubenites"(Deut. 4:43).'"

The treatment of Reuben is quite diverse, as we see, with several different explanations for where Rueuben had been and why he had acted as he did. The striking point is E, because of the success in linking the present detail to earlier ones. The actions of the progenitors of the tribes prefigure the history and distinction of the tribes to come. But there is another side to the matter. The tribes would suffer punishment because of the misdeeds of their ancestors.

LXXXIV:XX.

1. A. "Then Jacob tore his garments and put sackcloth upon his loins and mourned for his son many days" (Gen. 37:34):

   B. R. Phineas in the name of R. Hoshaiah: "The tribal fathers caused their father to tear his garments, and where were they paid back? In Egypt: 'And they tour their clothes' (Gen. 44:13).

   C. "Joseph caused the tribal fathers to tear their clothes. He was paid back in the case of the son of his son: 'And Joshua tore his clothes' (Josh. 7:6).

   D. "Benjamin caused the tribal fathers to tear their clothes. He was paid back in Shushan, the capital: 'Mordecai tore his clothes' (Est. 4:1).

   E. "Manasseh caused the tribal fathers to tear their clothes. He was paid back by having his inheritance divided into half, half on the other side of the Jordan, and half in the land of Canaan."

2. A. "...and put sackcloth upon his loins:"

   B. Said R. Aibu, "Because Jacob took hold of sackcloth, therefore sackcloth did not leave him or his children to the end of all generations:

   C. "Ahab: 'And he put sackcloth on his flesh and fasted' (1 Kgs. 21:27).

   D. "Joram: 'And the people looked, and behold, he had sackcloth within upon his flesh' (2 Kgs. 6:30).

   E. "Mordecai: 'And he put sackcloth and ashes' (Est. 4:1).

3. A. "...and mourned for his son many days:"

B. Twenty-two years. [Freedman, p. 785, n. 5: "Joseph was seventeen years old, and he was thirty when he stood before Pharaoh. To this must be added seven years of plenty, and Jacob's reunion with him took place after two years of famine."]

Nos. 1, 2 link the present conduct of Jacob to the future history of Israel, and No. 3 glosses.

LXXV:IX.

1. A. "[She said, 'What will you give me, that you may come in to me?' He answered, 'I will send you a kid from the flock.' She said, 'Will you give me a pledge, till you send it?'] He said, 'What pledge shall I give you?' She replied, 'Your signet and your cord and your staff that is in your hand:'" (Gen. 38:16-18):

B. Said R. Huniah, "The Holy Spirit flamed within her.

C. "'Your signet:' this refers to dominion, in light of this verse: 'Though Coniah the son of Jehoiakim, king of Judah were the signet upon my right hand' (Jer. 22:24).

D. "'...and your cord:' this refers to the sanhedrin: 'And that they put with the fringe of each corner a cord of blue' (Num. 15:38).

E. "'...and your staff:' this speaks of king-messiah: 'The staff of thy strength the Lord will send out of Zion' (Ps. 110:2)."

2. A. "So he gave them to her and went in to her, and she conceived by him" (Gen. 38:18):

B. "She conceived:" heroes, like him, and righteous men, like him.

3. A. "When Judah sent the kid [by his friend the Adullamite to receive the pledge from the woman's hand, he could not find her. And he asked the men of the place, 'Where is the harlot who was at Enaim by the wayside?' And they said, 'No harlot has been here.' So he returned to Judah and said, 'I have not found her, and also the men of the place said, 'No harlot has been here.' And Judah replied, 'Let her keep the things as her own, lest we be laughed at; you see, I sent this kid, and you could not find her'" (Gen. 38:20-22):

B. Said R. Judah bar Nahman in the name of R. Simeon b. Laqish, "'Laughing in his habitable earth, laughing always before him' (Prov. 8:31, 30).

C. "The Torah laughs at people.

D. "Said the Holy One, blessed be he, to Judah, 'You deceived your father with a goat-kid. By your life, Tamar will deceive you with a goat-kid.'"

The linking of the story at hand to the birth of the Messiah accomplished at No. 1 once more shows how the lives of the tribal founders prefigure the history of Israel. Nos. 2, 3 gloss, with a striking parallel drawn at No. 3. This has the further effect of tying the present story closely to the one interrupted by the narrative at hand.

XCII:III.

1. A. R. Joshua b. Levi interpreted the following verse to speak of the exiles: "'May God almighty grant you mercy before the man, that he may send back your other brother and Benjamin. If I am bereaved of my children, I am bereaved (Gen. 43:14):

    B. "'May God almighty grant you mercy:' 'He made them also to be pitied of all those that carried them captive' (Ps. 106:46).

    C. "'...before the man:' this refers to the Holy One, blessed be he: 'The Lord is a man of war' (Ex. 15:3).

    D. "'... that he may send back your...brother:' this refers to the ten tribal ancestors.

    E. "'...the other, and Benjamin:' this refers to the tribe of Judah and the tribe of Benjamin.

    F. "'...If I am bereaved of my children:' in the first destruction [of the Temple].

    G. "'...I am bereaved:' in the second destruction [of the Temple].

    H. "'If I am bereaved of my children:' in the second destruction of the Temple, 'I am not again going to be bereaved.'"

2. A. Another matter: "May God almighty grant you mercy before the man:" this refers to the government.

    B. "...that he may send back your brother:" Joseph.

    C. "...the other:" Simeon.

    D. "...and Benjamin:" as stated.

    E. "...If I am bereaved of my children:" specifically, Joseph.

    F. "...I am bereaved:" specifically, Simeon.

    G. "'If I am bereaved of my children:' specifically, of Simeon.

    H. "'I am not again going to be bereaved.'"

No. 1 finally links the statement of Jacob to the future of Israel, and No. 2 then goes over the statement in light of Jacob's own situation. Here at last we have a clear effort to broaden the narrative in the two anticipated dimensions, one outward toward Israel's history, the other inward toward the prior corners of the tale.

XCII:VIII.

4. A. "Then they tore their clothes, and every man loaded his ass, and they returned to the city:"

    B. R. Phineas in the name of R. Hoshaiah: "The tribal fathers caused their father to tear his garments, and where were they paid back? In Egypt: 'And they tour their clothes' (Gen. 44:13).

    C. "Joseph caused the tribal fathers to tear their clothes. He was paid back in the case of the son of his son: 'And Joshua tore his clothes' (Josh. 7:6).

    D. "Benjamin caused the tribal fathers to tear their clothes. He was paid back in Shushan, the capital: 'Mordecai tore his clothes' (Est. 4:1).

    E. "Manasseh caused the tribal fathers to tear their clothes. He was paid back by having his inheritance divided into half, half on the other side of the Jordan, and half in the land of Canaan."

Once more what the brothers did, their descendants had to pay for.

XCIII:II.

1. **A.** "For lo, the kings assembled themselves, they were angry together. They saw, forthwith they were amazed, they were frightened, they hastened away. Trembling took hold of them there, pangs as of a woman in travail" (Ps. 48:5-7):

B. "For lo, the kings assembled themselves:" this refers to Judah and Joseph.

C. "...they were angry together:" this one was filled with anger for that one, and that one was filled with anger for this one.

D. "They saw, forthwith they were amazed:" "And the men were amazed one with the other" (Gen. 43:33).

E. "...they were frightened, they hastened away:" "And his brothers could not answer him, for they were frightened at his presence" (Gen. 45:3).

F. "Trembling took hold of them there, pangs as of a woman in travail:" this speaks of the tribal founders, who said, "If kings contend with one another, what difference does it make to us? It is appropriate for a king to contend with another king [Judah, the founder of Israelite royalty, with the king of Egypt]."

G. "Then Judah went up to him and said, 'O my lord, let your servant, I pray you, speak a word in my lord's ears, and let not your anger burn against your servant, for you are like Pharaoh himself'" (Gen. 44:18).

2. **A.** "One is so near to another [that no air can come between them]" (Job 41:8):

B. This verse speaks of Judah and Joseph.

C. "...that no air can come between them:"

D. This refers to the tribal ancestors, who said, "If kings contend with one another, what difference does it make to us? It is appropriate for a king to contend with another king [Judah, the founder of Israelite royalty, with the king of Egypt]."

E. "Then Judah went up to him and said, 'O my lord, let your servant, I pray you, speak a word in my lord's ears, and let not your anger burn against your servant, for you are like Pharaoh himself'" (Gen. 44:18).

Nos. 1 and 2 go over the same ground, adducing in evidence different intersecting verses. Judah could approach the ruler of Egypt because, as the king of Israel, he constituted the counterpart. So Israel's history forms the counterweight to the history of the nations -- a large idea expressed in a small way.

XCVIII:II.

4. **A.** "Then Jacob called his sons and said, 'Gather yourselves together, that I may tell you what shall befall you in days to come:"

B. "Gather yourselves together" from the land of Israel, "and assemble and hear" in Raameses.

C. "Gather yourselves together" the ten tribes.

D. "And assemble and hear" the tribes of Judah and Benjamin.

E. He commanded them to treat the tribes of Judah and Benjamin with honor.

5.   R. Aha said, "'Gather together" means "purify' in line with this verse: 'And they gathered themselves together...and they purified themselves' (Neh. 12:28)."

6. A. Rabbis say, "It means that he commanded themselves about dissension. He said to them, 'All of you should form a single gathering.'

B. "That is in line with this verse: 'And you, son of man, take one stick and write upon it, "For Judah and for the children of Israel his companions"' (Ez. 37:16).

C. "What is written is 'his companion,' meaning, that when the children of Israel form a single assembly, then they prepare themselves for redemption.

D. "For what is written afterward? 'And I will make them one nation in the land' (Ez. 37:22)."

7. A. "Then Jacob called his sons and said, 'Gather yourselves together, that I may tell you what shall befall you in days to come:"

B. R. Simon said, "He showed them the fall of Gog, in line with this usage: 'It shall be in the end of days...when I shall be sanctified through you, O Gog' (Ez. 38:165). 'Behold, it shall come upon Edom' (Is. 34:5)."

C. R. Judah said, "He showed them the building of the house of the sanctuary: 'And it shall come to pass in the end of days that the mountain of the Lord's house shall be established' (Is. 2:2)."

D. Rabbis say, "He came to reveal the time of the end to them, but it was hidden from him."

E. R. Judah in the name of R. Eleazar bar Abina: "To two men the secret of the time of the end was revealed, but then it was hidden from them, and these are they: Jacob and Daniel.

F. "Daniel: 'But you, O Daniel, shut up the words and seal the book' (Dan. 12:4).

G. "Jacob: 'Then Jacob called his sons and said, "Gather yourselves together, that I may tell you what shall befall you in days to come. Assemble and hear, O sons of Jacob, and hearken to Israel, your father. Reuben, you are my first-born."'

H. "This teaches that he came to reveal the time of the end to them, but it was hidden from him."

I. The matter may be compared to the case of the king's ally, who was departing this world, and his children surrounded his bed. He said to them, "Come and I shall tell you the secrets of the king." Then he looked up and saw the king. He said to them, "Be most meticulous about the honor owing to the king."

J. So our father Jacob looked up and saw the Presence of God standing over him. He said to them, "Be most meticulous about the honor owing to the Holy One, blessed be he."

No. 4 interprets the language at hand both in its immediate context and in the larger setting of Israel's history. No. 5 goes over the same language., and No. 6 introduces, in the identical context, an eschatological dimension. No. 7 successfully carries forward this final theme, which surely is invited by the base verse, so that the personal history of the individual, dealt with at the opening compositions, gives way to the national history of Israel.

XCVIII:IX.

1. A. "Binding his foal to the vine [and his ass's colt to the choice vine, he washes his garments in wine, and his vesture in the blood of grapes; his eyes shall be red with wine, and his teeth white with milk]" (Gen. 49:8-12):

   B. R. Judah, R. Nehemiah, and rabbis:

   C. R. Judah said, "In the case of a vine which produces poorly, they tie an ass to it. Thus : 'Binding his foal to the vine.'

   D. "'...and his ass's colt to the choice vine, he washes his garments in wine:' in white wine.

   E. "'...and his vesture in the blood of grapes:' in red wine."

   F. R. Nehemiah said, "'Binding his foal to the vine:' God binds to the vine, that is Israel, his city, namely, 'the city which I have chosen.'

   G. "'...and his ass's colt to the choice vine:' the strong sons which are destined to arise from him."

   H. Rabbis said, "'I am bound to the vine and the choice vine' t[hat is Israel].

   I. "'Binding his foal to the vine and his ass's colt to the choice vine:' when the one concerning whom it is written, 'Lowly and riding upon an ass, even upon a colt of the foal of an ass' (Zech. 9:9).

   J. "'...he washes his garments in wine:' for he will link together words of Torah.

   K. "'...and his vesture in the blood of grapes:' for he will explain their errors to them."

2. A. Said R. Hanin, "Israel does not require the learning of the king-messiah in the age to come, as it is said, 'Unto him shall *the nations* seek' (Is. 11:1) -- but not Israel.

   B. "If so, why will the king-messiah come? And what will he come to do? It is to gather together the exiles of Israel and to give them thirty religious duties: 'And I said to them, If you think good, give me my hire, and if not, forbear. So they weighed for my hire thirty -pieces of silver' (Zech. 11:12)."

   C. Rab said, "These refer to thirty heroes."

   D. R. Yohanan said, "These refer to thirty religious duties."

   E. They said to R. Yohanan, "Have you not accepted the view of Rab that the passage speaks only of the nations of the world?"

   F. In the view of Rab, "And I said to them" speaks of Israel, and in the view of Israel, "And I said to them" speaks of the nations of the world.

   G. In the view of Rab, when the Israelites have sufficient merit, the greater number of the thirty heroes are in the Land of Israel, and the lesser number in Babylonia, and when the Israelites do not have sufficient merit, the greater number is in Babylonia and the smaller number in the Land of Israel.

Judah reads the view in a simple way. Nehemiah makes it allude to Jerusalem. It is rabbis' view that is interesting, because they introduce the messianic theme and work it out in an unusual way. Now the Israelites will not require the messiah to teach them the Torah. His job is only to reassemble Israel in the holy land. The secondary expansion reenforces rabbis' point.

XCIX:II.

1. A. "For the Lord God will do nothing unless he reveals his secret to his servants the prophets" (Amos 3:7).

B. Jacob linked two of his sons, corresponding to two of the monarchies, and Moses linked two of the tribes, corresponding to two of the monarchies.

C. Judah corresponds to the kingdom of Babylonia, for this is compared to a lion and that is compared to a lion. This is compared to a lion: "Judah is a lion's whelp" (Gen. 49:9), and so too Babylonia: "The first was like a lion" (Dan. 7:4).

D. Then by the hand of which of the tribes will the kingdom of Babylonia fall? It will be by the hand of Daniel, who comes from the tribe of Judah.

E. Benjamin corresponds to the kingdom of Media, for this is compared to a wolf and that is compared to a wolf. This is compared to a wolf: "Benjamin is a ravenous wolf, [in the morning devouring the prey, and at even dividing the spoil." And that is compared to a wolf: "And behold, another beast, a second, like a wolf" (Dan. 7:5).

F. R. Hanina said, "The word for 'wolf' in the latter verse is written as 'bear.' It had been called a bear."

G. That is the view of R. Yohanan, for R. Yohanan said, "'Wherefore a lion of the forest slays them' (Jer. 5:6) refers to Babylonia, and 'a wolf of the deserts spoils them' refers to Media."

H. [Reverting to E:] Then by the hand of which of the tribes will the kingdom of Media fall? It will be by the hand of Mordecai, who comes from the tribe of Benjamin.

I. Levi corresponds to the kingdom of Greece. This is the third tribe in order, and that is the third kingdom in order. This is written with a word that is made up of three letters, and that is written with a word which consists of three letters. This one sounds the horn and that one sounds the horn, this one wears turbans and that one wears helmets, this one wears pants and that one wears knee-cuts.

J. To be sure, this one is very populous, while that one is few in numbers. But the many came and fell into the hand of the few.

K. On account of merit deriving from what source did this take place? It is on account of the blessing that Moses bestowed: "Smiter through the loins of them that rise up against him": (Deut. 33:11).

L. Then by the hand of which of the tribes will the kingdom of Greece fall? It will be by the hand of sons of the Hasmoneans, who come from the tribe of Levi.'

M. Joseph corresponds to the kingdom of Edom [Rome], for this one has horns and that one has horns. This one has horns: "His firstling bullock, majesty is his, and his horns are the horns of the wild ox" (Deut. 33:17). And that one has horns: "And concerning the ten horns that were on its head" (Dan. 7:20). This one avoided kept away from fornication while that one cleaved to fornication. This one paid respect for the honor owing to his father, while that one despised the honor owing to his father. Concerning this one it is written, "For I fear God" (Gen. 42:18), while in regard to that one it is written, "And he did not fear God" (Deut. 25:18). [So the correspondence in part is one of opposites.]

N. Then by the hand of which of the tribes will the kingdom of Edom fall? It will be by the hand of the anointed for war, who comes from the tribe of Joseph.

O. R. Phineas in the name of R. Samuel b. Nahman: "There is a tradition that Esau will fall only by the hand of the sons of Rachel: 'Surely the least of the flock shall drag them away' (Jer. 49:20). Why the least? Because they are the youngest of the tribes."

This impressive theory of Israel's history finds a place here only because of E. Yet the larger relevance -- Jacob's predictions of the future -- justifies including the composition.

XCIX:III.

1. A. "Benjamin is a ravenous wolf, in the morning devouring the prey, and at even dividing the spoil" (Gen. 49:27):

B. The verse speaks of the judge that comes from Benjamin, that is, Ehud.

C. Just as a wolf seizes, so Ehud seized the heart of Eglon: "And Ehud came to him and he was sitting by himself alone in his cool upper chamber" (Judges 3:20).

D. "And he said, I have a secret errand for you, O king" (Judges 3:19):

E. He said to him, "Thus has the master of the world said to me, 'Take a sword and thrust it into his belly.'"

F. "And the dirt came out" (Judges 3:22):

G. This refers to his shit.

H. "Then Ehud went out onto the porch" (Judges 3:23):

I. R. Yudan said, "Out into the public square "

J. R. Berekhiah said, "There the ministering angels said all in a row."

2. A. Another matter: "Benjamin is a ravenous wolf, in the morning devouring the prey, and at even dividing the spoil" (Gen. 49:27):

B. The verse speaks of the king that comes from Benjamin, [that is, Saul].

C. Just as the wolf seizes, so Saul seized the monarchy, as it is said, "So Saul took the kingdom over Israel" (1 Sam. 14:47).

D. "...in the morning devouring the prey:" "And he fought against his enemies on all sides" (1 Sam. 14:47).

E. "...and at even dividing the spoil:" "So Saul died, and his three sons" (1 Sam. 31:6).

3. A. Another matter: "Benjamin is a ravenous wolf, in the morning devouring the prey, and at even dividing the spoil" (Gen. 49:27):

B. The verse speaks of the queen [that comes from Benjamin, [that is, Esther].

C. Just as the wolf seizes, so Esther seized the monarchy: "Esther was taken into the king's house" (Est. 2:8).

"D. "...in the morning devouring the prey:" "On that day did the king Ahasuerus give the house of Haman the Jews' enemy to Esther the queen" (Est. 8:1).

E. "...and at even dividing the spoil:" "And Esther set Mordecai over the house of Haman" (Est. 8:2).

4. A. Another matter: "Benjamin is a ravenous wolf, in the morning devouring the prey, and at even dividing the spoil" (Gen. 49:27):

B. The verse speaks of the land that belongs to Benjamin, [that is, Jericho].

C. Just as the wolf seizes, so the land of Benjamin seizes its crops [making them ripen fast].

D. "...in the morning devouring the prey: this speaks of Jericho, where the produce ripens first.

E. "...and at even dividing the spoil:" this speaks of Beth El, where the produce ripens last.

5. A. ["Benjamin is a ravenous wolf, in the morning devouring the prey, and at even dividing the spoil:"] R. Phineas interpreted the verse to speak of the altar: "Just as a wolf seizes, so the altar would seize the offerings.

B. "'...in the morning devouring the prey:' 'The one lamb you shall offer in the morning' (Num. 28:4).

C. "'...and at even dividing the spoil:' 'And the other lamb you shall offer in the evening' (Num. 28:45)."

The systematic reading of the reference to Benjamin links the blessing to successive events in the later history of Israel, the judge of Benjamin, then the king that Benjamin produced, then the queen, then the land, and, finally, the Temple, located as it was in Benjamin's territory. The clear intent of the compositors, to read Jacob's blessing in the light of future history, has attained realization time and again.

Chapter Fifteen

Rome in Particular

By this point readers must find themselves altogether at home in reading the book of Genesis as if it portrayed the history of Israel and Rome. For that is the single obsession binding sages of the document at hand to common discourse with the text before them. Why Rome in the form it takes in Genesis Rabbah? And how come the obsessive character of sages disposition of the theme of Rome? Were their picture merely of Rome as tyrant and destroyer of the Temple, we should have no reason to link the text to the problems of the age of redaction and closure. But, as we have repeatedly observed, now it is Rome as Israel's brother, counterpart, and nemesis, Rome as the one thing standing in the way of Israel's, and the world's, ultimate salvation. So the stakes are different, and much higher. It is not a political Rome but a messianic Rome that is at issue: Rome as surrogate for Israel, Rome as obstacle to Israel. Why? It is because Rome now confronts Israel with a crisis, and, I argue, Genesis Rabbah constitutes a response to that crisis. Rome in the fourth century became Christian. Sages respond by facing that fact quite squarely and saying, "Indeed, it is as you say, a kind of Israel, an heir of Abraham as your texts explicitly claim. But we remain the sole legitimate Israel, the bearer of the birthright -- we and not you. So you are our brother: Esau, Ishmael, Edom." And the rest follows.

Genesis Rabbah reached closure, people generally agree, toward the end of the fourth century. That century marks the beginning of the West as we have known it. Why so? Because in the fourth century, from the conversion of Constantine and over the next hundred years, the Roman empire became Christian -- and with it, the West. So the fourth century marks the first century of the history of the West in that form in which the West would flourish for the rest of time, to our own day. Accordingly, we should not find surprising sages' recurrent references, in the reading of Genesis, to the struggle of two equal powers, Rome and Israel, Esau and Jacob, Ishmael and Isaac. The world-historical change, marking the confirmation in politics and power of the Christians' claim that Christ was king over all humanity, demanded from sages an appropriate, and, to Israel, persuasive. response.

By rereading the story of the beginnings, sages discovered the answer and the secret of the end. Rome claimed to be Israel, and, indeed, sages conceded, Rome shared the patrimony of Israel. That claim took the form of the Christians' appropriation of the Torah as "the Old Testament," so sages acknowledged a simple fact in acceding to the notion that, in some way, Rome too formed part of Israel. But it was the rejected part, the Ishmael, the Esau, not the Isaac, not the Jacob. The advent of Christian Rome precipitated the sustained, polemical, and, I think, rigorous and well-argued rereading of beginnings in light of the end. Rome then marked the conclusion of human history as Israel had known it. Beyond? The coming of the true Messiah, the redemption of Israel, the salvation of the world, the end of time. So the issues were not inconsiderable, and when the sages spoke of Esau/Rome, as they did so often, they confronted the life-or-death decision of the day.

Let us begin with a simple example of how ubiquitous is the shadow of Ishmael/Esau/Edom/Rome. Wherever sages reflect on future history, their minds turn to their own day. They found the hour difficult, because Rome, now Christian, claimed that very birthright and blessing that they understood to be theirs alone. Christian Rome posed a threat without precedent. Now another dominion, besides Israel's, claimed the rights and blessings that sustained.israel. Wherever in Scripture they turned, sages found comfort in the iteration that the birthright, the blessing, the Torah, and the hope -- all belonged to them and to none other. Here is a striking statement of that constant proposition.

LIII:XII.

1. A. "[So she said to Abraham, 'Cast out this slave woman with her son, for the son of this slave woman shall not be heir with my son Isaac.'] And the thing was very displeasing to Abraham on account of his son" (Gen. 21:11):

   B. That is in line with this verse: "And shuts his eyes from looking upon evil" (Is. 33:15). [Freedman, p. 471, n. 1: He shut his eyes from Ishmael's evil ways and was reluctant to send him away.]

2. A. "But God said to Abraham, 'Be not displeased because of the lad and because of your slave woman; whatever Sarah says to you, do as she tells you, for through Isaac shall your descendants be named'" (Gen. 21:12):

   B. Said R. Yudan bar Shillum, "What is written is not 'Isaac' but 'through Isaac.' [The matter is limited, not through all of Isaac's descendants but only through some of them, thus excluding Esau.]"

3. A. R. Azariah in the name of Bar Hutah" "The use of the B, which stands for two, indicates that he who affirms that there are two worlds will inherit both worlds [this age and the age to come]."

   B. Said R. Yudan bar Shillum, "It is written, 'Remember his marvelous works that he has done, his signs and the judgments of his mouth' (Ps. 105:5). I have given a sign , namely, it is one who gives the appropriate evidence through what he says. Specifically, he who affirms that there are two worlds will be called 'your seed.'

   C. "And he who does not affirm that there are two worlds will not be called 'your seed.'"

No. 1 makes "the matter" refer to Ishmael's misbehavior, not Sarah's proposal, so removing the possibility of disagreement between Abraham and

Sarah. Nos. 2, 3 interpret the limiting particle, "in," that is, *among* the descendants of Isaac will be found Abraham's heirs, but not all the descendants of Isaac will be heirs of Abraham. No. 2 explicitly excludes Esau, that is Rome, and No. 3 makes the matter doctrinal in the context of Israel's inner life.

As the several antagonists of Israel stand for Rome in particular, so the traits of Rome, as sages perceived them, characterized the biblical heroes. Esau provided a favorite target. From the womb Israel and Rome contended.

LXIII:VI.

11. A. "And the children struggled together [within her, and she said, 'If it is thus, why do I live?' So she went to inquire of the Lord. And the Lord said to her, 'Two nations are in your womb, and two peoples, born of you, shall be divided; the one shall be stronger than the other, and the elder shall serve the younger'] " (Gen. 25:22-23):

B. R. Yohanan and R. Simeon b. Laqish:

C. R. Yohanan said, "[Because the word, 'struggle,' contains the letters for the word, 'run,'] this one was running to kill that one and that one was running to kill this one."

D. R. Simeon b. Laqish: "This one releases the laws given by that one, and that one releases the laws given by this one."

2. A. R. Berekhiah in the name of R. Levi said, "It is so that you should not say that it was only after he left his mother's womb that [Esau] contended against [Jacob].

B. "But even while he was yet in his mother's womb, his fist was stretched forth against him: 'The wicked stretch out their fists [so Freedman] from the womb' (Ps. 58:4)."

3. A. "And the children struggled together within her:"

B. [Once more referring to the letters of the word "struggled," with special attention to the ones that mean, "run,"] they wanted to run within her.

C. When she went by houses of idolatry, Esau would kick, trying to get out: "The wicked are estranged from the womb" (Ps. 58:4).

D. When she went by synagogues and study-houses, Jacob would kick, trying to get out: "Before I formed you in the womb, I knew you" (Jer. 1:5)."

4. A. "...and she said, 'If it is thus, why do I live?'"

B. R. Haggai in the name of R. Isaac: "This teaches that our mother, Rebecca, went around to the doors of women and said to them, 'Did you ever have this kind of pain in your life?'"

C. "[She said to them,] "'If thus:" If this is the pain of having children, would that I had not gotten pregnant.'"

C. Said R. Huna, "If I am going to produce twelve tribes only through this kind of suffering, would that I had not gotten pregnant."

5. A. It was taught on Tannaite authority in the name of R. Nehemiah, "Rebecca was worthy of having the twelve tribes come forth from her. That is in line with this verse:

B. "'Two nations are in your womb, and two peoples, born of you, shall be divided; the one shall be stronger than the other, and the elder shall serve the younger.' When her days to be delivered were fulfilled, behold, there were twins in her womb. The first came forth red, all his body like a hairy mantle, so they called his name Esau. Afterward his brother came forth...' (Gen. 25:23-24).

C. "'Two nations are in your womb:' thus two.

D. "'and two peoples:'thus two more, hence four.

E. "'...the one shall be stronger than the other:' two more, so six.

F. "'...and the elder shall serve the younger:' two more, so eight.

G. "'When her days to be delivered were fulfilled, behold, there were twins in her womb:' two more, so ten.

H. "'The first came forth red:' now eleven.

J. "'Afterward his brother came forth:' now twelve."

K. There are those who say, "Proof derives from this verse: 'If it is thus, why do I live?' Focusing on the word for 'thus,' we note that the two letters of that word bear the numerical value of seven and five respectively, hence, twelve in all."

6. A. "So she went to inquire of the Lord:"

B. Now were there synagogues and houses of study in those days [that she could go to inquire of the Lord]?

C. But is it not the fact that she went only to the study of Eber?

D. This serves to teach you that whoever receives an elder is as if he receives the Presence of God.

Nos. 1-3 take for granted that Esau represents Rome, and Jacob, Israel. Consequently the verse underlines the point that there is natural enmity between Israel and Rome. Esau hated Israel even while he was still in the womb. Jacob, for his part, revealed from the womb those virtues that would characterize him later on, eager to serve God as Esau was eager to worship idols. The text invites just this sort of reading. No. 4 and No. 5 relate Rebecca's suffering to the birth of the twelve tribes. No. 6 makes its own point, independent of the rest and tacked on.

LXIII:VII.

2. A. "Two nations are in your womb, [and two peoples, born of you, shall be divided; the one shall be stronger than the other, and the elder shall serve the younger]" (Gen. 25:23):

B. There are two proud nations in your womb, this one takes pride in his world, and that one takes pride in his world.

C. This one takes pride in his monarchy, and that one takes pride in his monarchy.

D. There are two proud nations in your womb.

E. Hadrian represents the nations, Solomon, Israel.

F. There are two who are hated by the nations in your womb. All the nations hate Esau, and all the nations hate Israel.

G. [Following Freedman's reading:] The one whom your creator hates is in your womb: "And Esau I hated" (Mal. 1:3).

3. A. "and two peoples, born of you, shall be divided:"

B.   Said R. Berekhiah,   "On the basis of this statement we have evidence that [Jacob] was born circumcized."

4.   A.   "...the one shall be stronger than the other, [and the elder shall serve the younger]" (Gen. 25:23):

B.   R. Helbo in the name of the house of R. Shila: "Up to this point there were Sabteca and Raamah, but from you will come Jews and Romans." [Freedman, p. 561, n. 8: "Hitherto even the small nations such as Sabteca and Raamah counted; but henceforth all these will pale into insignificance before the two who will rise from you.]

5.   A.   "...and the elder shall serve the younger" (Gen. 25:23):

B.   Said R. Huna, "If he has merit, he will be served, and if not, he will serve."

The syllogism invokes the base-verse as part of its repertoire of cases. No. 2 augments the statement at hand, still more closely linking it to the history of Israel. Nos. 3, 4, and 5 gloss minor details. The same polemic proceeds in what follows.

LXIII:VIII.

3.   A.   "The first came forth red:"

B.   R. Haggai in the name of R. Isaac: "On account of the merit attained by obeying the commandment, 'You will take for yourself on the first day...,' (Lev. 23:40),

C.   "I shall reveal myself to you as the First, avenge you on the first, rebuild the first, and bring you the first.

D.   "I shall reveal myself to you the First: 'I am the first and I am the last' (Is. 44:6).

E.   "...avenge you on the first: 'Esau, 'The first came forth red.'

F.   "...rebuild the first: that is the Temple, of which it is written, 'You throne of glory, on high from the first, you place of our sanctuary' (Jer. 17:12).

G.   "...and bring you the first: that is, the messiah-king: 'A first unto Zion will I give, behold, behold, them, and to Jerusalem' (Is. 41:27)."

LXIII:X.

1.   A.   "[When the boys grew up,] Esau was a skillful hunter, [a man of the field, while Jacob was a quiet man, dwelling in tents]" (Gen. 25:27):

B.   He hunted people through snaring them in words [as the Roman prosecutors do:] "Well enough, you did not steal. But who stole with you? You did not kill, but who killed with you?"

2.   A.   R. Abbahu said, "He was a trapper and a fieldsman, trapping at home and in the field.

B.   "He trapped at home: 'How do you tithe salt?' [which does not, in fact, have to be tithed at all!]

C.   "He trapped in the field: 'How do people give tithe for straw?' [which does not, in fact, have to be tithed at all!]"

3.   A.   R. Hiyya bar Abba said, "He treated himself as totally without responsibility for himself, like a field [on which anyone tramples].

B. "Said the Israelites before the Holy One, blessed be he, 'Lord of all ages, is it not enough for us that you have subjugated us to the seventy nations, but even to this one, who is subjected to sexual intercourse just like a woman?'

C. "Said to them the Holy One, blessed be he, 'I too will exact punishment from him with those same words: 'And the heart of the mighty men of Edom at that day shall be as the heart of a woman in her pangs' (Jer. 49:22)."

4. A. "...while Jacob was a quiet man, dwelling in tents" (Gen. 25:27):

B. There is a reference to two tents, that is, the school house of Shem and the school house of Eber.

5. A. "Now Isaac loved Esau, because he ate of his game:"

B. It was first rate meat and wine for Isaac's eating.

6. A. "...but Rebecca loved Jacob" (Gen. 25:28):

B. The more she heard his voice, the more she loved him.

Nos. 1-3 deal with the description of Esau, explaining why he was warlike and aggressive. Nothing Esau did proved sincere. He was a hypocrite, even when he tried to please his parents.

LXV:I.

1. A. "When Esau was forty years old, he took to wife Judith, the daughter of Beeri, the Hittite, and Basemath the daughter of Elon the Hittite; and they made life bitter for Isaac and Rebecca" (Gen. 26:34-35):

B. "The swine out of the wood ravages it, that which moves in the field feeds on it" (Ps. 80:14).

C. R. Phineas and R. Hilqiah in the name of R. Simon: "Among all of the prophets, only two of them spelled out in public [the true character of Rome, represented by the swine], Asaf and Moses.

D. "Asaf: 'The swine out of the wood ravages it.'

E. "Moses: 'And the swine, because he parts the hoof' (Deut. 14:8).

F. "Why does Moses compare Rome to the swine? Just as the swine, when it crouches, puts forth its hoofs as if to say, 'I am clean,' so the wicked kingdom steals and grabs, while pretending to be setting up courts of justice.

G. "So Esau, for all forty years, hunted married women, ravished them, and when he reached the age of forty, he presented himself to his father, saying, 'Just as father got married at the age of forty, so I shall marry a wife at the age of forty.'

H. "'When Esau was forty years old, he took to wife Judith, the daughter of Beeri, the Hittite, and Basemath the daughter of Elon the Hittite.'"

The exegesis of course once more identifies Esau with Rome. The round-about route linking the fact at hand, Esau's taking a wife, passes through the territory of Roman duplicity. Whatever the government does, it claims to do in the general interest. But it really has no public interest at all. Esau for his part spent forty years pillaging women and then, at the age of forty, pretended, to his father, to be upright. That, at any rate, is the parallel clearly intended by this obviously unitary composition. The issue of the selection of the intersecting verse does not present an obvious solution to me; it seems to me only the identification of Rome with the swine accounts for the choice. The contrast between Israel and Esau produced the following anguished observation. But here the Rome is not yet Christian, so far as the clear reference is concerned.

LXV:XXI.

3. A. Said R. Judah bar Ilai, "Rabbi would give the following exposition:

B. ""The voice is Jacob's voice," that is, the voice of Jacob crying out on account of what "the hands of Esau" have done to him.'"

C. Said R. Yohanan, "It is the voice of Hadrian, may his bones be pulverized, killing in Betar eighty thousand myriads of people."

The insistence upon reading the history of Israel into the biography of Jacob stands behind No. 3. The question then arises, why the enmity?

LXVII:VIII.

1. A. "Now Esau hated Jacob [because of the blessing with which his father had blessed him, and Esau said to himself, 'The days of mourning for my father are approaching; then I will kill my brother Jacob]'" (Gen. 27:41):

B. Said R. Eleazar b. R. Yose, "He turned into a vengeful and vindictive enemy of his, just as even today they are called 'senators' in Rome [with the word for 'senator' bearing the consonants that appear in the words for enemy and vindictive]."

LXXV:I.

1. A. "And Jacob sent messengers before him [to Esau his brother in the land of Seir, the country of Edom, instructing them, 'Thus shall you say to my lord Esau, "Thus says your servant Jacob, 'I have sojourned with Laban and stayed until now. And I have oxen, asses flocks, menservants and maidservants; and I have sent to tell my lord, in order that I may find favor in your sight'"]" (Gen. 32:4):

B. R. Phineas in the name of R. Reuben opened discourse by citing the following verse: "Arise, O Lord, confront him" (Ps. 17:13).

C. R. Phineas in the name of R. Reuben said, "There are five passages in the first book of Psalms in which David asks the Holy One, blessed be he, to rise: 'Arise O Lord, save me O my god' (Ps. 3:8); 'Arise, O Lord, in your anger' (Ps. 7:7); 'Arise, O Lord, O God, lift up your hand' (Ps. 10:12); 'Arise, O Lord, let not man prevail' (Ps. 9:20).

D. "'Arise, O Lord, confront him:'

E. "Said the Holy One, blessed be he, to him, 'David, my son, even if you ask me to rise a thousand times, I shall not arise. When shall I arise? When you see the poor oppressed and the needy groaning.'

F. "'For the oppression of the poor, for the sighing of the needy, now I will arise, says the Lord' (Ps. 12:6)."

2. A. ["For the oppression of the poor, for the sighing of the needy, now I will arise, says the Lord:"] R. Simeon b. Jonah said, "'Now I will arise.' As long as [Jerusalem] wallows in the dust, as it were. But when that day comes,

concerning which it is written, 'Shake yourself from the dust, arise, and sit down, O Jerusalem' (Is. 52:2), at that time, 'Be silent, all flesh, before the Lord' (Zech. 2:17).

B. "Why so? 'For he is aroused out of his holy habitation' (Zech. 2:17)."

C. Said R. Aha, "Like a chicken that shakes itself out of the dust."

3. A. "[Arise, O Lord,] confront him" (Ps. 17:13):

B. Confront the wicked before he confronts you.

C. "Cast him down" (Ps. 17:13):

D. into the scale of guilt.

E. "Break him," in line with this verse: "They are bowed down and fallen" (Ps. 20:9).

F. "Deliver my soul from the wicked, your sword" (Ps. 17:13):

G. "From the wicked person who comes with the power of the sword. "And by your sword shall you live" (Gen. 27:40).

4. A. Another interpretation of "Your sword:"

B. "[Esau] is your sword, because with it you punish the world."

5. A. R. Joshua of Sikhnin in the name of R. Levi: "Save my soul from that wicked man who is destined to fall by your sword: 'For my sword has drunk its fill in heaven, behold, it shall come down upon Edom' (Is. 34:5).

B. "Said the Holy One, blessed be he, to Jacob, 'Esau was walking along his solitary way, and you had to go and send word to him and say to him, 'Thus says your servant Jacob.'" [Freedman, p. 690, n. 1: "You would have had nothing to fear had you not drawn his attention to you, and the same applies to Jacob's descendants in their relations with Rome."]

No. 1 makes one point, No. 2 a different one. No. 1 stresses that God will rouse himself only to aid the poor and oppressed. No. 2 then maintains that God rouses himself to save Jerusalem at the end of time. These are distinct motifs. No. 3 works on the theme of the sword, in line with Gen. 27:40. No. 4 carries forward that same point of intersection. No. 5 makes the point articulated by Freedman, and that seems to me the upshot of the entire composition.

LXXV:II.

1. A. R. Judah b. R. Simon opened discourse by citing the following verse: "'As a troubled fountain and a corrupted spring, so is a righteous man who gives way before the wicked' (Prov. 25:26):

B. "Just as it is impossible for a fountain to be forever muddied and for a spring to be forever spoiled, so it is impossible for a righteous man to be forever humbled before a wicked one.

C. "And like a fountain that is muddied or a spring that is spoiled, so is a righteous man who is humbled before a wicked man.

D. "Said the Holy One, blessed be he, to him, 'Esau was walking along his solitary way, and you had to go and send word to him and say to him, 'Thus says your servant Jacob.'"

The same message is underlined, now interwoven with a different intersecting verse. Jacob should not have taken an initiative in dealing with Esau. The message of passivity in response to Rome, which Freedman underlined above, can be seen as the subterranean polemic.

LXXV:IV.

2. A. "And Jacob sent messengers before him:"

B. To this one [Esau] whose time to take hold of sovereignty would come before him [namely, before Jacob, since Esau would rule, then Jacob would govern].

C. R. Joshua b. Levi said, "Jacob took off the purple robe and threw it before Esau, as if to say to him, 'Two flocks of starlings are not going to sleep on a single branch' [so we cannot rule at the same time]."'

3. A. "...to Esau his brother:"

B. Even though he was Esau, he was still his brother.

4. A. "...in the land of Seir, the country of Edom:"

B. He was red, his food was red, his land was red, his mighty men were red, their clothing was red, his avenger will be red, and dressed in red. [Red symbolizes war.]

C. He was red: "And the first came forth ruddy" (Gen. 25:25).

D. ...his food was red: "'Let me swallow some of that red pottage, for I am famished'" (Gen. 25:30).

E. ...his land was red: "To Esau his brother to the land of Seir, the field of red" (Gen. 32:4).

F. ...his mighty men were red: "The shield of his mighty men is made red" (Nahum 2:4).

G. ...their clothing was red: "The valiant men are in scarlet" (Nahum 2:4).

H. ...his avenger will be red: "My beloved is white and ruddy" (Song 5:10).

I. ...and dressed in red: "Wherefore is your apparel red" (Is. 63:2).

No. 1 pursues a question important to the compositors, namely, the status of the "messenger" wherever such occurs. The point is that if angels served lesser figures, they surely accompanied Jacob. Nos. 2, 3 make a stunning point. It is that Esau remains Jacob's brother, and that Esau rules before Jacob will. The application to contemporary affairs cannot be missed, both in the recognition of the true character of Esau -- a brother! -- and in the interpretation of the future of history. No. 4 is familiar and simply works out the meaning of the color, red, of the land of Edom, the word meaning red. In what follows Rome is identified with Esau in a less negative context. Rabbi Judah the Patriarch, called simply "Rabbi" or "our holy master," and a Roman "emperor" called Antoninus are said to have maintained cordial relationships with one another. In that context the following story shows that Esau and Jacob still provided the generative paradigm.

LXXV:V.

1 . A. "... instructing them, 'Thus shall you say to my lord Esau, "Thus says your servant Jacob, 'I have sojourned with Laban and stayed until now:'"'"

B. Our master [Judah the Patriarch] said to R. Efes, "Write a letter in my name to our lord, King Antoninus."

C. He went and wrote, "From Judah the Patriarch to our lord, King Antoninus."

D. Rabbi took it, read it, tore it up, and had him write, "To our lord, the king, from Judah your servant."

E. He said to him, "My lord, why do you treat your own honor with contempt?"

F. He said to him, "Am I any better than my forefather? Did he not instruct them :'Thus shall you say to my lord Esau, "Thus says your servant Jacob, 'I have sojourned with Laban and stayed until now"''?"

2 . A. "I have sojourned with Laban and stayed until now:"

B. "Laban, the master of deceit, did I keep in my sleeve [having got the better of him (Freedman)], and as to you, how much the more so!"

3 . A.. "And why is it the case that 'I have stayed until now'?"

B. Because the adversary of Satan had not yet been born.

C. For R. Phineas in the name of R. Samuel bar Nahman: "It is a tradition that Esau will fall only by the hand of the descendants of the children of Rachel: 'Surely the youngest of the flock shall drag them away' (Jer. 49:20).

D. "[And why does Scripture call them 'the youngest of the flock'? Because they are] the youngest of the tribes."

No. 1 cites the base verse for its own purposes, thus showing how the patriarch followed the example of the patriarch, Jacob. No. 2 gives Jacob a more ominous message than does the biblical narrative. No. 3 goes over familiar ground. Esau, meaning Rome, will fall by the hand of the Messiah.

LXXV:IX.

1 . A. Someone else commenced discourse by citing this verse: "Do not grant, O Lord, the desires of the wicked, do not advance his evil plan" (Ps. 140:9).

B. "Lord of all ages, do not give to the wicked Esau what his heart has devised against Jacob."

C. What is the meaning of, "Do not advance his evil plan"?

D. He said before him, "Lord of the ages, Make a bit for the mouth of the wicked Esau, so that he will not get full pleasure [from anything he does]." [The word for "evil plan" and for "bit" use the same consonants.]

E. What sort of bit did the Holy One, blessed be he, make for Esau?

F. Said R. Hama bar Haninah, "These are the barbarian nations, the Germans whom the Edomites fear."

Sages clearly followed the news of the day and drew their own conclusions from the Romans' political problems.

LXXV:XI.

1. A. Another explanation of the statement, "And Jacob sent...:"

   B. Why did he send out messengers to him?

   C. This is what he was thinking, "I shall send messengers to him, perhaps he will return in repentence."

   D. And he said to them, "This is what to say to him: 'Do not suppose that the way that Jacob went forth from the house of his father is the way he is coming back.'"

   E. For it is said, "For with my staff I passed over this Jordan" (Gen. 32:11).

   F. [Reverting to Jacob's message:] "'For he did not take anything from his father. But it was for "my salary [the messengers are to repeat to Esau] that I have acquired all of these properties, through my own strength."'"

   G. For it is said, "And now I have become two camps" (Gen. 32:11).

2. A. At the moment that Jacob referred to Esau as "my lord," the Holy One, blessed be he, said to him, "You have lowered yourself and called Esau 'my Lord' no fewer than eight times.

   B. "I shall produce out of his descendants eight kings before your children [have any]: 'And these are the kings that reigned in the land of Edom before any king ruled the children of Israel' (Gen. 36:31)."

3. A. [In his message to Esau, Jacob said to him,] "If you are ready for peace, I shall be your counterpart, and if you are ready for war, I shall be your counterpart.

   B. "I have heroic, powerful troops, for I say something before the Holy One, blessed be he, and he grants what I ask: 'He will fulfill the desire of those who fear him' (Ps. 145:19)."

   C. Therefore David came to give praise and glory before the Holy One, blessed be he, for he helped him when he fled from Saul, as it is said, "For lo, the wicked bend the bow" (Ps. 11:2), then, "When the foundations are destroyed, what has the righteous done" (Ps. 11:3).

   D. He said to him, "Lord of the age, if you had been angry with Jacob and had forsaken him and not helped him, and he was pillar and foundation of the world, in line with this verse, 'But the righteous is the foundation of the world' (Prov. 10:25), then 'what has the righteous done' (Ps. 11:3)?"

   E. Concerning that moment it is said: "Some in chariots, some in horses, but we shall call on the name of the Lord our God" (Ps. 20:8). [Freedman, p. 697, n. 4: Jacob discomfited Esau by mentioning God, and David was saved from Saul by his trust in God.]

No. 1 supplies a message for the messengers in place of that given at Gen. 32:3-4. No. 2 responds to the statement, Gen. 32:3: "Thus you shall say to my lord Esau." The effect is to link Jacob's encounter with Esau to Israel's history with Edom/Rome. There are no surprises here. No. 3 works out a parallel between Jacob and David, as made explicit by Freedman.

LXXV:VII.

1. A. "And the messengers returned to Jacob, saying, 'We came to your brother Esau'" (Gen. 32:6):

B.   [They said to him,] "You treat him as a brother, but he treats you as Esau."

2. A.   "...and he is coming to meet you, and four hundred men with him" (Gen. 32:6):

B.   R. Simeon b. Laqish said, "'With him' means people equivalent to him himself.

C.   "Just as he has four hundred men with him, so each of them has four hundred men with him."

D.   R. Levi said, "He had gone and bought the right to collect duties. He thought to himself, 'If I can overcome him, well and good, and if not, I shall tax him and in doing so I shall kill him.'"

Here again sages refer to contemporary considerations in interpreting the sense of Scripture.

LXXVI:VI.

1. A.   "'Deliver me, I pray you, from the hand of my brother, from the hand of Esau, for I fear him:'"

B.   "From the hand of my brother, who comes against me with the strength of Esau" [which was the sword] (Gen. 27:40).

C.   That is in line with this verse: "I considered the horns, and behold, there came up among them another horn, a little one" (Dan. 7:8).

D.   This refers to Ben Neser [Odenathus of Palmyra].

E.   "Before which three of the first horns were plucked up by the roots" (Dan. 7:8).

F.   This refers to Macrinus, Carinus, and Cyriades.

G.   "And behold, in this horn were eyes like the eyes of a man and a mouth speaking great things" (Dan. 7:8).

H.   This speaks of the wicked realm, which imposes taxes on all the nations of the world.

I.   Said R. Yohanan, "It is written, "'And as for the ten horns, out of this kingdom shall ten kings arise' (Dan. 7:24), that is, the ten sons of Esau.

J.   "'I considered the horns, and behold, there came up among them another horn, a little one', meaning, the wicked realm.

K.   "'Before which three of the first horns were plucked up by the roots' speaks of the first three monarchies [Babylonia, Media, Greece].

L.   "'And behold, in this horn were eyes like the eyes of a man' alludes to the wicked realm, which looks enviously on someone's wealth, saying, 'Since Mr. So-and-so has a lot of money, we shall elect him magistrate,' 'Since Mr. So-and-so has a lot of money, we shall elect him councillor.'"

2. A.   "'...lest he come and slay us all, the mothers with the children. But you did say, "I will do you good and make your descendants as the sand of the sea, which cannot be numbered for multitude"'" (Gen. 32:12):

B.   "But you did say, 'You will not take the dam with the fledglings'" (Deut. 22:6).

C.   Another matter: "'...lest he come and slay us all, the mothers with the children. But you did say, "And whether it be cow or ewe, you shall not kill it and its young both in one day (Lev. 22:28)."'"

The explicit allusion at No. 1 to Rome in the time of Odenathus is puzzling, because, of course, Odenathus at Palmyra was an independent chief, not ruler of Rome (!). The reading of Daniel has three Roman generals fall before Palmyra. Now what this has to do with the power of one's brother, the power of the sword, I take it, is simple. Jacob is made to refer to wanting to be saved from someone who exercises the sort of power that Esau exercises, namely, from Palmyra. The message to Israel is that Palmyra, no less than Rome, exercises a kind of power from which Israel is to be delivered, not power Israel is itself to aspire to wield. Then the sense of Yohanan's statement is that the cited verse speaks of Rome, not Palmyra, and that at issue is Rome as successor to the first three monarchies. So Yohanan reads Daniel in the way in which rabbis generally did, and in his view, there is no point of contact with our base verse. It is a rather interesting construction therefore, in which a dispute on the meaning of Daniel has taken shape, only afterward to be brought into juxtaposition with our base verse. The reason the compositor chose the completed statement of course is the opening allusion, but that alone. No. 2 goes over familiar ground, drawing upon the setting of Jacob's address to call to God's attention the requirement of the Torah. The one who gave the Torah must see to it that its rule applies.

LXXVIII:XII.

1 . A. "Jacob said, 'No, I pray you, if I have found favor in your sight, then accept my present from my hand, for truly to see your face is like seeing the face of God, [with such favor have you received me. Accept, I pray you, my gift that is brought to you, because God has dealt graciously with me, and because I have enough.' Thus he urged him, and he took it]" (Gen. 33:10-11):

B. "Just as the face of God is judgment, so your face is judgment.

C. "Just as the face of God involves this statement: 'You will not see my face empty-handed' (Ex. 23:15), so as to you: I will not see your face empty-handed." [That is the meaning of the comparison Jacob has made.]

2 . A. "Accept, I pray you, my gift that is brought to you, because God has dealt graciously with me, and because I have enough:"

B. He said to him, "How much I suffered, how hard I worked, before this gift came to me, but to you it comes on its own."

C. What is written is not "which I have brought" but "[on its own] is brought to you."

3 . A. "... Thus he urged him, and he took it" (Gen. 33:11):

B. He acted as if to decline, but he put on his hands.

C. R. Judah b. Rabbi said, "'Every one submitting himself with pieces of silver' (Ps. 68:31) means, [Freedman:] 'he opens his hand and would be appeased with silver.' [Freedman, p. 723, n. 4: Esau meaning Rome demands money for appeasement.]"

4 . A. R. Simeon b. Laqish went up to pay his respects to our master [Judah the Patriarch]. He said to him, "Pray for me, because this kingdom is very wicked."

B. He said to him, "Do not take anything from anybody, and you will not have to give anything to anyone. [Stop collecting taxes.]"

C. While they were in session, a woman came along carrying a salver and a knife on it. He took the knife and gave her back the salver.

D. A royal representative came along, saw it, liked it, and took it.

E. In the evening, R. Simeon b. Laqish went up to pay his respects to our master [Judah the Patriarch]. He saw him sitting and laughing.

F. He said to him, "Why are you laughing?"

G. He said to him, "That knife that you saw -- a royal representative came along and took it away."

H. He said to him, "Didn't I tell you, 'Do not take anything from anybody, and you will not have to give anything to anyone.'"

5. A. A commoner said to R. Hoshaiah, "If I say something good to you, will you repeat it in my name in public?"

B. He said to him, "What is it?"

D. He said to him, "All the gifts that our father, Jacob, gave to Esau are the nations of the world destined to restore to the king-messiah in the age to come.

E. "What is the verse of Scripture that indicates it? 'The kings of Tashish and of the isles shall return tribute' (Ps. 72:10).

F. "What is said is not, 'bring,' but 'return.'"

G. He said to him, "By your life, that indeed is a good thing that you have said, and in your name I shall repeat it."

No. 1 amplifies Jacob's statement. No. 2 subjects the cited verse to an acute reading, producing the indicated exegesis. No. 3 is important because of its more general comment on Esau's rule, following Freedman, another instance of drawing from Jacob's life a lesson for the life of the people, Israel. I take it that No. 4 is tacked on because it underlines the judgment of No. 3 about Roman rule. No. 5 reverts to the theme of the gifts of Jacob to Esau, joins the tale to Israel's history, and imparts to it an eschatological dimension.

LXXXIII:I.

1. A. "These are the kings who reigned in the land of Edom before any king reigned over the Israelites: Bela the son of Beor reigned in Edom, the name of his city being Dinhabah" (Gen. 36:31-32):

B. R. Isaac commenced discourse by citing this verse: "Of the oaks of Bashan they have made your oars" (Ez. 27:6).

C. Said R. Isaac, "The nations of the world are to be compared to a ship. Just as a ship has its mast made in one place and its anchor somewhere else, so their kings: 'Samlah of Masrekah' (Gen. 36:36), 'Shaul of Rehobot by the river' (Gen. 36:27), and: 'These are the kings who reigned in the land of Edom before any king reigned over the Israelites.'"

2. A. ["An estate may be gotten hastily at the beginning, but the end thereof shall not be blessed" (Prov. 20:21)]: "An estate may be gotten hastily at the beginning:" "These are the kings who reigned in the land of Edom before any king reigned over the Israelites."

B. "...but the end thereof shall not be blessed:" "And saviors shall come up on mount Zion to judge the mount of Esau" (Ob. 1:21).

No. 1 contrasts the diverse origin of Roman rulers with the uniform origin of Israel's king in the house of David. No. 2 makes the same point still more forcefully. How so? Freedman makes sense of No. 2 as follows: Though Esau was the first to have kings, his land will eventually be overthrown (Freedman, p. 766, n. 3). So the point is that Israel will have kings after Esau no longer does, and the verse at hand is made to point to the end of Rome, a striking revision to express the importance in Israel's history to events in the lives of the patriarchs.

LXXXIII:II.

1. A. "These are the kings who reigned in the land of Edom before any king reigned over the Israelites: Bela the son of Beor reigned in Edom, the name of his city being Dinhabah" (Gen. 36:31-32):

B. Said R. Aibu, "Before a king arose in Israel, kings existed in Edom: "These are the kings who reigned in the land of Edom before any king reigned over the Israelites.'" [Freedman, p. 766, n. 4: "1 Kgs. 22:48 states, 'There was no king in Edom, a deputy was king.' This refers to the reign of Jehoshaphat. Subsequently in Jehoram's reign, Edom revolted and 'made a king over themselves' (2 Kgs. 8:20). Thus from Saul to Jehoshaphat, in which Israel had eight kings, Edom had no king but was ruled by a governor of Judah. Aibu observes that this was to balance the present period, during which Edom had eight kings while Israel had none. For that reason, Aibu employs the word for deputy when he wishes to say 'existed' thus indicating a reference to the verse in the book of Kings quoted above."]

C. R. Yose bar Haninah said, "[Alluding to a mnemonic, with the first Hebrew letter for the word for kings, judges, chiefs, and princes:] When the one party [Edom] was ruled by kings, the other party [Israel] was ruled by judges, when one side was ruled by chiefs, the other side was ruled by princes."

D. Said R. Joshua b. Levi, "This one set up eight kings and that one set up eight kings. This one set up Bela, Jobab, Husham, Samlah, Shaul, Hadad, Baalhanan, and Hadar. The other side set up Saul, Ishbosheth, David Solomon, Rehoboam, Abijah, Asa, and Jehoshaphat.

E. "Then Nebuchadnezzar came and overturned both: 'That made the world as a wilderness and destroyed the cities thereof' (Is. 14:17).

F. "Evil-merodach came and exalted Jehoiakin, Ahasuerus came and exalted Haman."

The passage once more stresses the correspondence between Israel's and Edom's governments, respectively. The reciprocal character of their histories is then stated in a powerful way, with the further implication that, when the one rules, the other waits. So now Israel waits, but it will rule. The same point is made in what follows, but the expectation proves acute and immediate.

LXXXIII:IV.

3. A. "Magdiel and Iram: these are the chiefs of Edom, that is Esau, the father of Edom, according to their dwelling places in the land of their possession" (Gen. 36:42):

B. On the day on which Litrinus came to the throne, there appeared to R. Ammi in a dream this message: "Today Magdiel has come to the throne."

C. He said, "One more king is required for Edom [and then Israel's turn will come]."

4. A. Said R. Hanina of Sepphoris, "Why was he called Iram? For he is destined to amass [a word using the same letters] riches for the king-messiah."

B. Said R. Levi, "There was the case of a ruler in Rome who wasted the treasuries of his father. Elijah of blessed memory appeared to him in a dream. He said to him, 'Your fathers collected treasures and you waste them.'

C. "He did not budge until he filled the treasuries again."

Nos. 3 presents once more the theme that Rome's rule will extend only for a foreordained and limited time, at which point the Messiah will come. No. 4 explains the meaning of the name Iram. The concluding statement also alleges that Israel's saints even now make possible whatever wise decisions Rome's rulers make. That forms an appropriate conclusion to the matter. Ending in the everyday world of the here and the now, we note that sages attribute to Israel's influence anything good that happens to Israel's brother, Rome. In our own day, even some of the children of Esau concede that point -- but that has come about only after Esau murdered nearly a third of Jacob's sons and daughters.

Index

Continued from back cover

140040	*Israeli Childhood Stories of the Sixties: Yizhar, Aloni, Shahar, Kahana-Carmon*	Gideon Telpaz
140041	*Formative Judaism II: Religious, Historical, and I̶̶ ̶ ̶ ̶S̶t̶u̶d̶i̶e̶s̶*	Jacob Neusner
140042	*Juda and*	Jacob Neusner
140043	*Supp Trac*	Roger Brooks
140044	*The Trac*	Louis E. Newman
140045	*Char Abra*	Jeffrey Fleck
140046	*Forn and*	Jacob Neusner
140047	*Phar in Rc*	Judith Baskin
140048	*The Back*	Matthew Black
140049	*Appl*	Marc Lee Raphael
140050	*Mysi*	William T. Miller
140051	*The Polic*	Eliezer Paltiel
140052	*Spar Anai*	Jack Martin Balcer
140053	*Herr*	William Kluback
140054	*Appl*	David R. Blumenthal
140055	*In th Trar*	Jacob Neusner
140056	*App*	Marc Lee Raphael
140057	*App*	David R. Blumenthal
140058	*App*	William Scott Green
140059	*The Amc*	Jack N. Lightstone
140060	*Maj Sym*	Jacob Neusner
140061	*Maj and*	Jacob Neusner
140062	*A History of the Jews in Babylonia. I: The Parthian Period*	Jacob Neusner
140063	*The Talmud of Babylonia: An American Translation. XXXII: Tractate Arakhin*	Jacob Neusner
140064	*Ancient Judaism: Debates and Disputes*	Jacob Neusner
140065	*Prayers Alleged to Be Jewish: An Examination of the Constitutiones Apostolorum*	David Fiensy
140066	*The Legal Methodology of Hai Gaon*	Tsvi Groner
140067	*From Mishnah to Scripture: The Problem of the Unattributed Saying*	Jacob Neusner
140068	*Halakhah in a Theological Dimension*	David Novak
140069	*From Philo to Origen: Middle Platonism in Transition*	Robert M. Berchman